GEOFFREY CHAUCER

LITERARY AND HISTORICAL STUDIES

GEOFFREY CHAUCER

LITERARY AND HISTORICAL STUDIES

HALDEEN BRADDY

KENNIKAT PRESS
Port Washington, N.Y. // London

GEOFFREY CHAUCER-LITERARY AND HISTORICAL STUDIES

© 1971 by Kennikat Press Inc.
All Rights Reserved
Library of Congress Catalog Card Number: 71-139351
ISBN 0-8046-9000-6

TO

JOSEPH ROYALL SMILEY

PREFACE TO *GEOFFREY CHAUCER STUDIES*

In assembling these multifarious items of Chauceriana, virtually all of my writings in this field have been included. Recent reissue of two kindred works of mine dictated their omission from the present volume. *Chaucer and the French Poet Graunson*, out of print for twenty years, was reissued in 1968 in a reprint incorporating an updating introduction (Kennikat Press, Port Washington, N.Y.). *Chaucer's "Parlement of Foules" in Its Relation to Contemporary Events* began its life as a doctoral dissertation in 1932. The Oxford University Press published the piece at the time as the second section of the full-sized book, *Three Chaucer Studies*. An American publishing house has now brought out *Chaucer's "Parlement of Foules"* as a separate volume featuring a new Preface, a new Introduction, and a Supplementary Bibliography (Octagon Books, New York, 1969). The later studies represent the scholastic writing of a regular faculty member carrying a full teaching schedule every year except 1963–64 (when I was a Research Professor on half-time teaching). Their completion would have been difficult except for support from the Institute of Organized Research, The University of Texas at El Paso. Modest grants from its funds have made possible travel, acquisition of materials and supplies, and part-time secretarial and editorial assistance. The last-named category has included underwriting the services of Student Assistant Corinne Peschka and of a special aide, Technical Assistant III Richard-Félicien Escontrías.

Grateful acknowledgement for permission to reprint these articles and notes is extended to the periodicals of first issue. In accord with convention, these publications have been credited individually in the book. The standard abbreviations used in *PMLA (Publications of the Modern Language Association)* characterize these bibliographical references. The dedication is to my friend Dr. Joseph Royall Smiley, savant, university president, and indefatigable sponsor of the ideals of scholarship.

Pass of the North   Haldeen Braddy
January, 1970

TABLE OF CONTENTS

TABLE OF CONTENTS (Cont)

GEOFFREY CHAUCER

LITERARY AND HISTORICAL STUDIES

1

THE PARLEMENT OF FOULES:
A NEW PROPOSAL

The purpose of this paper is to present certain facts relating to the historical and political conditions during a definite period of Chaucer's life, to demonstrate his intimate connection with events during this time, and to endeavor on the basis of these to fix the occasion of the contemporary allusions in the allegory of the *Parlement of Foules*.

Although several interpretations[1] of the *Parlement of Foules* had been suggested previously, the publication of Professor Koch's theory in 1877[2] was greeted as offering for the first time a satisfactory solution of the problem. Koch followed the lead of earlier scholars in recognizing that the allegory in Chaucer's poem rested upon some basis of historical fact, that the allusions to the bird-suitors reflected some contemporary situation in human affairs. But he rightly dismissed previous interpretations of the poem as failing to provide a likely occasion for its composition. In accordance with his theory, Anne of Bohemia represented the "formel" eagle, and Richard II, William of Bavaria, and Frederick of Meissen the three "tercel" eagle suitors.

This theory was accepted by Professor O.F. Emerson,[3] with certain modifications. Emerson felt that historical facts justified the rejection of William of Bavaria (Hainault) as a suitor,[4] and therefore moved Frederick of Meissen into second place, presenting Charles VI of France as the third "tercel" eagle. Thus amended, Koch's interpretation won general acceptance.

In 1913 Professor Manly presented a study of the poem with a thorough-going criticism of the Koch-Emerson theory.[5] He objected that the inconclusive ending of the poem did not refer to the marriage of Richard and Anne. Emerson attempted to meet this objection by pointing to a similar situation in Dunbar's *The Thistle and the Rose;* but inasmuch as the circumstances under which Dunbar's work was composed are unknown, this parallel cannot be considered a sufficient answer. Nor does it satisfactorily explain Chaucer's failure to make any reference to the nuptials of Richard and Anne to say that we can only "wonder that he did not go a step further."[6] The failure of the Richard-Anne interpretation at this vital point is so serious as to call into question the basis of the theory.

3

Manly observed, moreover, that the intended compliment of the poem is unexplained. To reply, as Emerson did, that it is unnecessary to be specific at this point is illogical,[7] for to consider the poem in the light of its inconclusive ending as the celebration of the royal couple's marriage must be regarded as a rather untactful (if not positively uncomplimentary) reference to the actual relationship between Richard and Anne.

Nor does the historical evidence supporting the Koch-Emerson theory justify or explain the "formel's" delay in accepting the proposal offered her. The suggestion that "maidenly coyness" deterred her[8] is hardly in keeping with Anne's character. The situation is not saved by proposing, conversely, that Chaucer departed from facts to avoid a tactless reference to this very lack of diffidence in Anne's behavior when accepting Richard's offer.[9] Obviously neither of these explanations can be regarded as a satisfactory answer.[10]

Manly's objections remain, in spite of the repeated endeavors by supporters of the Koch-Emerson theory to refute his conclusions.[11] If the poem refers to Richard and Anne, the allusion to seeing Venus in the north-north-west must fix its date in 1382, as Manly has shown by astronomical evidence.[12] It would then become the celebration of their nuptials, but this interpretation is manifestly unsuited as an explanation of the suitor-scene in the *Parlement of Foules*.

The recognition of the justice of Manly's objections to the Koch-Emerson theory makes necessary a reconsideration of the historical occasion for the poem. One must not overlook, in this survey of critical opinion, the argument by Farnham that the *Parlement of Foules* was constructed on the basis of a widespread formula story of "The Contending Lovers."[13] But fully conceding the force of these considerations, one is not compelled to abandon the likelihood that there were historical circumstances which provided the occasion of the poem.

In Miss Rickert's recent article on the *Parlement of Foules*,[14] although she makes a spirited attack on the older theories, she tacitly discards Manly's view that the poem has no historical foundation by bringing forward a new occasion for the poem. The way is still open, it would appear, for an interpretation of the poem which will avoid the objections raised by the Koch-Emerson theory and at the same time provide a plausible historical occasion for its composition.

In making such an attempt, the most promising clew would appear to be the fact, long ago noted in the *Life-Records*, that Chaucer was himself associated on some three commissions which discussed marriage alliances as well as treaties. Accordingly, in the present paper I shall inquire into the history of these negotiations. But before taking up the record of the commissions in which Chaucer was personally concerned, it will be necessary to review briefly the series of diplomatic negotiations which began in 1370, in the effort to restore peace between France and England.

By 1370 the political situation had vastly changed from the victorious period of the Black Prince's successes at Crécy and Poitiers. France was beginning to reassert its power on the battlefield, and England became anxious over the eventual outcome of the war. Edward III hoped, however, to be able to negotiate a satisfactory settlement with Charles V.

In desiring to effect an agreeable treaty with France, Edward relied upon the assistance of Pope Gregory, whose energy was frequently devoted to the task of bringing the nations peace. Edward must have felt somewhat reassured when in 1372 the Pope was able to arrange a conference with the French. But Charles was not at this time ready to come to an agreement, and the conference ended in failure. In 1373 Edward accordingly attempted to continue the struggle, "avec plus d'énergie, que de succès."[15] The Pope, however, continued to insist that the two kings treat for peace; and his legates accompanied the English envoys in their journey to France. At Bordeaux, in 1374, representatives of the two nations met. The Duke of Lancaster, who represented the hopes of England, was there presented with excellent opportunities for arranging a satisfactory treaty; but because of his too ambitious claims the conference ended with a mere agreement to suspend hostilities for some two months. When he returned to England shortly afterward, his father and eldest brother, who had expected a favorable treaty, were quite disconcerted by the result of his campaign and the temporary agreement with France.[16]

The truce lasted not quite two months, and Edward was once more in an uncomfortable predicament. The victories of Du Guesclin and the illness of the Black Prince increased his anxiety. Nothing could be done except to arrange for another truce.

The friendly intervention of Gregory XI in 1375 was responsible for the series of truces and partial treaties which followed, one being concluded at Bourboug on February 11, 1375, and another more general treaty being later effected at Bruges. But when the Count of Flanders soon entered the negotiations in favor of Charles V, the previous agreements were practically nullified, as Edward was then presented with the difficulty of meeting both the demands of France and Flanders.[17]

The legates of the Holy See, whose efforts to effect a reconciliation between the two monarchs had been uniformly unsuccessful, attempted now to induce the powers of England, France, and Flanders to treat for peace. Edward accordingly dispatched the Duke of Lancaster to Calais, there to confer with Charles V's representatives. Lancaster, having been persuaded to less ambitious designs, promised to aid in "l'avancement du traité." The envoys of the respective nations met at Bruges, the Duke of Bourgogne and the Bishop of Amiens representing the French, and the Duke of Lancaster, the Count of Salisbury, and the Bishop of London being sent by the English. A treaty was drawn up and signed by the envoys on June 27, 1375, it being agreed that peace should continue until May 1, 1376. An interesting contemporary document contains Edward's full approval of this treaty.[18]

Toward the end of the year 1376, conferences held between the French and English prolonged the existing peace and proposed details to be ratified in a later treaty. As yet, however, the final decision had not been made.

As it was frequently the procedure of opposing sovereigns in similar situations to reach their final settlements through betrothals, it is not surprising to find Edward interested in promoting a marriage alliance with France. Although it is difficult to state exactly when such an alliance was first broached, it was certainly under consideration in 1376; for in that year, at Buenen and later at Bruges, the ambassadors reopened conferences to treat not only of peace but chiefly of the marriage of Marie, daughter of Charles V, and Richard, son of the Black Prince. The account by Froissart contains further details about the meeting at Bruges, and relates that the King of England, "aprés la fête Saint Michel," formally invested young Richard as his successor; and "en ce temps" dispatched Lord Cobham, the Bishop of Herford and the Dean of St. Pauls, London, to Bruges, where they conferred with the French for a considerable time on the subject of the aforementioned marriage.[19]

The marriage alliance, we see from the foregoing statements, was discussed as early as 1376. An allusion to these 1376 negotiations appears in one of the items of Charles V's instructions to his envoys in 1377, wherein the French King states that the marriage alliance is not to be considered as his proposal; but if, as he expects, the English mention it, he charges the envoys to listen to their proposals and afterward report these to him.[20] Charles V's expectation that the English would bring up the subject was, of course, based upon his knowledge of its discussion at the earlier meetings of 1376.

We may now inquire into Chaucer's activities during the latter part of 1376. It is well known that he was sent abroad on King Edward's secret affairs in the company of Sir John de Burley, Captain of Calais, on

December 23, 1376, although the record of this fact indicates neither their object nor proposed destination.[21] It is significant, however, that in 1378 Chaucer was associated with this same John de Burley in a mission to Lombardy, the subject of which was to treat of, among other matters, the proposed alliance of King Richard and Caterina, daughter of the Duke of Milan.[22] Is it not, then, a reasonable inference that in December, 1376, Chaucer and John de Burley were associated on a similar mission? The same conclusion, I believe, is to be drawn from a record dated May 10, 1377, which refers to Chaucer as *often* abroad on the King's service.[23] Another record, dated April 11, 1377, also speaks of him as completing *"divers voyages"* to France.[24] Inasmuch as at the time of these entries Chaucer had apparently made only one journey to France, namely from February 17 to March 25,[25] the journey made by the poet and Burley in 1376 would seem to be one of these included in the phrase "divers voyages."

At all events Chaucer, who was himself associated in 1377 with several of the commissioners represented in the several 1376 conferences, must have known that the marriage alliance was being considered late in 1376. There is little reason to believe that these affairs were not generally known by men at court; and Chaucer may have been more intimately acquainted with them. We may therefore conclude his interest in the alliance to date from 1376.

On February 12, 1377, as we know from the *Life Records,* letters of protection were granted to Chaucer who was about to go abroad on the King's services; and by February 17 of the same year he was in France.[26] Richard Stury also was sent to France on February 17 and returned on March 25, — dates of departure and return being the same as those of Chaucer: Stury, like Chaucer, was sent "in obsequio regis."[27] Neither is mentioned, however, in the first royal commission of February 20, 1377; and it would appear that they were sent on a confidential mission, which differed in some respects from that of the official deputation. At all events it would be reasonable to suppose that Stury and Chaucer were engaged on the same errand.

This supposition is confirmed by the direct testimony of Froissart, who also supplies detailed information as to the subject of their negotiation.

> Environ le quaremiel se fist une secrés treti(é)s entre ces François et ces Englès, et deurent li Englès leurs trettiés porter en Engleterre, et li François en France, cascuns devers son signeur le roy, et devoient retourner, ou aultre commis que li roy renvoirent, à Moustruel sus

mer; et sus cel estat furent les triewes ralongies jusques au premier
jour de may. Si en alèrent li Englès en Engleterre, et li François
(revinrent) en France, et raportèrent leurs trettiés, et recordèrent sus
quel estat il estoient parti l'un de l'autre. Si furent envoiiet à
Moustruel sus mer, dou costé des François, li sires de Couci, li sires de
Riviere, messires Nicolas Brake et Nicolas le Mercier, et dou costé des
Englès, messires Guichars d'angle, messires Richars Sturi et Joffrois
Cauchiés. Et parlementèrent cil signeur et ces parties grant temps sus
le mariage dou jone Richard, fil dou prince, et de ma damoiselle
Marie, fille dou Roy de France, et revinrent arrière en Engleterre, et
raportèrent leurs trettiés, et ossi le François en France, et furent les
triewes ralongies un mois.[28]

This statement by Froissart has been, however, the subject of some
controversy. Nicolas believed that this passage related to the negotiation of
January, 1378, in which Chaucer likewise figured as commissioner, and
accordingly that Froissart inserted the reference to the marriage proposals
out of its proper place. Skeat, on the other hand, rejected Nicolas'
interpretation and accepted Froissart's account as referring to the year
1377. Both commentators, however, failed to perceive that Froissart in his
complete account reports two negotiations for the hand of Marie.[29] The
commission of 1378, which is not recorded by the chronicler, was for the
hand of Marie's sister. The dates of the two meetings which Froissart
mentions are approximately from February 14 to April 1, and from May 1
to June 1, 1377. These dates coincide closely with those of the two official
deputations of February 20 and April 26; and the connection between
them is no longer doubted.[30]

Historians now accept Froissart's statement that an agreement
concerning the marriage alliance was made between the French and English
commissioners, and declare that a treaty was apparently signed on this
basis, the negotiators agreeing to meet each other May 1, as Froissart
stated, between Montreuil and Calais, to ratify it.[31] (In a later paragraph
the meeting in May, already referred to, is discussed.) As one authority
puts it, the commissioners had every reason to anticipate that this marriage
agreement would result in securing a permanent peace.[32]

Chaucer and his associates then returned to England to report this
agreeable news to their King, and await his official approval and advice as
to the final ratification of the treaty. They may have justifiably felt
satisfied with the success of their endeavors; for whereas previous
commissioners had been able to bring back only *news* of war (even the
Duke of Lancaster being unsuccessful in his early campaign and receiving
"a cold welcome from his indignant father")[33] they could now inform
their King of the most successful results that had been achieved since 1372.

No more likely or important occasion for poetic treatment could be found than the very affair we have been considering here. Chaucer, as we have seen, was interested in the marriage alliance as early as 1376, and his journeys to France in 1377 would serve to increase his interest in its later developments. As the agreement had been signed with the understanding that Richard and Marie were to marry shortly after its ratification in May, 1377, Chaucer might reasonably be said to have seen an opportune occasion to anticipate their nuptials by celebrating the alliance in poetic allegory.

This is the new suggestion which I offer to explain the occasion of the *Parlement of Foules;* but before proceeding to apply the theory it is necessary to discuss briefly the type of poem we are studying.

It was an established convention in the court poetry of the fourteenth century to employ bird and beast allegory, and under this veil to discuss contemporary events, political situations, love-matches, and related subjects.[34] The allegory which Chaucer used in his *Parlement of Foules* was a conventional device, and the allusion to actual historical figures would be apparent to contemporary readers.

The poem, as Manly has said, is of the "demande d'amours" type. The setting for the suitor-scene Chaucer took not from Alan de Lille's *De Planctu Naturae,* but from folk-tales dealing usually with only three suitors, a maiden and an arbiter or judge. This folk-tale Farnham has aptly designated "The Contending Lovers." Farnham recognized the possibility of the poem's having an historical basis but remarked that any historical interpretation must be considered in the light of this conventional tale.[35]

Although Chaucer must have had this type in mind when writing his poem, he did not follow the pattern slavishly; but, as in many other cases, altered details here and there. He here alters the more pedestrian scheme of the folk-tale so as to throw chief stress upon the first suitor. The question in the *Parlement of Foules* is clearly not why the "formel" accepts *one* of the rival suitors rather than another, but why she postpones her final decision in favor of the first tercel eagle.

The second eagle is somewhat individualized. He declares that he has served the "formel" longer in his degree. A similar situation is found in the historical negotiations which we are considering, for Richard was not without a rival. In 1377 Marie was still affianced to William of Bavaria, their betrothal having been formerly agreed upon by Charles V and Duke Albert of Bavaria in March, 1375.[36] William of Bavaria accordingly had served Marie two years longer than his rival Richard by 1377. This is exactly the situation in the *Parlement of Foules.*

Or atte leste I love her as wel as ye;
And lenger have served hir, in my degree. (PF. ll. 452–53.)

For the third "tercel eagle" however, I have not found a historical figure, though there may have been one. But we are not necessarily required to find him; for Chaucer was following "The Contending Lovers" type, in which we have a formula situation of three suitors and a maiden.[37] The presentation of the suit of a third lover, at all events, would obviously not have been uncomplimentary to Marie.[38]

In accordance with this proposal, the historical figures are young Richard, presumptive heir to the throne of England, who represents the first tercel eagle; William of Bavaria, the second eagle, who has served longer in his degree; and Marie, daughter of Charles V, who is distinguished as the "formel."

The poem alludes to the proposals for the marriage of Richard and Marie, and was intended as an anticipation of the union to be celebrated after the ratification of the treaty at the conference of May, 1377. The poem may have been begun in 1376, and could easily have been written in the interval of time between Chaucer's return to England in March and his second journey to France.

To proceed with the later stages of the historical negotiations, the commissioners returned to France; and the conference was reopened; but toward the end of May, when the treaty was in the process of being ratified, the young princess Marie suddenly died.[39] The negotiators were thus left in a quandary and their efforts to prolong the treaty on a different basis failed. These unexpected developments, together with the death of Edward III, on June 21, 1377, were the chief causes which led to the rupture not only of this conference but also of the Treaty of Bretigny.[40]

England, however, despite these reverses, continued the effort to effect a marriage alliance with France, thereby affording further evidence of the seriousness with which the earlier proposal had been urged. Early in 1378, another commission was sent to France, in which Chaucer was again represented.[41] This commission was empowered to treat of marriage between King Richard II and the daughter of the King of France, in this case the Princess Isabel.[42] It is significant to observe in this connection that all three of Charles V's surviving daughters became at different times the objects of marriage proposals from England.

The English ambassadors were in Flanders from January 26 to May 30, 1378, to treat of peace between the two kings and arrange the marriage. Edward de Berkely, in whose train Chaucer figured, shortly followed them thither.[43] Although the negotiations were scheduled to open January 26, the commissioners were unable to arrange a meeting because the Duke of Bourgogne, occupied in welcoming his uncle the Emperor Charles IV, declined to proceed with the treaty. All plans for persuading the French to continue the treaty were nullified by the death of Isabel, February 23, 1378.[44]

Although negotiations with the French concerning treaties and marriage alliances continued up until as late as 1380, historians have recognized only one of these conferences as productive of actual results after the settlements of the Treaty of Bretigny. This conference of 1377 was the one in which Chaucer figures, and which we have previously discussed. When in 1378 the English sent their negotiators to Lombardy on a similar mission,[45] it was only after trying repeatedly to perfect an alliance with France. The papal schism, however, had the effect of severing Anglo-French relations, and the later negotiations for the hand of Anne of Bohemia were directly instigated by the intervention of Pope Urban, who wished to keep England from associating itself with the supporters of his rival, Pope Clement of Avignon; and it was not until 1398 that Richard chose a French princess for his queen.

In the foregoing discussion, in which it has been necessary to compress important historical details, it should be clear that in this stage of the Hundred Years' War England was primarily interested in forming a marriage alliance between its royal house and that of France; but that the 1377 conference was the most successful of the several negotiations for this purpose.

We may now turn to questions which might arise as to the appropriateness of this new proposal for the occasion of Chaucer's poem. We may well agree that no more likely and distinguished occasion for its writing can be found. The outlook which Chaucer had during his stay in England, after returning from France, March 25, 1377, could not have been other than bright; and when we take into consideration that there are reasons to believe he was interested in the marriage alliance even earlier, the assumption that he wrote a courtly poem to celebrate these negotiations seems altogether reasonable.

The indefinite conclusion of the poem, a battleground of much controversy, is thus presented as a true reflection of the historical facts. The marriage alliance was not to be formally concluded until after the final ratification of the treaty in May, 1377, as Chaucer certainly knew. The indefinite conclusion to the poem indicates there is no reference to a completed project; and Chaucer presented this situation as true to the historical case as the conventions he was employing would permit. In "The Contending Lovers," to follow the similarity, the maiden is given freedom of choice, a circumstance which is justified both artistically and historically in Chaucer's poem. The poet's unerring artistic sense impels him to grant the maiden that freedom of choice which is characteristic of the manner of courtly love and the best social custom; and it is justified historically by the fact that the English were first to suggest the subject of the marriage alliance, the French being granted freedom to discuss the question at their will before giving a final decision.

The formel's request for a year in which to form her decision was recognized by Manly as a conventional device of Valentine-day poetry. This postponement of her final decision until the next meeting of the bird-parliament on the following Valentine day may be considered as an allusion to the fact that Chaucer was aware that another conference was yet to be held before the celebration of Richard and Marie's nuptials. The formel merely postpones her final decision until the next meeting of the birds, at which, in accordance with the historical theory her favorable answer would be expected. In asking for a respite the formel declares:

> I wol noght serven Venus ne Cupyde
> For sothe *as yet,* by no manere wey.

When one considers that Marie was born February 26, 1371 and was accordingly in her seventh year[46] when these negotiations were proceeding, the phrase "as yet" will be seen to be peculiarly appropriate to her case. Anne of Bohemia, on the other hand, was born in 1360 and was therefore twenty-one years of age at the time of her espousal to Richard. Obviously there would have been less reason for such a statement on her part.

Dame Nature's advice to the "formel," her intuitional direction to the "formel" eagle to accept the royal "tercel's" proposal may be considered in its actual historical light as embodying an expression of Chaucer's own wish. From one point of view it is a symbol of the desire of all England that the unnatural, tedious, and wasting war might be forever ended by the union of the royal couple. Dame Nature, as a part of the convention, it is hardly necessary to add, is the eternal symbol of union between the sexes; and her advice is directed in allegory as in reality toward the consummation of this particular end.

The appropriateness of the St. Valentine day device as an allusion to the historical scene must not be overlooked. Chaucer was first associated with the conference in February; and according to Froissart the time of this negotiation was almost exactly February 14, 1377.[47] The conference, we know, continued throughout the spring, and the conventional background of springtime in the poem finds close approximation to the historical facts of the case.

As for Chaucer's synopsis of Cicero's *Somnium Sciponis,*[48] which Moore rightly regarded as a veiled expression of desire for some form of reward or remuneration,[49] no more satisfactory interpretation may be desired than the fact that Chaucer's plea was answered when King Edward, on April 11, 1377, presented him with a gift of £20. This gift to Chaucer, it is to be noted, was made in addition to other payments for his travelling expenses, and the poet's veiled petition was probably a partial occasion for its being given. This appears more likely when we consider that no one of Chaucer's associates seems to have been rewarded in like manner.

This theory receives striking confirmation from the accepted interpretation of the astronomical allusion in l. 117 of the poem. Early computations included 1377 as one of the dates for the occurrence described in the following line: "As surely as I saw thee in the north-north-west." Recent investigations confirm, in general, the results of earlier researches.[50] Between 1372 and 1384, however, there were only three years when Venus could appear as an evening star to an observer in England in the direction of the northwest,[51] these years being 1374, 1377, and 1382. In 1377 Venus could be seen in this position only near the beginning of the evening star period. In March, 1377, Venus would be in the correct position but much fainter than in April or May, either of which two months is acceptable for the present interpretation of the poem.[52]

In accordance with this new theory the *Parlement of Foules* refers to the proposed marriage alliance of Richard and Marie. The poem was therefore written in 1377.

NOTES

[1] On the subject of earlier interpretations see Hammond, *Bibliography,* p. 389 f.
[2] Koch, *Engl. Stud.* I, 288; trans. in *Ch. Soc. Essays,* pp. 406 ff. Cf *Engl. Stud.* XV, 399 ff.
[3] Emerson, *Mod. Phil.* VIII, 45–62.
[4] Professor Samuel Moore gave further reasons for rejecting William of Bavaria. (*Mod. Lang. Notes* XXVI, 8–12.)
[5] Manly, *Festschrift für Lorenz Morsbach. (Stud. zur Englischen Phil.,* L, 278 ff.)

[6] Emerson, *Jour. Eng. & Gmc. Phil.*, XIII, 578 ff.

[7] Emerson, *JEGP*, XIII, 570. Cf. J. N. Douglas, *MLN* XLIII, 380.

[8] Emerson, *JEGP*, XIII, 573 f.   [9] Lange, *Anglia*, XL, 395 f.

[10] Koch also shifts repeatedly in his date for the poem. In 1877 he favored 1381; in 1880 he preferred 1380, emending *west north west;* 1381 was again chosen in 1903; and finally in 1921 he selected April, 1382. (Cf. Brusendorff, *The Chaucer Tradition*, p. 389, n.3.)

[11] Douglas suggests that to tell of the outcome of Richard and Anne's marriage would be contrary to the rules of the type. (*MLN*, XLIII, 380.) But it would not be contrary to the facts of the case. The Richard-Anne relation fails to explain the "formel's" decision, and we should desire a more reasonable interpretation.

[12] Manly, *Festchrift für Morsbach*, p. 287 f.

[13] Farnham, *PMLA*, XXXII, 492–518.

[14] Rickert, *Mod. Phil.*, XVIII, 1 ff. As the new theory put forward by Miss Rickert has not met acceptance, it is not discussed here.

[15] In this historical discussion I have relied for the most part on the following authorities. Paulin-Paris, *Les Grands Chroniques de France*, VI, 346 ff; Petitot, *Les Mémoires de Du Guesclin*, 156 ff; E. Cosneau, *Les Grands Traités de la Guerre de Cent Ans*, 69 ff.

[16] G. Clement-Simon, *La Rupture du Traité de Bretigny*, 90 ff. Cf. Barante, *Hist. des Ducs. de Bourg.*, pp. 144–45.

[17] H. Moranville, *Chron. Reg. Franc.*, p. 360 ff.

[18] L. Gilliodts-Van Severen, *Le Cotton Manuscrit Galba B.I.* "Annexes, 3 F.," p. 518 ff. (*Acad. Roy. des Sciences de Belg.*, 1896.)

[19] Gilliodts-Van Severen, *op. cit.*, p. 488 f. Cf. Buchon, *Les Chron. de J. Froissart*, VI, 101. Cf. *Bibl. de l'Ecole des Chartes*, LX, 177–214, "Les Ambassades Anglaises," Nos. cclxxviii, ccclxxxvi, ccclxxv.

[20] Skeat erroneously suggested the marriage proposal originated with the French. (*Intro., Minor Poems*, xxix f.) Cf. Delachenal, *Chron. des regnes de Jean II et de Charles V*, III, 207.

[21] *Life Records*, No. 98.

[22] *Life-Records*, No. 143. But cf. Hulbert, *Chaucer's Official Life*, p. 48. Cf. Rymer, *Foedera*, Rec. ed., IV, 60.

[23] *Cal. of Pat. Rolls* 1374–1377, 51 Edw III Memb. 14 p. 462. Cf. S. Moore, *Mod. Phil.*, XVIII, 497 f.

[24] *Life-Records*, No. 103.   [25] *Life-Records*, No. 101.

[26] *Life-Records*, Nos. 99–101.

[27] *Bibl. de l'Ecole des Chartes*, LX, 196, No. ccxci. In this place Mirot and Deprez have published other excerpts from the *Exchequer Accounts*. Several of these have been copied for me from the originals now in the British Museum. Space hardly permits my introducing this material in the present article, but I may say that it corroborates the evidence presented here.

[28] S. Luce, *Chroniques de Froissart*, VIII, 225–226.

[29] Cf. Skeat, *Intro. Minor Poems*, p. xxix ff. Cf. W. Longman, *Edward III and His Times*, pp. 271–272.

[30] Rymer, *Foedera*, III, pt. II, 1073, and 1076. Cf. W. Longman, *op. cit.*, pp. 271–272. Cf. J. A. Buchon, *Les Chron. de Froissart*, VI, 101 ff. and notes.

[31] Simonde de Sismondi, *Hist. des Français*, XI, 224 f.

[32] Clement-Simon, *La Rupture du Traité de Bretigny*, pp. 91–92.

[33] Clement-Simon, *ibid.*, p. 89.

[34] Deschamps' *La Fiction de l'Aigle* is a satire of the court of Charles VI. (Cf. Rickert, *MP,* XVIII, 4.) Machault used bird-allegory in the celebration of a love match in *Le Dit de L'Alerion.* (Cf. Hoepffner's ed., *Soc. de Anc. Textes Franc.,* II, 239 ff.) Froissart's *Le Temple d'Amour* is accorded a similar historical interpretation. (Cf. Brusendorff, *The Chaucer Tradition,* 158–62.

[35] Cf. Farnham, *PMLA,*XXXII, 492–518; also *PMLA,* XXXV, 247–323; as well as *Univ. of Wis. Studies in Lang. and Lit.,* No. 2, 341 ff.

[36] Devillers, *Cartulaire des Comtes de Hainaut,* VI, pt. I, 393 ff. Cf. L. Lalanne, *Œuvres de Brantome,* VIII, 53.

[37] Farnham, *PMLA,* XXXII, 492–518.

[38] Douglas has remarked that the suit of the latter two lovers was flattering whether they existed as historical figures or not. (*MLN,* LXIII, 382.)

[39] A letter of Charles V, dated May 30, 1377, indicates that Marie died toward the end of this month. Cf. Delisle, *Mandements et Actes Divers de Charles V,* No. 1377, p. 708 (*Coll. de Doc. inedits* 1874). The statement of Froissart (Buchon, *Les Chron. de Froissart,* VI, 105) that the death of Marie occurred shortly *after* that of Edward III is therefore erroneous.

[40] *Les Mémoires de Du Guesclin,* p. 157. Cf. Clement-Simon, *La Rupture du Traité de Bretigny,* p. 92.

[41] Cf. Skeat's account of Rymer's evidence. (*Intro., Minor Poems* xxvii ff.)

[42] Ward suggested Marie. (*Chaucer,* p. 77, in English Men of Letters.) Coulton distinguishes the daughter as "one of poor little Marie's sisters." Marie, however, died before 1378; Catherine was not born until February 4, 1378, and Isabel remained the only daughter to receive a proposal in January, 1378. Cf. Anselme, *Hist. généalogique,* I, 110D. Delisle, *Le Cab. des MSS. de la Bibl. Nat.,* III, 337 ff. Delachenal, *Chron. des reg. de Jean II et de Charles* V, II, pp. 258, 272, 282, and notes.

[43] Skeat, *Intro., Minor Poems,* xxvii ff. But cf. Kervyn de Lettenhove, *Œuvres de Froissart,* IX, 582, and notes.

[44] Barante, *Hist. des Ducs. de Bourg.,* I, 70. Secousse, *Hist. de Charles le Mauvais,* I, pt. II, 177. Anquetil, *Hist. de France,* v, 48. S. Luce, *Chron. des Quatre Premiers Valois,* p. 265 f. (*Soc. de l'Hist. de Fr.* 1862.)

[45] There is no means of knowing what occurred at this meeting, but it obviously ended without producing results. Cf. Rymer, *Foedera,* Rec. ed., IV, 60.

[46] According to the "Table des Nativités" as quoted by L. Delisle (*Recherches sur la Librairie de Charles V,* I, 268–9), the year of Marie's birth is 1370, but this is Old Style reckoning. In this paper I have given the dates uniformly according to the New Style. Anselme (*Hist. généalogigue,* I, 110 D) erroneously gives the date as "le 27 février."

[47] Froissart: "Environ le quareme." In 1377 the first day in Lent was February 11. Buchon dates Froissart's account as the middle of February.

[48] Cf. *Parlement of Foules,* ll. 109–102, 167–168.

[49] S. Moore, *MLN,* XXVI, 11.

[50] Koch, *Chronology,* p. 37 f. Cf. Manly, *Festschrift für Morsbach,* p. 289 f.

[51] Venus is never visible technically NNW. The planet appears in several other years as evening star between 1372 and 1384, but would not be visible in the correct position in the northern hemisphere.

[52] These computations were undertaken for me by Dr. Harlow Shapley and Miss Jennie Mohr, of the Harvard College Observatory. I wish to acknowledge also a like indebtedness to Professor P. H. Graham, of New York University.

Those skilled in mathematics may find it convenient to consult *"Astronomical Papers,"* VI, pt. III, pp. 271–382. (Washington. 1895).

Reprinted from *PMLA,* XLVI (1931), 1007-1019.

2

NEW DOCUMENTARY EVIDENCE CONCERNING CHAUCER'S MISSION TO LOMBARDY

It has long been known through the Foreign Accounts, published in *Life-Records,* that Geoffrey Chaucer departed from London May 28, 1378, on his second Italian journey, being "sent in the retinue" of Sir Edward de Berkeley to the parts of Lombardy "as well to the Lord of Milan (Bernabo Visconti), as to (Sir) John Hawkwood, for certain affairs touching the expedition of the King's war."[1] The French Roll, in the same publication,[2] adds that Chaucer received on May 10, 1378, the letters of protection for his voyage abroad. More recently, Professor Manly has discovered a document which states that Chaucer, in making preparation for his absence from England, appointed Richard Baret on May 16 as his lieutenant at the office of Controller.[3] Still another entry in *Life-Records*, also from the French Roll, relates that on May 21, a few days later, Chaucer gave power of attorney to John Gower and Richard Forester, "during his absence."[4]

In addition to these published records, there is a writ in the Exchequer Accounts,[5] not hitherto printed, which supplies further information as to the number of persons in the commission and the route they followed in travelling to Italy. Although Chaucer's name is not mentioned, this document deals with his Italian journey. The dates are the same (i.e., May 28 to September 19); furthermore, we know that Chaucer was sent in Sir Edward de Berkeley's retinue. The present document relates also to Sir Edward's trip to Flanders in 1379, but for our purpose only the portions referring to the Lombardy mission need to be quoted.

> Particule compotis Edwardi de Berkele militis euntis in quodam viagio per ipsum facto in seruicio Regis versus partes Lumbardie anno primo Regis Ricardi Necnon particule compoti eiusdem Edwardi de quodam alio viagio per ipsum facto in dicto seruicio Regis versus villam de Bruges in Flandria anno secundo. Berkele.
> Membrane 1. xxviii die Maii anno primo Pasche.
> Edwardo de Berkele militi misso in Nuncio Regis versus partes Lumbardie tam ad dominum de Melan quam ad Johannem de Hawkwode pro certis negociis expedicionem guerre tangentibus in denariis per ipsum receptis de Willelmo Walworth & Johanne Phelipot Receptoribus denariorum pro guerris Regis super vadis suis cxxxiii li. vi s.

. . . .

Membrane 4.

Particule compoti Edwardi de Berkeleye militis de Receptis vadiis & custibus suis eundo in quodam viagio per ipsum facto in seruicio Regis versus partes Lumbardie anno primo Regis.

Idem onerat se de cxxxiii li. vi s. viii d. receptis de Thesaurario & Camerario ad Receptam Scaccarii per manus Willelmi de Walworth & Johannis Philipote receptorum denariorum pro guerra Regis super vadiis suis missos versus dictas partes Lumbardie tam ad dominum de Melan quam ad Johannem de Hawkewode pro certis negociis expedicionem guerre tangentibus xxviii^0 die Maii predicto anno primo termino Pasche. Summa Recepte cxxxiii li. vi s. viii d.

Idem computat in vadiis suis euntis in seruicio Regis in viagio predicto ad partes predictas Lumbardie ex ordinacione predicti consilii ipsius Regis ob causam supradictam videlicet a xxviii die Maii predicto anno primo quo die recessit de Civitate Londonie super dicto viagio versus partes supradictas usque xix^m diem Septembris proxime sequentem quo die reuenit ad eandem civitatem scilicet per cxv dies utroque die computato capientis per diem xx s. cxv li.

Summa vadiorum cxv li.

Et in passagio & repassagio maris ipsius Edwardi X hominum & X equorum suorum cum hernesiis suis videlicet inter Douerram in Anglia & Caleysiam Francie infra idem tempus x marce.

Summa totalis vadiorum
& expensarum cxxi li. xiii s. iiii d.
Et debet xi li. xiii s.
iiii d.

This newly printed record, it is to be observed, makes it certain that the expedition travelled *via* Calais and thence overland to Italy. This appears from the fact that the commissioners were provided with horses for the trip from Calais. The document printed in *Life-Records*, on the other hand, mentions merely "le passage du dit Geffrey, et son repassage de la meer."[6] Chaucerians have not known whether the entire journey was made by sea or not. The present record also states that ten persons, and not Chaucer alone, figured in Sir Edward's company. This circumstance, while it tends to increase the official dignity of the embassy, corrects the impression, received from *Life-Records*, that the undertaking was entrusted to Sir Edward and Chaucer alone. Who these other persons were, I have been unable to discover. Further search in the Public Record Office might bring to light records of some of the other commissioners.

The same entry in *Life-Records* (from the Issue Roll) which recounts that on May 28 Chaucer and Sir Edward were advanced wages for their Italian mission relates also that at this same date the army of John of Gaunt was paid some £4000 for service in the wars.[7] It is possible, therefore, that the nine other members of the embassy sent to Lombardy were recruited from the personnel of Gaunt's forces. At least, it is interesting to observe that Sir Guischard d'Angle is mentioned in the document as a knight in John of Gaunt's service.

In this connection, we may inquire into Chaucer's diplomatic activities earlier in the year 1378. On March 6, 1381, according to the Issue Roll,[8] Chaucer received payment for a mission abroad on which he had been sent in the time of Edward III and also for going to France in the reign of Richard II to negotiate a marriage between the English King and a French Princess (i.e., Isabel). On the basis of this record, Skeat plausibly suggested that Chaucer had been connected in some capacity with the royal deputation appointed January 16, 1378 (as in the French Roll),[9] to treat in regard to this marriage, although Chaucer is not named as one of these ambassadors. The commissioners named are Sir Guischard d'Angle, Dr. Walter Skirlawe, and Sir Hugh Segrave. We find definite record in the Exchequer Accounts of the departure of the first two on this mission January 26, and they remained until May 30, 1378;[10] but Segrave is not mentioned, nor is there any record that he actually went on this mission. In fact, we have positive evidence that Segrave was in England on March 15, since on this date he appeared as a witness to the "grant of the reversion of the manor of Padeworth co. Berkes" to William of Wykeham, bishop of Winchester.[11] This leads one to suspect that Segrave after being appointed was replaced or for some reason was unable to join the expedition.[12] If this be the case, the substitution of Chaucer for Segrave would explain why Chaucer's name is not included in the royal commission of 1378 and why he later received payments for making the journey. Added interest is attached to this explanation, for Sir Guischard d'Angle, as I have recently shown,[13] was one of Chaucer's friends and was earlier associated with the poet in several other diplomatic errands.

NOTES

[1] R.E.G. Kirk, *Life-Records of Chaucer,* Part IV (*Chaucer Society Publications,* 1900), No. 122, pp. 218–19. See also "Forewords," p. xxix.
[2] No. 118, pp. 215–16.
[3] J. M. Manly, "Chaucer as Controller," *Modern Philology,* XXV (1928), p. 123.
[4] No. 120, p. 216.

5 Q. R. E. 101/318/7. This writ is in a white leather pouch in the Public Record Office. Miss Edith Scroggs, of London, kindly sent me a transcript of the writ.

The following account of this document has been printed by Mirot and Déprez, "Les Ambassades Anglaises," *Bibl. de L'École des Chartes,* LX (1899), No. CDIX, p. 199. "1378, 28 mai-19 septembre.—Compte de Édouard de Berkeleye, chevalier, envoyé en Lombardie « tam ad dominum de Milan quam ad Johannem de Hawkwode, pro certis negociis expedicionem guerre tangentibus ». Depart: Londres. Dépenses, 121 livres 14 sous 4 deniers. Gages 20 sous par jour."

6 "Additions," No. 8, pp. 338–39. Professor Tatlock states *(JEGPh,* XII [1913] 121) that the duration of Chaucer's second visit to Italy would have allowed him time to become familiar not only with the language but also with the country, "which many travelers find stimulates an interest in its literature." Added interest accrues to this suggestion in the light of our new evidence that Chaucer's journey from Calais to Lombardy was made overland.

7 No. 121, pp. 216–17.

8 *Life-Records,* No. 143, pp. 230–31. Payments were not made to Chaucer for the balances of his expenses in the journey to Lombardy until November 28, 1380. See *Life-Records,* No. 140, pp. 228–29.

9 See Rymer's *Foedera* (Record Edition), IV, 28.

10 Sir Guischard was employed from January 26 to May 30, Dr. Skirlawe from January 22 to May 31. See Mirot and Déprez, "Les Ambassades Anglaises," *Bibl. de L'École des Chartes,* LX (1899), Nos. CDIV and CDVI, pp. 198–99.

11 *Calendar of Close Rolls* (1377–1381, Ric. II), p. 126.

12 A strikingly analogous case of another man who was appointed but who, due to some last minute arrangement, did not go occurred in February, 1377, when Sir Thomas Percy was replaced by Sir Richard Stury. Chaucer's fellow-associate in the mission to Flanders and France was, then, Sir Richard Stury. See the following footnote.

13 *Three Chaucer Studies,* II (Oxford University Press, 1932), pp. 28 ff., 34–39.

Reprinted from *MLN,* XLVIII (1933), 507–511.

3

SIR PETER AND THE "ENVOY TO BUKTON"

Professor E.P. Kuhl[1] has recently presented some very convincing evidence that Chaucer's "Envoy to Bukton" was addressed to Sir Peter Bukton. As this interpretation has won almost complete acceptance,[2] it is clear that new information coming to light about Sir Peter may be considered not without significance—especially when this information seems to give further support to the view generally held.

Accordingly, I wish to call attention to the newly discovered "Kirkstall Chronicle, 1355-1400," which has been edited by M.V. Clarke and N. Denholm-Young.[3] This chronicle is important to us for three reasons. First of all, it is a contemporary record of events: the editors state that it "seems to have been composed in part shortly before and in part shortly after the deposition of Richard II."[4] In the second place, it is certain that this is the same Bukton whom Kuhl has discussed, since the Peter Bukton of the chronical was a Yorkshireman. Finally, the chronicler was himself associated with Yorkshire and there is thus good reason to accept the statement of the editors that "When the *compilator* describes Peter de Bucton as *probus homo* he was appraising a man of whom he must have had personal knowledge."[5]

In this chronicle we find that Sir Peter appears in connection with the events which immediately followed the deposition of Richard II and specifically in the provisions made by the supporters of Henry regarding the custody of the king.

> Soluto igitur parliamento et recedentibus dominis singulis ad sua, dominus Ricardus quondam rex Anglie dictus ductus est sub custodia domini Peter de Bucton ad castellum de Knaresburgh et deinde post unum mensum elapsum quo transferebatur inter communes et wlgares penitus ignoratur. Set etiam a quibusdam quad sit mortuus suspiciatur. Hic rex Ricardus renovavit et sumptuosissime perornavit magnam aulam Westmonasterii intus et extra subtus et supra anno Christ 1398.[6]

The important information afforded by this passage is that when Richard was confined at Knaresborough castle,[7] he was committed to the hands of Peter Bukton. Obviously, it should be significant to have still further details about this hitherto unknown[8] part which Bukton played in aiding Henry to advance his claims to the English throne. We should be particularly interested in knowing just how he performed the office of custodian of the royal prisoner. But, unfortunately, the chronicle does not provide us with these data; and we are obliged to content ourselves with the conclusion drawn by the editors:

> No doubt the writer had knowledge of what befell Richard when Bucton brought him to the county, but beyond the fact that a month was spent at Knaresborough before the removal to Pontefract he is too cautious to write more than "in quadam turre castelli [i.e., Pontefract] . . . solitare inclusi et qualiter ibidem mortui deus novit...[9]

We can not clearly determine whether Peter actually had a hand in the death of the king,[10] for the evidence does not appear strong enough to warrant a safe inference. But, in any case, the fact that Bukton accepted the custody of Richard gives convincing testimony that he was a partisan of Henry of Bolingbroke. This fact appears to have a significant bearing upon the question whether Sir Peter is to be identified with Chaucer's "maister Bukton," inasmuch as we now appear to have positive proof that he was devoted to the cause of the Lancasters.

In the case of such a notable example of political allegiance,[11] we should naturally expect certain royal favors to follow. And this, apparently, was the case; for the new king in 1399 granted to Peter Bukton for life the office of Steward of the lordship of that district which Chaucer describes in the *Summoner's Tale* as "merrshy Holdernesse."[12] About a year later, in May 1400, Henry expressed further appreciation by appointing him constable of Knaresborough castle.[13] These two appointments, we suspect, may have had a special significance; for, as we have just observed, the scene of Richard's imprisonment was near "merrshy Holdernesse"; and according to this chronicle, it was in Knaresborough castle that Sir Peter held Richard under guard before he was removed to Pontefract, where the unfortunate king met his end.

Chaucer's affiliations with Henry of Bolingbroke have long been recognized, because it is to this new king that the "Complaint to his Empty Purse" is addressed. The evidence presented here would seem to suggest that Chaucer may have sponsored the cause of Henry a little earlier than we have supposed.

NOTES

[1] *PMLA*, XXXVIII (1923), 115ff.

[2] In reviewing the case for Peter and Robert Bukton, Professor Robinson (in explanatory notes, p. 980) states that "the approaching marriage of one of them—probably of Peter—was doubtless the occasion of the *Envoy*."

[3] *Bulletin of the John Rylands Library*, XV (1931), 100–37.

[4] *Ibid.*, p. 103.

[5] *Ibid.*, p. 106.

[6] *Ibid.*, p. 134.

[7] According to the *Dict. Natl. Biog.* (XLVIII, 155), Richard was "confined successively at Henry's castles of Pickering, Knaresborough and Pontefract." The chronicle, moreover, is thus corroborated by this statement.

[8] So far as I know. Compare the accounts given by other chronicles. H. Wallon, *Richard II*, II (1864), 367–74.

[9] *Op. cit.*, p. 109; the text of the Latin quotation is on p. 135.

[10] Professor J. L. Hotson (*PMLA*, XXXIX [1924], 762 ff.) has called attention to the significant strictures on homicide in the *Nun's Priest's Tale* and sees in them an allusion to the assassination of Gloucester in September, 1397. But allusions to homicide might equally well have suggested to the reader the murder of Richard II, and the question is whether Chaucer as a Lancastrian would wish to risk a reference at that date which could be thus misinterpreted. This would seem to imply that his lines on "homycides" were written before this period.

[11] The editors we have been referring to point out (p. 134, n. 3) that Peter Bukton "in the *Chronicle of Melsa*" (III, 298–299) ... is called 'nostre et compatrioto, qui maxime familiaris dicti domini regis [i.e., Henry of Bolingbroke] extitit praedilectus ... dicto domino regi in applicatione apud Ravenzer Spurne ob exilio ...' "

[12] As noted by Kuhl, *op. cit.*, p. 122.

[13] *Ibid.*, p. 120.

Reprinted from *PQ*, XIV (1935), 368–370.

4

THE TWO PETROS IN THE "MONKES TALE"

The chronology of the "Monkes Tale" has been often discussed,[1] and there are widely divergent views regarding its composition. Skeat and others have suggested that it was an independent work of Chaucer's, written early as the beginning of a collection after the form of the *De Casibus*.[2] More recently, Professor Robinson has suggested that Chaucer's model was the *Roman de la Rose*, which provided not only the source for some of the stories but the connecting link of the Fortune Moral as well. If Chaucer did use the *Roman de la Rose*, the "Monkes Tale" may very well have been written early, at a time, indeed, when the French influence on Chaucer was still strong. For this reason and others, Professors Robinson and Kittredge regard the poem as an early composition.[3] On the other hand, Professor Tatlock[4] has argued that the poem was written expressly for the *Canterbury Tales* and at a time when this project was already well under way.

A complicating factor in dating the "Monkes Tale" is, however, the series of tragedies, conveniently termed the Modern Instances. These tragedies deal with mediaeval figures, whereas the other stories are drawn from biblical and ancient literature. Accordingly, the Modern Instances are considered by some scholars as having been later appended to the "Monkes Tale." In any case, the account of Bernabo could not have been written earlier than 1386, since he was slain in December, 1385.[5] It is notable, however, that this tragedy differs in two ways from the others. First, it lacks formal reference to the moral concerning Fortune, which is the central theme of the poem as a whole. In the second place, as Professor Kittredge[6] has pointed out, the stanza bears every indication of being an afterthought, because Chaucer makes the query ($B^2 3591$): "Why sholde I nat thyn infortune acounte...?"

In considering the date of the Modern Instances, however, we reckon with the fact that in the manuscripts these occupy two alternate positions in the "Monkes Tale." Twenty-seven manuscripts[7] introduce them immediately following Zenobia, while fifteen[8] place them at the end, following the tragedy of Croesus. Regard for chronology would, of course, favor the latter arrangement; but the Monk in his prefatory lines ($B^2 3178$)

expressly announces that he does not propose a chronological arrangement for his tragedies: "But tellen hem som bifore and some bihynde." In the light of this statement, Chaucer's authority would rather favor the middle position. Furthermore, as Professor Robinson remarks, the fact that the account of Croesus closes with a definition of tragedy makes it "a natural ending of the whole tale."[9]

Before drawing any conclusion in regard to this, it is necessary to note also an important difference in the text of the "Nun's Priest's Prologue" which immediately follows the "Monkes Tale"; and which seems to have some connection with the order of the tragedies. Whereas in twenty-nine manuscripts[10] the "Nun's Priest's Prologue" appears in its full form, in no less than ten manuscripts[11] a passage of twenty lines ($B^2 3961-80$) is lacking. It appears significant, now, that when one reads the prologue with these lines omitted, the connection is in no wise impaired. Moreover, with these lines omitted the Knight continues as the speaker down to line $B^2 3995$, while the Host comes into the dialogue with the line, "Thanne spak oure Hoost with rude speche and boold ($B^2 3998$)." It would be indeed singular if a scribe could have omitted this passage and left the text so perfectly connected. What is most significant of all, however, is that in this passage we have the statement, "He spak how Fortune covered with a clowde ($B^2 3972$)," which refers back to the last line of Croesus: "And covere hire [Fortune's] brighte face with a clowde ($B^2 3956$)." This proves conclusively that when this passage was written the Modern Instances did not stand at the end.

It might possibly be argued that the Modern Instances stood at the end in the first draft and that Chaucer then put them back into the middle at the time when these lines were inserted to bind the two together. This would supply a possible reason for transferring them from one position to the other. But there are only four manuscripts which have the Modern Instances at the end followed by the shorter prologue, and these manuscripts are of doubtful or unreliable authenticity.[12] Had such a change been made, we would expect a considerable group of such manuscripts.

The more probable explanation of the Modern Instances at the end is scribal tinkering. The reason for placing them at the end is obviously chronological, since these tragedies ranged from 1288 to 1385.

We appear to have, therefore, three stages in the arrangement of this material: (1) with the Modern Instances in the middle followed by the shorter form of the "Nun's Priest's Prologue;"[13] (2) with the Modern Instances in the middle followed by the expanded form of the prologue[14]

—a stage also no doubt attributable to Chaucer; and (3) probably as the result of scribal arrangement, with the Modern Instances at the end and the expanded prologue following.[15] Chaucer may himself have made this shift, but whoever is responsible failed to notice that it resulted in breaking the connection between "Fortune" and the "clowde" and the last line of the tragedy of Croesus. The recognition of these three stages has important implications for the general problem of manuscript relations in view of the fact that this third stage is the arrangement followed, not only by Ellesmere, but by every one of the nine manuscripts which Manly designates as Class I.[16]

From the foregoing discussion, one point stands out: the Modern Instances were written, not as a postscript, but as a part of the fabric of the "Monkes Tale." The chronology of this group of stories carries with it, therefore, the date of the tale as a whole.

In this connection, the stories of the two Pedros ("Petros," Chaucer calls them) are clearly significant; for both Peter of Spain and Pierre of Cyprus died in 1369.[17] This fact gives the year 1369 as the earliest possible date for the composition of the poem. Contemporary references of this kind would be, moreover, less likely to have point long after the events themselves. It is reasonable to suppose, therefore, that Chaucer wrote these tragedies while the facts were still fresh in his mind. Indeed, the two Pedros are so definitely of contemporary interest that we may inquire if the materials concerning them upon which Chaucer drew do not give indications of an early date.

It is notable that in introducing Don Pedro Chaucer addresses him as "O noble, O worthy Petro, glorie of Spayne."[18] But in thus presenting him in a favorable light, Chaucer appears unique; for all other contemporary writers,[19] even Ayala of Spain,[20] anathematized Don Pedro. Skeat has endeavored to explain this unusual view of Chaucer's on the ground that "our Black Prince fought on the side of Pedro against Enrique at the battle of Najera...."[21] But Skeat fails to note that this very battle marked the beginning of a rupture between the English Prince and Don Pedro over Pedro's treatment of prisoners,[22] which developed later into a quarrel between the two over the payment for the Prince's military services.[23] Indeed, when the Black Prince returned to his home in Aquitaine, he was still unreconciled with Pedro.[24] Accordingly, if Chaucer had intended to represent the attitude of the Prince, his account of Pedro would have been unfavorable. As another possible explanation for Chaucer's sympathetic view of Pedro, Skeat[25] reminds us that Pedro's daughter, Constance of Castille, was later married to John of Gaunt.

Besides this, there is the still more important question as to how Chaucer received the same story as Ayala, whose statement of the tragedy appears to be the true one. This fact was first observed by Dr. Furnivall, who stated that "Chaucer is a witness for the truth of the Spanish chronicler Ayala as against the French writers Froissart, Cuvelier, and others...."[26] We know quite a lot about Chaucer's relations to Froissart,[27] with whom we would normally expect him to be in agreement. It is therefore surprising that Chaucer, who elsewhere turns to Froissart,[28] felt obliged in this story to refer to an outside source. There are serious chronological difficulties, moreover, in supposing Chaucer read Ayala.[29] How, then, are we to explain that both writers agreed in the details?

The solution which I wish to offer is that the story was transmitted to Chaucer through his friend, Sir Guichard d'Angle.[30] It is to be observed that Ayala, according to his own statement,[31] had been captured by the English at the battle of Nagara in 1367[32] and kept in prison until after the death of Pedro in March, 1369.[33] Sir Guichard, we may add, was also a participant in the Spanish campaign.[34] Indeed, at the battle of Nagara, he and his two sons, according to the Herald of Chandos,[35] distinguished themselves for their valor. Moreover, as Sir Guichard was the Black Prince's Marshal of Aquitaine,[36] it is clear that he would have heard the details. We can readily understand, therefore, how Sir Guichard and Ayala would receive the same report of Pedro's death.

Indeed, this interpretation seems more reasonable than any that has been suggested. An alternative view, however, is that the story came to Chaucer through Philippa.[37] But this suggestion, likely as it might seem, leaves unexplained a second important point in Chaucer's account. For in the second stanza Chaucer emphasizes the treachery of Don Enrico and the baseness of du Guesclin and de Mauny, who aided him in the conspiracy to murder Pedro.[38] Why should Chaucer in an additional stanza have been obliged to censure them? Now, if we suppose the poem to represent Sir Guichard's attitude, Chaucer's strong feeling against the conspirators is easily explained. In the first place, Chaucer's disapprobation of Enrico would be accounted for, because Sir Guichard, who had been captured by Enrico's forces in 1372, was compelled for two years to suffer the tortures of a Spanish dungeon.[39] While they were imprisoned, the English captives were on one occasion led before certain visiting Frenchmen, whom they prayed: "Noble gent de France et doulce, se nous fussions voz prissoniers, vous ne feussons pas si villainement menez ni si durement traictiez comme nous sommes."[40] One month after the capture (i.e, in July) of Sir Guichard and his colleagues, Owen de Galles saw the prisoners (i.e., those who were not killed or wounded after their capture) "liés ou enchainés deux par deux, comme des chiens tenus en laisse."[41] In the light of these facts, it is clear that Sir Guichard would have represented Enrico unfavorably.

Furthermore, with regard to du Guesclin and de Mauny, Sir Guichard had equally good reasons for being embittered. For while he was imprisoned in Spain, these French generals persecuted Sir Guichard's wife. Dame d'Angle was, in fact, forced to surrender her castle of Achart. She received a safe-conduct, however, and fled to the Duke of Berry.[42] She made a personal appeal to the Duke, which we have in her own words:

> Monsigneur, vous savés que je sui une seule femme à point de fait ne de deffense, et veve de vif mari, s'il plaist à Dieu; car mon signeur, messires Guichars [Guichard d'Angle], gist prisonniers en Espagne, ens es dangiers dou roy Henri. Si vous vorroie priïer en humilité que vous me feissiés celle grasce que, tant que mon signeur sera prisonniers en Espagne, mi chastiel et ma terre, mon corps et (mes biens, avec) mes gens, puissent demorer en pais, par mi tant que nous ne ferons point de guerre, et on ne nous en fera point ossi.[43]

The plea touched the Duke's heart and he swore to place his aid in her behalf. Strong inducements, in the form of bribes and assurances to exchange prisoners, were accordingly made to Bertrand du Guesclin and Oliver de Mauny. At length, the Frenchmen were persuaded, not only to desist their persecutions of Dame d'Angle, but to effect in 1374–75 the release of Sir Guichard and his colleagues.[44] Therefore, in explaining Chaucer's denunciation of the French generals, the evidence points again to Sir Guichard as the informant.

According to the present interpretation, we have, therefore, not only an explanation of Chaucer's agreement with Ayala, but the source of his view of the conspirators who brought about the murder of Don Pedro. Nor is it necessary to call in (as have Skeat and others) either Gaunt or Constance, or much less Philippa, to account for Chaucer's taking the part of Don Pedro because the Duke married Constance of Castille. Obviously Phillippa would have been informed only by hearsay. And there would be little reason for Chaucer to turn to Gaunt, especially when he could have received the story more directly from his friend. For Sir Guichard had been throughout a promoter of this particular marriage. It was he, indeed, who suggested to John of Gaunt the policy of a marriage with Constance of Castille. Moreover, he was entrusted with and succeeded in the negotiations for the marriage alliance. Afterwards, he was present when the nuptials of the Duke and Constance were solemnized at Rochefort. This clearly reveals, of course, the regard in which the Duke held him. It is to be observed, moreover, that he attended Lancaster and his bride to England, where the company was received by King Edward, "who, at the feast of St. George...1372, admitted our heroic knight into the order of the Garter...."[45] As another evidence of the high regard in which Sir Guichard was held by the English court, we may note that when King Edward III was asked in 1374 whether he preferred to rescue from the Spaniards Otto de Granson or Sir Guichard, he replied "que il s'enclinot plus à monseigneur Guichart d'Angle que à monsigneur Othe."[46] On the basis of these facts, it will be seen that Sir Guichard had every reason to represent the murder of the father of the new Duchess of Lancaster in sympathetic terms.

It remains to be noted that Sir Guichard was personally associated with Don Pedro. According to Froissart,[47] it was Sir Guichard who was appointed in 1367 to escort Pedro to Burgos, capital of Old Castille. It is also significant that Sir Guichard witnessed in 1366 the famous conference between Don Pedro and the Black Prince, where he would have heard of Pedro's having been forced to flee for his life to Bordeaux.[48] It is to this very flight, in fact, that Chaucer appears to refer in the statement "Out of thy land thy brother made thee flee."[49] Accordingly, the tragedy of Don Pedro of Spain is best explained and most fully accounted for on the basis that Sir Guichard d'Angle was Chaucer's informant.

It is easier to understand Chaucer's interest in the second "Petro" than the first, for Pierre of Cyprus had visited England on at least two occasions. In fact, it is possible that Chaucer in 1358, while retaining a position in the household of Prince Lionel, may have seen Pierre's father, Hughes IV, who attended the banquet given by King Edward.[50] Chaucer, however, had the opportunity of hearing from his friends of Pierre's own activities. For the King of Cyprus was present at the tournament which celebrated the birth of the first son of the Black Prince, where he would have seen or met Guichard d'Angle, who participated in this festival.[51] Sir Guichard was also present in 1364 at the meeting of Edward III and Pierre at Bordeaux.[52] The year before (i.e., 1363) the King of Cyprus had made a celebrated visit to England in the interest of organizing a new crusade,[53] and prominent among the company sent to welcome the King was Chaucer's friend, Sir Richard Stury. It was Sir Richard, indeed, who assisted in conducting Pierre through the city of London and to his lodging.[54]

In taking up the tragedy of Pierre of Cyprus, however, the case is considerably simplified, because for this story we have a literary source. The striking fact about Chaucer's stanza on Pierre is that it is historically inaccurate in every detail.[55] It is significant to note, accordingly, that Machaut's *La Prise d'Alexandrie,* a poetic biography of Pierre, is also unhistorical.[56] Moreover, Machaut's poem, though longer than Chaucer's, contains the same mistakes in statement.

Both Machaut and Chaucer, for example, praise the valor of the King and describe him as little short of a martyr. In the record of history, however, Pierre appears in a different light. His injustice in dealing with his subjects aroused public indignation,[57] and the cruelty of his treatment of Marie de Giblet led directly to his assassination.[58] Chaucer, on the other hand, says Pierre was slain "for no thing but for thy chivalrye" by "thyn owene liges."[59] Similarly, Machaut, after extolling the virtues of his royal patron, states: "Mais ceus qui ces ouevres faisoient //Tous ces hommes liges estoient."[60] Machaut then goes on with the emphatic statement: "Et en ce despit//Lors en son lit fus [?sus] li coury..."[61] with which we may compare Chaucer's description: "They in thy bedde han slayn thee."[62] But here history again reports that when Pierre was murdered he was not only standing "upright and outside his bed" but "in the adjoining apartment."[63] Finally, both poets agree in giving an inaccurate statement as to the time of the assassination. Pierre was in reality murdered at midnight, January 17–18, 1369.[64] But Machaut gives the time as "a l'aube crevant"[65] and Chaucer as "by the morwe"[66] (i.e., early in the morning).

In the light of these facts, we may readily accept *La Prise d'Alexandrie* as the source of the tragedy of Peter of Cyprus. It was perfectly natural, of course, for Chaucer to turn to Machaut. For Chaucer, as has long been known, made use of several poems of Machaut in writing certain passages of the *Book of the Duchess.*[67] Professor Lowes[68] has shown, moveover, that Machaut's *Dit de la Marguerite* influenced Chaucer in the "Prologue" of the *Legend of Good Women.* This new evidence provides, therefore, an addition to the influence of Machaut on Chaucer.

In this connection, we may return to the chronology of the "Monkes Tale." We have already noted 1369, the year both "Petros" died, as the earliest date for the poem. Moreover, *La Prise d'Alexandrie* is dated by French chronologists as about 1369.[69] The indebtedness of the stanzas on Ugolino to Dante[70] suggests as a convenient date 1374, the period of Chaucer's introduction to Italian literature. Also, since Sir Guichard was Chaucer's informant, the story of Pedro of Spain would antedate 1380, the year Sir Guichard died.[71] This chronology, furthermore, favors the suggestion made by Professor Kittredge: "...we may feel pretty safe in inferring for the tribute to Constance's father, Pedro of Castile, the date of 1373 or 1374. The royal title which John of Gaunt had recently assumed, by right of his wife, made such a tribute especially timely."[72] In the light of this evidence, the composition of the "Monkes Tale" would appear to belong to the neighborhood of 1374 or 1375; that is, at a date shortly following Chaucer's first Italian journey.

NOTES

[1] I wish to express my gratitude to Professors Cirot, of the University of Bordeaux, and Oliver Towles, of New York University, for answering my inquiries regarding Spanish and French literature, respectively. My chief indebtedness is to Professor Carleton Brown, whose assistance throughout this investigation and especially in the study of manuscripts has been most generous. Other detailed obligations are expressed in their proper places.

[2] Skeat, *Complete Works...* (Oxford, 1900), III, 427 f.

[3] Robinson, *Complete Works...* (Camb. ed., 1933), p. 14; and Kittredge, *Date of Chaucer's Troilus...* (Chaucer Soc., 1909), p. 46.

[4] *The Dev. and Chron...* (Chaucer Soc., 1907), pp. 164-172.

[5] See Skeat,*Oxf. Chaucer,* v, 240-241; and Robinson's note, p. 856.

[6] *Op. cit.,* pp. 44-46.

[7] B_o^1, B_w, C_p, E_n^2, F_i, G_1, H_a^2, H_a^4, H_t, I_i, L_a, L_o, L_d^1, M_c, M_g, M_m, N_1, P_h^2, P_h^3, P_w, R_a^1, R_y^1, R_y^2, S_1^1, S_1^2, T_c^1, and T_o^2.

[8] Ad^1, Ad^3, C_h, C_n, D_d, D_s, E_1, E_n^1, E_n^3, G_g, H_g, L_n, M_a, P_y, and Se.—These data were garnered from Sir William McCormick's *The Manuscripts of Chaucer's Canterbury Tales* (Oxford, 1933).

[9] P. 853. Professor Robinson also suggests another means for accounting for the arrangement; but since this explanation "involves a complicated series of assumptions...," he prefers "to regard the order with Croesus at the end as the one intended by Chaucer at the outset."

[10] Ad^1, Ad^3, B_o^1, B_w, C_h, C_n, D_d, D_s, E_1, E_n^2, E_n^3, F_i, H_a^2, H_a^4, H_t, L_a, L_c, L_d^1, L_n, M_g, M_m, N_1, P_h^2, P_h^3, R_y^1, R_y^2, S_1^1, and T_o.

[11] C_p, H_g, I_i, M_a, M_c, P_w, P_y, Se, S_1^2, and T_c^1.

[12] The manuscripts in question are H_g, M_a, P_y, and Se. Manly in the introduction to his edition lists M_a as Class I, P_y as II_a, and both H_g and S_e as Very Irregular.

[13] For these six MSS, I give in parentheses Manly's classification, as follows: C_p (II_b), $I_i(II_c)$, $M_c(II_a)$, $P_w(II_c)$, $S_1^2(II_b)$, and $T_c^1(II_a)$.

[14] Nineteen MSS are represented in this second stage: $B_o^1(II_a)$, $B_w(II_c)$, $E_n^2(II_c)$, $F_i(II_c)$, $Ha^2(II_c)$, $Ha^3(II_c$ for this portion), $H_t(II_c)$, $L_a(II_b)$, $L_c(II_a)$, L_d^1 (Very Irregular), $M_g(II_c)$, $M_m(II_c)$, $N_l(II_a)$, $Ph^4(II_a$ for this portion), $Ph^3(II_c)$, $R_y^1(II_c)$, $R_y^2(II_c)$, $Sl^1(II_c)$, and T_o (Very Irregular).—Two MSS, G_1 and R_a, lack the prologue, but have the Modern Instances in the middle.

[15] There are ten MSS to show the third stage: $Ad^1(I)$, $Ad^3(I)$, C_h (Very Irregular), $C_n(I)$, $D_d(I)$, $D_s(I)$, $E_l(I)$, $E_n^1(I)$, $E_n^3(I)$, $L_n(II_a)$.

[16] E_l, G_g, D_d, D_s, E_n^1, Ad^1, E_n^3, M_a, C_n.—Brusendorff, *The Chaucer Tradition* (Oxford, 1925), p. 492, n. 2, would have these tragedies at the end as Chaucer's own arrangement.—In discussing the "Nun's Priest's Prologue," Miss Hammond (*Bibliography*, pp. 242-243; cf. Robinson's note, p.857) suggests that the first intention was to have the Host make the interruption (in 1.2767 four MSS, Ad^1, E_n^3, T_c^2, Cx^1, read *Hoste* and *Knyght*); but that Chaucer then perceived he would have the Host, not only interrupting before the *Melibee*, but here as well; and that, to avoid this repetition, he substituted the Knight, and added the Croesus passage. But the interruption in the case of the Host could hardly be considered monotonous repetition, since his speech occurs at the end of *Sir Thopas*, which is separated from the "Nun's Priest's Prologue" by both the tale of *Melibee* and that of the *Monk*. Moreover, the statement (B 3998): "Thanne spak oure Hoost with rude speche and boold" would seem to introduce him for the first time as speaker in this short prologue.

[17] Pedro of Spain was murdered in 1369, shortly after the battle of Monteil (Alfred Morel-Fatio, "La Donation du Duché de Molina à Bertrand du Guesclin," *Bibl. de l'Ecole des Chartes*, LX (1899), 147). Pierre of Cyprus was assassinated in January, 1369. See N. Jorga, *Philippe de Mézières* (Paris, 1896), p.390,n.5.

[18] $B^2$3565.

[19] Notably, Froissart, *Chroniques de J. Froissart*, ed. S. Luce, (Paris, 1888), VIII, and Deschamps, *OEuvres Compl. de E. Deschamps*, ed. Marquis de Saint-Hilaire-(Paris, 1880), II, 327-328; III, 1882, 100. For this second reference, I am indebted to the kindness of Professor Carleton Brown.

Edward Storer, *Peter the Cruel* (New York, 1911), p.204, states that Villani and Machaut also severely criticized Don Pedro. Alfred Morel-Fatio, *Bibl. de l'Ecole des Chartes*, LX (1899) 151, n. 2, has pointed out that in the *Cancionero de Baena* (no. 304) Pedro is made the subject of a vicious rhyme. And George Ticknor, *History of Spanish Literature* (New York, 1849), p. 182, n. 15, found several Spanish ballards denouncing Don Pedro for his murder of Leonor de Guzman as well as for his cruelty in imprisoning Queen Blanche.

All these literary detractions were of course not without a basis in fact. For example, in the case of Queen Blanche, just referred to, the actions of the King appear thoroughly reprehensible; because at the time Pedro married Blanche he was still enamored of Maria di Padilla. Indeed, H. D. Sedgwick, *The Black Prince* (Indianapolis, 1932), p. 205, states that for this reason Pedro deserted Blanche on the Wednesday following their marriage on Monday. The case, however, appears even worse, for Blanche wrote the Pope she was deserted on the very day of the wedding

(George Daumet's *Innocent VI et Blanche de Bourbon*, rev. by L. Mirot, *Bibl. de L'Ecole des Chartes*, LX, [1899], 654-655). The French, as a matter of fact, suspected Pedro of having murdered Blanche in 1361 (Prosper Merimée, *Hist. de don Pedre, roi de Castille* [Paris, 1865], p. 265; E. Lavisse, *Hist. de France*, pt. I, ed. A. Coville [1902], p. 178; H.D. Sedgwick, *Spain, A Short History* [Boston, 1925], p. 99). It was just such unprincipled actions as these that won for Don Pedro the name of the Cruel (T. Morgan, *Jour. Engl. Arch. Ass.*, XLVII [1891], 177).

On the fairness of the contemporary accounts, see Ticknor, *op. cit.*, p. 183, n. 17; J.B. Sitges, *Las Mujeres del rey don Pedro I de Castille* (1910), p. 53; and C. E. Chapman, *History of Spain* (New York, 1918), p. 116.

[20] The first volume of Ayala's *Crónicas de los Reyes de Castilla* (Madrid, 1779) is concerned with the reign of Don Pedro. For an explanation of Ayala's attitude, see Ticknor (I, 176-178) and R. Altamira y Crevea, *Historia de España y de la Civilización Española* (Barcelona, 1929), pp. 10-12.

[21] Skeat, *Oxford Chaucer*, VI, 238.

[22] Edward Storer, *Peter the Cruel* (New York, 1911), pp. 309-310.

[23] *Ibid.* Cf. J. Leslie Hotson, "The Tale of *Melibeus* and John of Gaunt," *SP*, XVIII (1921), 432.

[24] J. R. Moreton Macdonald, *A History of France* (London, 1915), I, 254-255.–At an earlier period, the relations between England and Spain were more friendly. In fact, Edward III, who had once congratulated Alphonso XI on the conquest of Algezir (J. M. Manly, *Trans. and Proc. of the Am. Phil. Ass.*, XXXVIII [1907], 92), planned a marriage between Princess Joan and Don Pedro; but the project was abruptly terminated in 1348 when the English princess succumbed to the Black Death on the way to Castille (T.F. Tout, *Political History of England* [New York, 1905], III, 370). Later, in 1362, Edward III, in order to insure his hold on Aquitaine, concluded with Pedro an alliance offensive and defensive (J. R. Green, *Hist. of the English People*, p. 100).

[25] *Oxford Chaucer*, v, 238.

[26] J.J. Furnivall, "A Chaucer Difficulty Cleared Up," *Notes & Queries*, 4 S, VIII (1871), 449–450.

[27] See G. L. Kittredge, "Chaucer and Froissart," *Engl. Stud.*, XXVI (1899), 321-336.

[28] R.D. French, *A Chaucer Handbook* (New York, 1929), pp. 88, 129.

[29] The first edition of Ayala's chronicle was printed at Seville, October 8, 1495 (A. Paulau y Dulcet, *Manual del Librero Hispano-Americano* [Barcelona, 1926], IV, 261). For this reference, I have to thank Professor E. Herman Hespelt, of New York University.

[30] On Chaucer's relation to d'Angle, see the present writer's account in *Three Chaucer Studies* (Oxford, 1932), pt. II, pp. 28ff., 34-39; and in *MLN*, XLVIII (1933), 510-511.

[31] In the *Rimado de Palacio*. My attention was first drawn to this in reading George Ticknor's *Hist. of Sp. Lit.*, I, 100. See also D. Marcelino Menéndez y Pelayo, *Antología de Poetas Líricos Castellanos* (Madrid, 1918), IV, p. xii.

The poem may be consulted in the following editions: A. F. Kuersteiner's *Poesia del canciller Pero Lopez de Ayala,* Hispanic Society of America, New York, 1920; *Biblioteca hispanica,* vols. 21-22, also *Biblioteca de autores españoles* (Madrid, 1864), LVII, 425-476. For these references, I am indebted to the kindness of Mr. J. R. Spell, of the Univ. of Texas.

One manuscript states Ayala was imprisoned in "Inglaterra," but the others report Gascony as the place. See Wm. J. Entwistle's essay in *Spain, A Companion to Spanish Studies,* ed. E. Allison Peers, New York, 1929), p. 112.

[32] Ayala was released when Enrico succeeded to the throne after the death of Pedro I. See Ticknor, *Hist. of Sp. Lit.,* I, 178-179.

[33] The date of March 23 for the murder of Don Pedro as given by Skeat, Robinson, and others appears to be inexact. R. Amador de los Rios ("Los Restos Mortales del Rey don Pedro de Castilla," *Revista de Archivos, Bibliotecas y Museos,* X [1904], 113) states in this connection that: "Aunque ni acuerdo en que la fecha existe, parece, la alevosa muerte de don Pedro acaecio en la noche del 22 al 23 de Marzo de 1369..."

[34] Sir Guichard, in fact, is reported by the Herald (*The Life of the Black Prince,* ed. M K. Pope and E. C. Lodge [Oxford, 1910]) as one of "les hautez officers du trenoble Prince":

> Primerment Iohn Chaundos fust Conestable
> Et apres sa mort le Captawe sanz fable
> Mons Guichard dangle fut Mareschall (4197-99).
> Et la fut bons Guicharz d'Angle,
> Qui ne se tenoit pas en l'angle;
> Avoecques li ot ses deux filz
> Et d'autres chevaliers de pris,
> Qui bien fesoient lour devoir (3239-43).

[35]

[36] The title of Marshal of Aquitaine was given to Sir Guichard as reward for his loyalty and fidelity to the English cause. R. Delachenal, *Histoire de Charles V* (Paris, 1928), IV, 21.

[37] F. N. Robinson, *The Complete Works of Geoffrey Chaucer* (Cambridge edition, 1933), pp. 855-856.

[38] Chaucer (in $B^2$3573-80) alludes to du Guesclin by referring to the heraldric emblems on his coat of mail; to de Mauny by punning on his name in the phrase "wikked nest" (OF. *mau ni;* i.e., MnF. *mal nid).* Brusendorff (*The Chaucer Tradition* [Oxford, 1925], p. 489) has suggested that Chaucer drew upon a ballade on du Guesclin attributed to Deschamps in writing his description of Bertrand's coat of arms.

[39] *Chroniques de J. Froissart,* ed. S. Luce (Paris, 1888), VIII, pp. 38-42, 295-299. Ayala mentions (*Crónicas de los Reyes de Castilla,* II, 12 ff.) Guichard d'Angle by name as one of the prisoners captured at Rochelle.

[40] *Chronique des Quatre Premiers Valois,* ed. S. Luce (Paris, 1862), p. 235.

[41] R. Delachenal, *Histoire de Charles V* (Paris, 1928), IV, 416.

[42] The substance of the foregoing paragraph is drawn from G. F. Beltz, *Memorials of the Order of the Garter* (London, 1841), pp. 184-186.

43 *Chroniques de J. Froissart,* ed. S. Luce (Paris, 1888), VIII, 116.

44 Du Guesclin and his nephew Oliver de Mauny, it appears, had received from Enrico certain lands in Spain as reward for their services. The estate of Soria in Castille du Guesclin surrendered for the Earl of Pembroke; Mauny, his estate of Agreda for Sir Guichard and other Englishmen captured at Rochelle. Beltz (pp. 186-187) explains another phase of the transaction as follows: "It happened that a rich French knight, the sire de Roye, a prisoner in England, had an only daughter whom Oliver de Mauni desired to espouse." But Beltz appears incorrect in representing Oliver as the suitor, for it is established by other evidence that the knight was Alain de Mauny (*Chron. de J. Froissart,* ed. Luce, VIII, xcviii, note 4).–Beltz gives 1374 as the date of the prisoners' release; the time was in the early months of 1375 (Paul Guérin, *Archives Historiques du Poitou,* XIX [1888], 173, n. 2).

45 The facts made use of in the foregoing paragraph are drawn from G.F. Beltz, *Memorials of the Order of the Garter* (London, 1841), pp. 184-186.

46 *Chroniques de J. Froissart,* ed. Luce, VIII, 166.

47 The French chronicler (VII, 50) recounts the story as follows: "Tantost apriès messe et boire, li rois dan Pietres monta à cheval, et li contes Sanses ses frères et li mestres de Caletrave et tout cil qui si homme estoient devenu, et li doi mareschal messires Guiçars d'Angle et messire Estievenes de Cousentonne et bien cinq cens hommes d'armes, et se partirent, de l'ost et dou prince et chevaucierent viers Burghes."

48 Beltz, *op. cit.,* pp. 184-186.   Don Pedro had repaired to Bordeaux to enlist the services of the Black Prince. He came, however, with promises rather than with gold. But despite this, and the hesitancy among the Gascons in the Prince's council, Don Pedro prevailed upon the Black Prince to undertake the campaign. At length, in February, 1367, the English Prince, whose coffers were now replenished with gold from Navarre and whose forces had been augmented by divisions under John of Gaunt, crossed the Pyrenees. T. Morgan, *Jour. British Arch. Ass.,* XLVII (1891), 178-182; A. E. Prince, *English Hist. Rev.,* XLVI (1931), 353-371; and Walter of Peterborough's poem, "Prince Edward's Expedition into Spain ... " *Political Poems and Songs* (Rolls Series, 1859), I, 97-122.

49 $B^2 3568$

50 R. Morris, *Chaucer: Prologue, Knightes Tale,* &c. (Clarendon Press Series, 1903), p. vii, note C.

51 N. Jorga, *Philippe de Mézières* (Paris, 1896), p. 184.

52 Beltz, *Mem. of the Order of the Garter,* p. 184.

53 J. L. Lowes, *PMLA,* XIX (1904), 594, notes 4-6.

54 N. Jorga, *op. cit.* p. 179. Sir Richard's colleague was Gautier de Mauny, whose name is not to be confused with that of the French family. Gautier's last name is variously spelled; he is referred to in a royal letter as "nostre cher et foial Wauter de Manny" (B. Wilkinson, *Eng. Hist. Rev.,* XLII [1927], 250).

55 This was first noted, so far as I know, by Professor Lowes: "Chaucer's statement of the case in the *Monk's Tale* is curiously at variance with what seem to be the facts" (*PMLA,* XIX [1904], 597 f:, note 2).

[56] My attention was first called to this in reading L. de Mas-Latrie's "Guillaume de Machaut et *La Prise d' Alexandrie," Bibl. de l'École des Chartes,* XXXVII (1876), 445-463. Machaut received the story from Gautiers de Conflans, a knight of Champagne: "Vesci sa parole & son dit,//Si comme Gautiers le me dit" (*La Prise d'Alexandrie* [ed. Mas-Latrie, Geneva, 1877], vv. 8285-86).

[57] In one instance, without the sanction of high court, Pierre assumed the right to pass judgment against a knight; and in another he exerted private authority in condemning a poor vassal to prison and exile. See L. de Mas-Latrie,*Bibl. de l'École des Chartes,* XXXVII (1876), 445-465.

[58] Machaut mentions in *La Prise d'Alexandrie* (ed. Mas-Latrie, pp. 268-269) Jacques d'Ibelin, Sire d'Arsur, Jean de Gaurelles, and Henry de Giblet as the murderers. The name of Pierre de Mimars is added in *Chronographia Regum Francorum* (ed. R. Moranville Paris, 1893), II, 304.–Henry de Giblet, Marie's father, seems to have been drawn into the conspiracy as a result of King Pierre's animosity toward his family; the dissension arose over the following ridiculous matter: "Le 8 janvier 1369, Henry de Giblet chassait avec deux beaux levriers turcomans qu'il avait donnés à son fils Jacques, quand le jeune comte de Tripoli, fils du roi Pierre, voyant passer ces chiens en lut envie et les fit demander au fils du vicomte, qui les lui refusa en accompagnant son refus de paroles blessantes pour le prince et la famille royale. Le roi, informé de cet événement, fit demander les chiens à Henry de Giblet, qui, prenant le parti de son fils, ne voulut pas les lui remettre. Le roi fit prendre les levriers, et il en résulta un incident à la suite duquel le roi enlevait à Henry de Giblet la charge de vicomte de Nicrosie et l'envoyait à Baphe, pendant qu'il faisait mettre auz fers Jacques de Giblet, son fils, et l'obligeat à travailler aux fossés de la tour Marguerite. Marie de Giblet, fille d'Henry et soeur de Jacques, alors veuve de Jean de Verny, fut obligée de se réfugier au monastère de Notre-Dame de Tortose, pour echapper au roi qui voulait le remarier à un tailleur, serf de Raymond de Rabin, nommé Caras; sans égard pour l'asile, le roi l'en fit arracher et mettre à la torture." See E. Rey, "Les seigneurs de Giblet," *Revue de L'Orient Latin,* III (1895), 420. In attempting to force Marie, a lady of the nobility, to marry a serf, Pierre was obviously opposing the feudal code. Compare the story by Saxo Grammaticus (*The Danish History* . . . , trans. Oliver Elton [1905], II, 374-380) of Helga's (Ingeld's sister) attachment to a low-born goldsmith and of the wrathful vengeance of Starcad.

[59] B²3584-85.

[60] VV.8756-57.

[61] The meaning of the passage is clear from the following longer quotation concerning the assassination of Pierre:

Devant son lit sont arresté	Faus garson, traitre, parjur.
De mal faire tuit apresté.	Qui vous fait entrer en ma chambre?"
Li sires d'Absur la courrine,	Et li respondi sans attendre:
Qui de soie estoit riche & fine,	"Je ne sui mauvais ne traites,
Tira, pour le roy mieux veoir,	Mais tel estes vous, com vous dites;
Et pour son cop mieux asseoir.	Dont vous morrez, sans nul respit,
Et si tost comli roys le vit,	De mes mains." Et en ce despit
De son lit gisant li dist:	Lors en son lit fus [?sus] li coury
"Estes vous la, sires d'Absur,	Et ij. cos ou iij. le fery. . . vv. 8686-703.

[62] B²3586.

[63] As translated from L. de Mas-Latrie, *Bibl. de l'École des Chartes*, XXXVII (1876), 461-462.

[64] N.Jorga, *op. cit.*, p.390, n. 5.

[65] V.8636.

[66] B²3586.

[67] Kittredge, *PMLA*, XX (1905), 1-24.

[68] *PMLA*, XIX (1904), 593 ff.

[69] L. de Mas-Latrie, editor of *La Prise d'Alexandrie* (Geneva, 1877), p. viii; and V. Chichmaref, *G. de Machaut, Poésies Lyriques* (Paris, 1909), I, p. lxvii.

[70] Skeat, *Oxford Chaucer*, VI, 241. Tatlock (*Dev. and Chron. of Chaucer's Works*, pp. 164-165 and notes) points out that Chaucer "quotes Dante also in the account of Nero; and [that] the Italian influence is also plain in the form of the names which he gives to Zenobia's sons."

[71] *Three Chaucer Studies* (Oxford, 1932), pt. II, p. 36.

[72] *The Date of Chaucer's Troilus and Other Chaucer Matters* (Chaucer Society, 1909), p. 46.

Reprinted from *PMLA*, L (1935), 69−80.

5

THE HISTORICAL BACKGROUND OF THE
PARLEMENT OF FOULES

An eminent scholar,[1] in reviewing recently my study, " The *Parlement of Foules* in its Relation to Contemporary Events,"[2] undertakes to demolish my argument that Chaucer's poem had for its occasion a proposed marriage between Richard of England and Marie of France by questioning the date of Marie's death. He assembles evidence to show that the death of the princess occurred prior to the conferences reported by Froissart for her marriage with Richard. If he is right in his opinion that Marie died in December, 1376, or January, 1377, then there is nothing further to be said regarding the marriage negotiations in the spring of 1377.

But let us see what evidence he brings forward in support of his opinion. In the first place, he presents a document,[3] dated January 26, 1378, reciting an order of January in the preceding year, laying out a budget for clothing for the royal family for 1377. In this document we have a warrant of 2,000 francs of gold for payments of a group in the royal household mentioned by name:"...nostre très chiere compaigne la royne, Charles, nostre ainsné filz, et aussi Loys et Ysabeau de France, nos enfanz, et aussi Charles de Lebret, compaignon de nostre dit ainsné filz, et aussi Henri de Bar, nostre nepveu, . . ." The fact that Marie is not named among the other royal children Professor Manly construes as evidence that in January, 1377, she was no longer living.

Since this document recites an order twelve months before, the omission of her name from the document of January, 1378, might conceivably have been due to the occurrence of her death during the year which had elapsed since the original order was issued.

Professor Manly, however, regards such an explanation as impossible in view of a second piece of evidence. This is an order (No. 1311) for gloves, dated January 9, 1377, in which again all the royal children except Marie are mentioned. If the omission of her name in this document supports Professor Manly's inference, this document would carry the date of her death back into the preceding December, because the expenditures for which payment was then made were incurred on December 8 and Christmas Eve.[4] On the other hand, Marie's name does occur, as Professor Manly himself notes, in an order (No. 1306) dated January 5, 1377, though this *mandement,* like the other, had to do with robes for the preceding Christmas season.[5] In other words, of these two documents which record payments for the same occasion, Christmas Eve, 1376, one mentions Marie whereas the other does not. This in itself should make one cautious about basing any conclusion on the omission of Marie's name in one of them.

Indeed, pursuing exactly the same line of argument, Professor Manly might have carried Marie's death back to a much earlier date. For there is another *mandement* (No. 1193) dated January 4, 1376, for clothing, which is similar in every respect to the one which he quoted. In this *mandement* Marie's name does not appear, although mention is made of ". . . nostre très chier et ainsné filz Charles, . . . nostre nepveu Charles de Lebret, . . . Ysabel, nostre fille, . . . Loys nostre filz, . . . nostre nepveu Loys de Lebret, . . . filz du conte d'Armignac, . . . " But this is not all. For it is to be observed that this document of January 4, 1376, recites an order for "le premier jour de l'an derrenierement passé . . ."; namely, March 25, 1375. Accordingly, applying Professor Manly's own reasoning we should now be forced to conclude, not that Marie died as early as December, 1376, but that she was already deceased March 25, 1375. Such a conclusion, however, would conflict flatly with established historical facts. We have two documents[6] later than this date which mention her as living. In the first of these, her father, Charles V, under date of June, 1375, "s'engage à remplir les conditions du traité de mariage entre sa fille Marie et Guillaume, fils aîné du duc Albert de Bavière, relativement à la dot de cent mille francs d'or, par lui promise à cette princesse. . . ." In a second set of letters, also dated June, 1375, "le même souverain renonce, pour et au nom de sa fille Marie, à toutes les pretentions qu'il pourrait avoir, à cause de ce mariage, sur les comtés de Hainaut, de Hollande et de Zélande, et sur la seigneurie de Frise, en exceptant toutefois l'adhéritement qui devait être fait en faveur de Guillaume de Bavière, de la moitié du comté de Hainaut, ainsi que le douaire de la princesse. . ." Thus we see that the negotiations for Marie's marriage to William of Bavaria were in progress in June, 1375, and consequently that the omission of her name in the *mandement* for March cannot be used as evidence that she had died. The peril of the *argumentum ex silentio* could hardly be more forcibly illustrated.

But, fortunately, in dealing with Professor Manly's inferences as to Marie's death, it is not necessary to rest the case on negative evidence. Marie's name actually appears in a document a fortnight later than the order of January 9, 1377, on which Professor Manly bases his inference she was no longer living. This is *mandement* No. 1325[7], dated January 24,

1377, in which "Charles V ordonne de payer à son amé vallet de chambre et pelletier Jehan Maudole[8] une somme de 239 francs un quart, à lui due 'pour cause de certaine pelleterie bailliée par lui de nostre comandement, pour nous et nostre très chère et amée fille Marie, à Jehan Noel, nostre vallet pelletier." It is obvious that if Marie were still living January 24, 1377, no argument can be based on the omission of her name in the earlier *mandement* of January 9.

Furthermore, Professor Manly puts forward his conclusion as to the date of Marie's death in direct contradiction with the statements of earlier authorities. Anselme, the compiler of the *Histoire généalogique. . .*, states that Marie "mourut jeune en 1377."[9] Anselme consistently uses old style, according to which the calendar year began on March 25, so that his statement rules out a date prior to March 25, 1377. Froissart also in recording the death of Edward III (June 21, 1377) adds the remark: "Assez tôt après tréspassa madame Marie ains-née fille du roi de France."[10]

We are left, therefore, with the document I originally cited as affording the closest approximate date of Marie's death. This is the *mandement* of May 30, 1377 (No. 1377), directing payment to be made for her pall. Professor Manly thinks one should "inquire how long she had been dead when the bill for her *poille* was paid." According to his view of the case, the interval between her death and this payment would have been not less than five or six months. Let us see what evidence the *mandements* afford in this matter. Though few payments for similar expenditures are recorded in 1377, in three definite instances (cf. Nos. 1306, 1311, 1385) payment seems to have followed within two or three weeks after the date of purchase. In the case of this payment on May 30 to Martine la Thierre, it should be noted further that a previous payment to this same person had been ordered on April 18 (No. 1361), and that no less than five subsequent payments to her (Nos. 1439, 1440, 1507, 1508, 1545) were authorized within the next half year, viz. on August 21, August 28, two on November 7, and December 13. The *mandement* of May 30 would therefore seem to relate to goods purchased later than the previous payment made to her on April 18. Accordingly, it may be concluded with reasonable probability that Marie's death occurred within the month of May, 1377.

It remains to consider Professor Manly's somewhat desperate attempt to set aside Froissart's explicit statements in regard to the marriage negotiations. Professor Manly makes much of the fact that my quotations from Froissart's text are taken in one instance from the edition of Buchon and in another from that of Luce; and in this matter I plead guilty to reprehensible inconsistency, although this was an inadvertence on my part and was not a device adopted, as he charges, "in order to make out his [Braddy's] case." In point of fact, the use of one edition rather than the other does not affect my argument, inasmuch as in the points under discussion they show no essential disagreement. Neither in this nor in my "neglect" of still a third redaction[11] does he bring proof against the authority of the chronicler. On the other hand, it becomes the more significant that Froissart in thrice revising his statements chose to retain in each redaction his account of the marriage negotiations. If any conclusion is to be drawn from this evidence, it is not that Froissart was "changing his mind" about these meetings, as Professor Manly states, but that in the course of correcting details he was careful to preserve the essentially important statement that Chaucer figured in the conferences of 1377.[12]

As a notable instance of Froissart's unreliability, Professor Manly contrasts his statements in regard to the commissioners with those in the French official documents:

> On the French side we have the *mandement* of Charles V dated August 11, 1377 (No. 1425), authorizing payment to Nicolas Braque for three journeys to Montreuil and Boulogne; but the commissioners therein named do not agree with any of Froissart's lists.

This, however, conveys the wholly erroneous impression that Froissart's account is in essential disagreement with the official records. By way of reply, one need only place side by side the names in Froissart's account and in the official document. The French *mandement* names as the companions of Nicolas Braque on his first voyage "nostre cousin le seigneur de Coucy et nostre amé et feal chevalier et premier chambellen Bureau sire de la Riviere, . . ." Froissart[13] refers to the first meeting as follows: "Si furent envoiiet à Moustruel sus mer, dou costé des Francois, li sires de Couci, li sires de Rivière, messires Nicolas Brake et Nicolas[14] le Mercier,. . ." The only discrepancy between the two accounts, it will be seen, consists merely in the occurrence of le Mercier's name in Froissart's list but not in the other. It should be further noted that the commissioners whom Froissart names as from the English side, Chaucer, Stury, d'Angle, are confirmed by the official records.

It is obviously necessary for Professor Manly to explain Froissart's statements; and this he undertakes to do by suggesting that Froissart really refers to the negotiations for the marriage of Richard and Marie's younger sister Isabel, which took place in 1378. In this Manly revives the earlier opinion of Nicolas which Skeat has already corrected.[15] But let us consider what this explanation would involve. If Froissart was actually referring to the negotiations of 1378, he not only committed a serious chronological error in dating the meetings a year too early, but he was also guilty of the incredible blunder of naming Marie instead of Isabel[16] as the princess concerned.

Finally, before impugning Froissart's testimony on the ground that it is not supported by other contemporary authority, one should bear in mind that Froissart was personally acquainted with Chaucer,[17] and that quite possibly he may have been speaking from personal knowledge.

In this brief review, it is only possible to deal with the points which have been challenged by Professor Manly. For the positive arguments advanced in favour of my interpretation of the *Parlement of Foules*, anyone who is interested may refer to the text of my study.

NOTES

[1] John Matthews Manly, *The Review of English Studies*, x. (July, 1934).

[2] *Three Chaucer Studies*, No. II, New York and London, Oxford University Press, 1932.

[3] *Mandements... de Charles V*, ed. Delisle, No. 1618.

[4] "Tout ce dessus livré le dit VIIIe jour de decembre. Et pour quatre autres paires de gans de chamois, doublez de chevrotin et brodez, livrez la vigille de Noel passé,...."

[5] "... pour la veille et feste de Noel darrenierement passé,..."

[6] *Cartulaire des comtes de Hainaut*, ed. Devillers, vi., pt. I, 395-96.

[7] It is surprising that Professor Manly overlooked this document, which is duly entered under Marie's name in the index although some of the others are omitted.

[8] Jean Maudole was the same person to whom payment for robes for Marie had previously been ordered on January 5, 1377 (No. 1306).

[9] I, IIOD. Anselme's statement is repeated in the *Dictionnaire de Moreri*, vii., 247. See on the subject of old style dates A. Giry's *Manuel de Diplomatique*, 107 f.

[10] According to one redaction: Buchon, *Les Chron. de Froissart*, VI, 105.

[11] Luce states (i, vi): "Enfin, une dernière rédaction, que tout le monde s'accorde à regarder comme la troisième, ne subsiste que dans le célèbre manuscrit de Rome." Kervyn, who separately edited this manuscript (*Le Premier Livre des Chron. de J. Froissart*, 2 vols.) calls this a fourth redaction. Regarding the redaction to which Manly refers to as the third, Kervyn states (i., pt. 3, 355): "Le récit des années 1372 à 1379 est emprunté à la narration developpée, cest-à-dire au manuscrit d'Amiens (texte de la première redaction)."

[12] In seeking to discredit Froissart, Professor Manly invokes the authority of Siméon Luce to show that Froissart was "often mistaken both as to dates of important events and the persons concerned." We may, therefore, fairly appeal to the statement of this editor in settling the question raised by Professor Manly. Luce points out that Chaucer was not a member of the official deputation, but he doubts that Froissart is incorrect in naming the poet, and believes that among the records there must be some trace of Chaucer's mission. Significantly, Luce next states: "Nous apprenons précisément par un de ces articles qu'un payement fut fait, le 17 février, à Geoffroi Chaucer qu'Édouard III avait chargé d'une mission en Flandre" (viii., cxxxix, n. 3). The French editor, moreover, is apparently drawing a distinction, which Manly ignores, between the official deputation and the confidential embassy entrusted to Chaucer.

[13] S. Luce, *Chron. de J. Froissart,* VIII, 225-26.

[14] Very likely an error for "Jean." In his introductory summary, Luce refers (viii., cxxxix) to this commissioner as 'Jean le Mercier,' whose name frequently occurs in the *mandements* in connection with these peace negotiations (Nos. 1374, 1411, 1413, 1490).

[15] Skeat,*Oxford Chaucer,* i,xxix ff. I have discussed the error of Nicolas at length in *Three Chaucer Studies,* No. II, pp. 20-22, 49-50.

[16] Less likely Katherine, who was not born until February 4, 1378.

[17] G.L. Kittredge, *Englische Studien,* xxvi (1899), 321–36. See also F.S. Shears, *Froissart, Chronicler and Poet,* p. 19.

Reprinted from *RES*, XI (1935), 204–209.

6

THE ORIENTAL ORIGIN OF CHAUCER'S
CANACEE–FALCON EPISODE

In his essay, 'On the Magical Elements in Chaucer's *Squire's Tale*',[1] W.A. Clouston long ago demonstrated that the setting and also numerous details of the story derive from the literature of the East. Some fifteen years later additional evidence of Oriental influence upon the *Squire's Tale* was supplied by Professor Lowes, who pointed out clear indications of its contacts with the legends of *Prester John*.[2] Furthermore, in Chaucer's description of the horse of brass, as Dr. Pollard has observed,[3] we are dealing with Oriental material closely resembling the tale of the Ebony Horse in the *Arabian Nights*. Indeed, it has recently been argued that this type of tale also served as the basis for the episode of Algarsif and Theodora which the Squire proposed to relate in the course of his Tale.[4]

The purpose of the present paper is to carry the argument for the Oriental origin of the *Squire's Tale* still further by examining the episode of Canacee and the falcon.[5] Though this episode comprises approximately one-half of the fragmentary tale which has come down to us, its source has not thus far been identified[6] and even its significance for the narrative has never been satisfactorily explained, nor is there entire agreement as to its interpretation.[7] Most scholars believe that for his story of the falcon Chaucer depended upon some source, but no such pertinent analogues for it have been discovered as in the case of the other Oriental material. The explanation advanced by Clouston is as definite as any which has been proposed:

> That Chaucer had before him, or in his memory, a model for his story of the Falcon is not only possible but highly probable. There exists a somewhat analogous ancient Indian tale of two birds—a male parrot and a hen maina, a species of hill starling—in which, however, it is the male bird who is distressed at the female's treachery, and is about to cast himself into the midst of a forest fire, when he is rescued by a benevolent traveller, to whom he relates the story of his woes.[8]

Here, however, we have simply an instance of unfaithfulness among birds; and since the conditions in this particular example are the very opposite of what we find in the *Squire's Tale*, we are compelled to turn elsewhere for the source materials Chaucer drew upon.

For this episode, as for others in the Chaucerian fragment, the *Arabian Nights* affords a close parallel. The Arabian story represents a definite type of tale in which the subsequent behaviour of a princess is motivated by a dream experience. In this dream, animals are usually represented as birds are in the *Squire's Tale*, and the vision serves to warn the princess that men are unfaithful. It is thus interpreted as picturing in the plight of a forsaken bird or beast what might occur to the princess if she accepted at face value the promises of a suitor. This simple plot, using an animal fable to foreshadow an identical situation in human affairs, is obviously folklore material. That the plot was popular in Oriental fiction appears certain on the basis of the *Arabian Nights* alone, in which collection this conventional machinery is employed no less than three times.

One of the three stories treating this plot follows the type in most respects; but it does not use birds for the purpose of influencing the princess to hate men,[9] and may accordingly be dismissed from present consideration. The remaining two stories, however, contain the essentially important bird episode as a part of the framework of the dream. These stories are so similar as to be nothing less than two redactions with minor differences of an almost identical plot;[10] one has to do with Tāj al-Mulūk and Princess Dunyā; the other, with Ardashīr and Hayāt al-Nufūs.

Since the first-mentioned tale not only appears in the larger number of editions, but chances to be the one which offers closest resemblance to Chaucer's account, I give a brief summary of the plot concerned from Burton's translation.

> In a dream, Princess Dunyā sees two pigeons, a male and a female. The male bird is caught in a snare; and all the birds about him fly away except his mate, who returns to rescue him. A fowler then readjusts his snare, and after a time the birds assemble again. This time the female bird is caught in the trap. Her mate, however, flies away with the others; and he does not return to rescue her. The princess awakes and declares: 'All men are, like this pigeon, worthless creatures; and men in general lack goodness to women.' When Tāj al-Mulūk, who is trying to win the love of the princess, hears from the governess an account of this dream, he strikes upon a plan whereby Princess Dunyā and her attendants are to be led into a garden where the scene is differently created in pictures on the pavilion. In the first, the female bird is shown rescuing her mate; in the second, the male pigeon, deserting her; and in the third, the male pigeon is depicted as

being prevented from returning to the rescue by a huge Raptores that has seized him in his talons. When Princess Dunyā later enters the garden and sees the paintings, she exclaims: 'Exalted be Allah! This is the very counterfeit presentment of what I saw in my dream.' After gazing in wonder at the figures of the birds, she concludes: 'O my nurse, I have been wont to blame and hate men, but look now at the fowler how he hath slaughtered the she-bird and set free her mate;[11] who was minded to return and aid her to escape when the bird of prey met him and tore him to pieces.'[12]

The main points of Chaucer's falcon episode may be accounted for in the light of this Arabian tale. In the *Squire's Tale*, it will be remembered, Canacee, like the Arabian princess, awakes after her first sleep and declares that she has 'hadde a visioun'(v. 372). She thereupon summons a group of her attendants[13] and they walk into the garden. Here Canacee finds a falcon[14] bitterly lamenting because she has been deserted by her mate. The falcon, like Princess Dunyā, concludes that men resemble this false tercelet, for both follow after 'newefangelnesse' (v. 610) in love.

The setting is the same in both accounts: that is, a garden adjoining a palace. Furthermore, Canacee, like Princess Dunyā, repairs to the 'park' accompanied by her 'maistresse'.

It appears worthy of notice, finally, that this Arabian story enables us to explain two minor details. In Chaucer's incomplete account, the purpose of the two passages is not immediately clear; but these lines appear less disconnected with the plot when viewed in the light of the story of Tāj al-Mulūk. First of all, Chaucer's description of the falcon's 'mewe' as painted with emblematic colours, in one case suggesting the constancy of bird lovers and in the other their infidelity, finds a general counterpart in the pictures on the pavilion, which in one instance reveal the male bird as a true lover and in another as a false mate in deserting her. In the second place, when Canacee prepares to visit the garden, she has about her 'wommen a greet route,. . . well a ten or twelve' in attendance; but she actually proceeds 'Nat but with fyve or sixe of hir meynee' (v. 391). This decision of Canacee in favour of a select company[15] finds no parallel in the story of Tāj al-Mulūk; but in the second redaction of this Arabian tale we find that the princess concerned similarly discriminates when she dismisses the body of her attendants and chooses for her companions only the nurse and 'two of her hand-maids who were most in favour with her'.[16] As I have just remarked, Chaucer gives no indication as to why Canacee selected individual ladies; but the reason for the discrimination in the Arabian version is that the nurse has privately secreted the prince in the garden and does not wish to frighten him away by bringing forth a host of attendants.

The Arabian Nights is a compilation of stories which was itself too late to serve as a source for Chaucer;[17] but since the tale of birds told here accounts for the very details which have hitherto been unexplained, it is reasonable to suppose that the Canacee-falcon episode reflects similar Oriental influences. It seems probable, therefore, that the original of this Arabian version supplied the ultimate basis for Chaucer's story. Although I cannot undertake to trace this fable to its origin, or to define precisely the stages in its transmission to Western Europe, I can offer evidence in early Oriental fiction of this situation in which princesses have visions of forsaken birds and refer the plight of the birds to their own affairs.

There is an early version of the *Kathā Sarit Sāgara*,[18] which may represent the original of the fable involving birds. This is the story of Princess Karpūrikā, who hated men and refused marriage because in a previous incarnation[19] she had been a swan, and her mate, the male swan, had shown himself heartless towards her. The prince who woos her pretends he is the repentant male swan reincarnated. The seventh-century Hindu romance, *Vásavadattá*, by Subandhu,[20] also contains certain features reminiscent of the situation in the Canacee-falcon episode. In this early romance, Kandarpaketu, son of Chintámani, King of Kusumpapura, sees in a dream a beautiful maiden of whom he becomes so desperately enamoured that he immediately sets out with his attendants to search for her. While resting beneath a tree, his confidant, Makaranda, hears[21] two birds conversing, and from their dialogue learns that Princess Vásavadattá has rejected all suitors because she saw Kandarpaketu in a dream[22] and even learned his name. It so happens that the princess, in turn, had sent her confidante in search of the prince; and this person Makaranda discovers in the same forest. The confidante delivers a letter to the prince from her mistress, and escorts him to the king's palace, where he is happily united with the princess. An analogue more closely approximating the conditions of the *Squire's Tale* is found, however, in the Persian collection entitled *Tūti Nāma*. According to one of the stories, the Emperor of China falls hopelessly in love with a beautiful princess whom he saw in a dream, and he sends his vizier to search for her. The vizier at length discovers her in the person of the Princess of Rúm. But at the same time he also learns from a traveller that she is averse to marriage because of the following experience:

> Once on a time the queen was sitting in a summer house situated in a garden, where, on the top of a tree, a peahen had deposited her

eggs. Suddenly the tree was struck with lightning, which burnt all the trees; when, the flames approaching that tree, the peacock, unable to support the heat of the fire, inhumanely quitted the nest; but the hen, from her affection for the eggs, remained with them and was burnt. When the queen saw this want of feeling in the male, she exclaimed: Men are very faithless! I vow myself never to speak of a man![23]

Having learned the cause of the lady's dislike for men, the vizier determines to correct her opinion by showing her a number of paintings of animals, among which is the picture of a male deer sacrificing his life to save his mate and their fawn. The princess is astonished at this; and when she next learns that the emperor had conceived an aversion for women because he witnessed the incident in this painting,[24] she conquers her dislike completely, and the emperor is thus made happy.

The two stories in the *Arabian Nights* were adapted,[25] it appears clear, from some such version as is presented in the *Tūti Nāma*. The frame story of the collection entitled the *Thousand and One Days*,[26] which is considered later than the *Arabian Nights*,[27] is also quite obviously based on this Persian story of the Emperor of China and the Princess of Rúm. The only difference between the account in the *Thousand and One Days* and in the Arabian tale is that the figures used are not birds, but a stag and a doe, while in the *Tūti Nāma* the allegorical representation involves both birds and beasts.[28] It is possible to add still other, much later, versions of this latter order—for example, a story of Turkish extraction.[29] But without going into these, we may suppose that in the migration of this tale to Western Europe there appeared some manuscript version with which Chaucer became familiar. In any case, although lacking the exact model, we have significant analogues of the falcon episode in the *Tūti Nāma* and the *Arabian Nights*.

The story of Tāj al-Mulūk and Princess Dunyā affords the closest analogue; and since the bird episode in this Arabian tale is employed simply as a device to unite the two human lovers, it may be suggested that the falcon-tercelet incident was composed with a similar intention in mind. The reader feels that Chaucer must have intended the incident of the falcon in the *Squire's Tale* to have some further bearing on the fortunes of Canacee. Though the fragmentary narrative does not fully disclose the course of his plot, certain hints in the extant text indicate the general direction in which it was to move. If these hints are studied in the light of the Oriental type of tale here discussed, it is possible to make some fairly definite conjectures as to Chaucer's aims.

The Host, it will be recalled, requests the Squire to 'sey somwhat of love; for certes ye/Konnen theron as muche as any man'. The Squire, modestly disclaiming any such extensive acquaintance with love, indicates his willingness to obey the Host's request: ' "Nay, sire," quod he, "but I wol seye as I kan." ' This byplay between the master of ceremonies and the proposed narrator establishes the type of tale which the reader is to expect. When Canacee at the beginning of the narrative is described as surpassing in beauty,[30] we have at least a generic counterpart of that same merciless beauty which Princess Dunyā possessed in common with other typical heroines of romance.

Now if the *Squire's Tale* represents a variation of the plot found in the Arabian story, we should expect the fable of the birds to motivate the human drama. This would seem to be precisely the method that Chaucer adopted; for the 'faucon peregryn...Of fremde land' (vv. 428–9) declares that her purpose in relating her experience to Canacee was

> . . . for noon hope for to fare the bet,
> But for to obeye unto youre herte free,
> And for to maken othere be war by me.   (vv. 488–90.)

We know, then, that Canacee was to draw a moral from the plight of the bird. Moreover, the falcon is explicit in stating exactly wherein Canacee must 'be war'. The bird advises her that 'alle thyng, repeirynge to his kynde,/Gladeth hymself' (vv. 608–9), and that in following a new love, 'So ferde this terclet'. Canacee was not permitted to interpret this fickleness of character as applying to birds alone; for the falcon gives a more general application to her warning in the statement which immediately follows:

> Men loven of propre kynde newefangelnesse
> As briddes doon that men in cages fede.   (vv. 610–11.)

The purpose of these passages is now obvious: the fable of birds was intended to carry over to the affairs of human beings. Thus, after hearing the tragic predicament of the falcon, Canacee would readily draw the conclusion that men are perfidious. Accordingly, in consequence of her dream, Canacee probably would, like Princess Dunyā, conceive an aversion for men.

If Chaucer intended a romantic story, how was he to complete it? In the type of tale we are considering, it devolves upon the hero in every case to conquer the aversion of the princess by some exceptional or remarkable feat. Tāj al-Mulūk, for example, wins Princess Dunyā by the effective device of presenting in pictures the very scene which the princess had seen in a dream. Chaucer in his fragmentary account of the subject does not disclose so exactly the strategy to be practised in the *Squire's Tale;* but in stating that Cambalo had to fight

> ...in lystes with the bretheren two
> For Canacee er that he myghte hire wynne   (vv. 668–69)[31]

he does reveal that Cambalo must have had to prove that he deserved Canacee's love.

The present interpretation, it should be noted, accords with still other passages in the *Squire's Tale.* That the falcon-tercelet incident was, in point of fact, designed to show Canacee the falseness of men is foreshadowed in the description of the magic mirror, because Canacee's mirror possessed the special power that

> ...if any lady bright
> Hath set hire herte on any maner wight,
> If he be fals, she shal his tresoun see,
> His newe love, and al his subtiltee,
> So openly that there shal no thyng hyde.   (vv. 137–41.)

And Canacee had herself demonstrated the efficacy of this mirror when

> ...In hire sleep, right for impressioun
> Of hire mirour, she hadde a visioun.   (vv. 371–72.)[32]

Moreover, the suggestion that Canacee was led to suspect men seems to harmonise admirably with the impression we receive as to her modest deportment or demeanour. She attended the banquet given by her father Cambyuskan and participated in the revels; she met the strange knight 'And on the daunce he gooth with Canacee'. She did not disport herself until a late hour and have to retire after 'muchel drynke.... And with a galpyng mouth', as did the others. 'For of hir fader hadde she take leve,/To goon to reste soone after it was eve.' On the basis of this description, it is easy to suppose that the plight of the falcon would have served to increase her diffidence; for Canacee was, as Chaucer expresses it, 'ful mesurable'.

Accordingly, we seem to have in the *Arabian Nights,* not only an analogue of the falcon-tercelet incident, but the type of story which Chaucer apparently intended to relate. This promised story, according to the present interpretation, would reveal Canacee, like all the princesses in the Oriental stories here discussed, as suspicious of men because of the dream in which she had seen a forsaken falcon. This suggestion receives support from an entirely different quarter. Spenser, using Chaucer's text alone, arrives at a similar conclusion.

Cambelloes sister was fayre *Canacee* . . .
She modest was in all her deedes and words,
And wondrous chast of life, yet lou'd of Knights and Lords.
Full many Lords, and many Knights her loued,
Yet she to none of them her liking lent...
So much the more as she refused to love
So much the more she loued was and sought.   (*F.Q.*, iv, ii, 35–37.)

Finally, in attempting to view the large issue by way of the small, it may be suggested that the story of Tāj al-Mulūk seems to shed some new light on the question of the *Squire's Tale* as a whole. According to the view expressed by Professor Manly,[33] the *Squire's Tale* was based on a single model. But since such parts of the narrative as deal with the messenger and the gifts, the Ebony Horse, and the Canacee-falcon episode appear to have different origins, it may be more safely concluded that Chaucer in attempting to write a romance drew upon multiple or composite sources,[34] and that one of the important episodes of the finished romance was intended to hinge on the influence of birds' infidelity on the behaviour of a princess toward her suitors.

NOTES

[1] Chaucer Soc. Publ., Second Ser. (1890), No. 26, pp. 269-469.

[2] J. L. Lowes, *Modern Philology* (1905),III, 1 ff.; and *Washington University Studies,* I (1913), pp. 3 ff.

[3] A. W. Pollard, ed. *Squire's Tale,* London (1926) (1st ed. 1899), p. xiii.

[4] J. Bolte and G. Polívka, *Anmerkungen. . .Hausmärchen der Brüder Grimm,* Leipzig (1915) II, pp. 134 ff. and n. 1. See also Professor Robinson's explanatory notes in the Student's Cambridge Edition of *Chaucer,* p. 822.

[5] To Professor Margaret Schlauch, of New York University, I am indebted for suggesting the subject of this investigation, which I began as a student of her seminar in Mediaeval Romance. Both Miss Schlauch and Professor Carleton Brown have been kind enough to read this paper in manuscript, and to them I wish to express my thanks for several improvements in the statement of the argument.

[6] In the *Cléomadès,* a work to which Chaucer was possibly indebted for some suggestions, 'there is', according to Professor H. S. V. Jones (*P.M.L.A.* (1905), xx, 352), 'nothing corresponding to the incident of Canacee and " the falcon peregrine" '.

[7] Lowes (*Washington University Studies* (1913), I, p. 16) seems to follow Skeat (*Oxford Chaucer*, I, p. 78) in believing that Chaucer was working out a theme of his own in the case of the falcon story. According to Professor Frederick Tupper (*P.M.L.A.* (1921), XXXVI, pp. 196 ff.) this episode in the *Squire's Tale*, as well as the *Anelida and Arcite*, was concerned with an actual love-triangle in contemporary England. But this interpretation has not won acceptance: see Robinson's *Chaucer*, p. 822.

[8] *Op. cit.,* p. 462.

[9] No. 218 in Victor Chauvin's *Bibliographie des ouvrages arabes* (Liége 1902), VI, pp. 52-3. This is the story of Ibrāhīm and Gamila.

[10] The appearance of doublets in the *Arabian Nights* is not uncommon, as A. Müller has noted (*Beiträge zur Kunde der indogermanischen Sprachen* (1888), XIII, p. 234 and n. 1).

[11] It is interesting to note that in John Lane's continuation of the *Squire's Tale*, Chaucer Soc. Publ., Second Ser. (1888),No. 23, p. 230, the magic glass of Canacee shows the tercelet the image of his falcon as dead (pt. xii, vv. 443-53).

[12] *The Book of the Thousand Nights and a Night*, trans. by Sir Richard F. Burton, Medina edition, n.d., III, pp. 31 ff.

[13] Canacee's governess is obviously somewhat paralleled by Princess Dunyā's nurse; but what was to be the office of Canacee's 'maistresse' in the continued story is not clear. In the Arabian tale, the nurse serves as confidante to Princess Dunyā and as pandar for the prince.

[14] The female bird in the tale of Ardashir and Hayāt al-Nufūs is called both pigeon and *falcon* (Burton, VII, pp. 209 ff.).

[15] Clouston (*op. cit.,* p. 273) seems not to have observed that Canacee selected her company, because he states that she 'roused half a dozen of her attendants [and] went forth with them into the park'.

[16] Burton, VII, p. 240.

[17] *The Arabian Nights* appears not to have been known in Europe as a collection in the fourteenth century, although, as H. Zotenberg points out (*Histoire d'* *'Alâ Al-Dîn, . . ., Paris, 1888, p. 2),* 'l'un de nos manuscrits remonte au XIVᵉ siècle'.

[18] *The Ocean of Story:* C. H. Tawney's translation of Somadeva's *Kathā Sarit Sāgara*, ed. by N. M. Penzer (London, 1925), III, pp. 259 ff. In his notes to this tale (III, p. 291 f.) and to the story of Ratnavatī, daughter of king Vīraketu, who disliked the male sex so greatly that she did not desire even Indra for a husband (VII, pp. 35–9, 217), Penzer refers to these two Arabian accounts as later versions of the situation.

[19] Pollard (*op. cit.,* p. viii) refers to Canacee's falcon as 'perhaps an enchanted princess'.

[20] See Colebrooke's analysis in *Miscellaneous Essays . . .,* ed. by E. B. Cowell (London, 1873), II, pp. 121 ff.; reprinted from *Asiatic Researches* (1808), X, pp. 450 ff. See especially L. H. Gray's ed., Columbia University Indo-Iranian Series, VIII, 1913.

[21] According to Maurice Bloomfield (*American Journal of Philology* (1920), XLI, 309-35), birds are most frequently represented in the overhearing-motif in Hindu fiction; but Bloomfield does not here adduce an example similar to the one now under discussion.

[22] The literature dealing with falling in love in consequence of a dream is extensive, as the following references (which I have consulted from Chauvin's more complete list, *op. cit.,* V, p. 132) show: J. Bédier, *Les Fabliaux* (Paris, 1893), pp. 84–5; J. Dunlop and F. Liebrecht, *Geschichte der Romane . . .* (Berlin, 1851), pp. 474–5; *Histoire des Rois des Perses,* trans. by H. Zotenberg (Paris, 1900), pp. 246 ff.; and E. Rohde, *Der griech. Roman. . .* (Leipzig, 1876), pp. 44–51.

[23] *The Tooti Nameh, or Tales of a Parrot* (London, 1801), p. 157.

[24] But the emperor had fallen in love with the princess when he saw her for the first time in a dream, and the animal fable is not alluded to until a late point in the story. For another example in which animals are represented in one way or another in the framework of a dream, see the story of the Bird of Sorrow in *Forty-Four Turkish Tales,* trans. by I. Kunós (London, 1913), pp. 150 ff. Tāj al-Mulūk falls in love when he sees a design of two gazelles which Princess Dunyā had drawn, and the animals in this picture, interestingly enough, are likewise so depicted as to show that men are faithless and unkind.

[25] Clouston (*Popular Tales. . .* (London, 1887), II, p. 228) refers to the *Thousand and One Days* as an adaptation of the *Tūti Nāma*; but neither in this reference nor in a second statement (*Flowers from a Persian Garden* (London, 1894), pp. 132–6) does he mention the two Arabian tales.

[26] Trans. by J. C. McCarthy (London, 1892), I, 1–6; II, 255–6.

[27] Cf. Édouard Montet, *Le Conte dans l'Orient Musulman* (Paris, 1930), pp. 16, 22.

[28] In the *Turkish Evening Entertainments* (trans. by J. B. Brown (New York, 1850), pp. 166–8) there is an episode concerning animals which is not applied to the affairs of human beings. It may be that these bird and beast stories find their origin in a simple fable which was later added to a major plot as a means of motivating a tragic human drama. In any case, this particular fable furnishes a similar situation in narrating how a stag and doe are reunited after being separated by hunters. The circumstances led the doe to believe her companion forsook her in 'thinking only of gratification and enjoyment'; but when she reproached him, the stag stated that he fell 'a prey to misfortune in the hands of a huntsman'. The gazelles are thus reconciled and become as good friends as before.

[29] *The Story of Jewād,. . .,* trans. by E. J. W. Gibb (New York, 1888), pp. 76 ff. and 206 ff. This tale is little more than a repetition of the one in the *Thousand and One Days*, and in both cases it is the frame story which contains the animal fable. The only originality of this Turkish collection, indeed, seems to lie in the title; for it was the usual practice to employ the '1001' phrase, as the numerous occurrences of this nomenclature in Oriental fiction show (see Sir Wm. Ouseley, *Travels in Various Countries of the East* (London, 1821), II, p. 21, n. 16).

[30] Vv. 33 ff. All quotations are from Robinson's edition.

[31] The original that Chaucer followed probably provided this deviation from the formula appearing in the Arabian tale; but since the passage refers to the more chivalric Western custom of winning the lady fair 'in lystes' instead of by the form of trickery featured in the Oriental account, it is not impossible that Chaucer himself invented the variation. In any case, Canacee and Princess Dunyā would seem to have made it obligatory for the suitor to prove his mettle before he should be accepted;

and there is at least one feature in the Canacee-falcon episode which suggests the device practised by Tāj al-Mulūk, who convinces the princess of the fidelity of men, it will be remembered, by representing the male pigeon as desiring to return to his mate. Chaucer likewise promises to tell how Cambalus restored to the falcon 'hire love ageyn/Repentant' (vv. 654–55).

[32] In this 'visioun', Canacee hears the story of the falcon peregrine, which supplies the bird-allegory as a counterpart of the scene to be unfolded by the magic mirror. That is, after understanding the treachery of the tercelet, Canacee when presented with 'any maner wight. . .shal his tresoun see'.

[33] *P.M.L.A.* (1896), XI, p. 362.

[34] Chaucer's phrase, 'as the storie telleth us' (v. 655), would seem to indicate that he followed a specific model for the falcon-tercelet incident; and I think it is altogether the most likely view that the poet depended on a single source for the main features of the *Squire's Tale*, but he unquestionably also relied upon other materials as well.

Reprinted from *MLR*, XXXI (1936), 11–19.

7

THE DATE OF CHAUCER'S *LAK OF STEADFASTNESSE*

The traditional and long-accepted view as to the chronology and occasion of *Lak of Stedfastnesse*[1] was first challenged by Dr. A.W. Pollard, who ascribed the balade to the year 1389. This new interpretation won immediate favor with a large circle of readers, and when the Globe edition of Chaucer's works appeared in 1907, Dr. Pollard's associates quoted his arguments with approval. More recently, Professor F.N. Robinson, in re-evaluating the data available, has also questioned the older view by preferring to assign the poem to the late eighties—a date some ten years earlier than Skeat's. Before proposing new evidence for dating the balade in the nineties, it would therefore appear not inappropriate first to consider the arguments against Skeat's position.[2]

Professor Robinson says:

> ...most scholars have assigned the ballade to the last years of Richard's reign (1397–99). But the immediate occasion is quite uncertain, and both the characterization of the age and the admonition to the sovereign would have been equally appropriate between 1386 and 1390. In fact there is a familiar passage of similar import in the *Prologue to the Legend* (F, 373 ff., G, 353 ff.). The association of *Lak of Stedfastnesse* with the Boethius group also counts somewhat in favor of the earlier date.[3]

The connection with the *Prologue to the Legend* can not be denied, although here, as the God of Love, Richard's "tyrannye" is not altogether the same as his political instability described in *Stedfastnesse*. Moreover, it would be difficult to arrive at a chronological datum on these grounds since similar criticisms at widely separated dates are far from uncommon.[4] Indeed, as Professor Root has observed, in criticizing the times "Chaucer is at one with Langland, with Wiclif, and with Gower."[5] Robinson's principal argument would thus appear to be the relation he suggests between *Stedfastnesse* and the *Consolation* by Boethius.

One may immediately question, however, whether Chaucer's balade is sufficiently indebted to the *Consolation* to justify its inclusion in a Boethian cycle. If the poem is compared with Book II, Metre 8, of Chaucer's translation, which it is supposed to follow, one will discover that

54

the two passages have little in common. Both do discuss mutability, but this is about all. Besides, the examples of mutability are not the same, and there are no verbal parallels between the two. Professor Root seems to have noted these discrepancies, since he states that "the indebtedness, if any, was very slight."[6] More recently, Professor French has scouted the whole theory; he says: "Skeat's suggestion that the *Balade* was based upon Boethius, Book II, Metre 8, seems unnecessary."[7] And even Professor Robinson admits that the "relation to the *Consolation* is not close."[8] Accordingly, it hardly seems necessary to associate Boethius with Chaucer's balade.[9]

Indeed, a more likely source for Chaucer's whole conception is Deschamps. As recently observed by the late Professor Brusendorff,[10] there are no less than three balades by Deschamps which contain similar features. Moreover, these French poems resemble the English balade rather closely both in content and in style. For example, all three poems by Deschamps not only discuss evil conditions at court but also enumerate the characteristics of an unsteadfast age. Particularly arresting is balade No. 209, which describes how times have changed because of the governance of unwise lords. In the opening verses Deschamps says:

> Je voy tout changer condicion,
> Et que chascuns de sa regle se part.
> Li sers viennent en dominacion,
> Seignourie des seigneurs se depart,
> Lasche hardi, et li hardi couart,
> Li sage foul, et li foul se font saige,
> Et li donneur veulent tout mettre a part:
> Dont puet venir au jour d'ui tel usaige?[11]

Still another balade (No. 234) yet more closely approximates the English version, for here the French poet clearly ascribes the ills of the time to unstable governorship. More significantly, this French poem contains an envoy very much like Chaucer's: it is addressed to the sovereign (in this case, Charles VI of France) and is admonitory in tone[12] –

> Prince, qui veult vivre en temps et saison
> Pour son hostel face sa garnison,
> De gens d'oneur et prodommes se farde,
> Ce qu'il en fault, n'on pas trop grant foison;
> S'autrement fait, lors en perdicion
> Tout se destruit et par default de garde.[13]

One should note especially that the English refrain, "That al is lost for lak of stedfastnesse," appears to follow pretty closely the French, "Tout se destruit et par default de garde."

Brusendorff's suggestion that Chaucer drew upon Deschamps would thus seem on analysis altogether acceptable. But if further evidence is needed, I may call attention to still another balade by Deschamps, which has not hitherto been cited in this connection—

Quant se pourra tout reformer? Qui fais les choses mal aler?
Quant sera paix et vraie amour? Qui nous a fait tant de dolour?
Quant verray je l'un l'autre amer? Les foulz es estas eslever,
Quant verray je parfaicte honnour? Les saiges laisser en destour
Quant aura congnoissance tour, Les vaillans mettre au cul du four,
Verite, loy, pite saison? Faire injustice et desraison,
Quant-sera justice en raison, Couvoitise, orgueil, traison,
Que les mauvais pugnis seront? Et trop d'officiers, qui yront
Quant aura Roys juste maison? A honte et a perdicion
Quant les saiges gouverneront. Quant les saiges gouverneront.

L'en queurt aus estas demander;
C'est au requerant deshonnour,
Qui n'est digne de l'exercer:
L'en doit eslire sanz favour   L'Envoy
Prodonme qui soit de valour
Sanz son sceu; telle election Prince, pour la grant charge oster
Fait bon fruict: sanz destruction Du peuple, vueillez moderer
Les princes par ce regneront Sur tant d'officiers qui trop sont
Et leur peuple en vraye union, Et a droit nombre ramener;
Quant les saiges gouverneront. Lors ne pourra que bien aler,
            Quant les saiges gouverneront.[14]

Besides discussing covetousness, pride, lack of truth and pity, Deschamps here tells how princes may hold their people in true union. Many of Deschamps' statements are thus analogous to Chaucer's; moreover, in the envoys both poets similarly advise their sovereigns. No one of these French balades affords an exact model, but each contains suggestive parallels. It would thus appear that Chaucer was following Deschamps, rather than Boethius.[15]

The acceptance of the French poems as the source materials which Chaucer used has a direct bearing upon the chronology of *Stedfastnesse,* since the Marquis de Saint-Hilaire, Deschamps' editor, assigns the first balade (no. 31), presumably the earliest of the four,[16] to the year 1390. He points out the Deschamps is referring to the notorious behavior of King Charles and his court in 1389.[17] According to this datum, and there seems no reason to question it, Chaucer before 1390 could not possibly have made use of these French balades.

In suggesting Deschamps as a more likely model than Boethius for the type of balade Chaucer wrote, it remains to consider when Chaucer could first have access to the French poems. Here, of course, one deals with probabilities, but fortunately not without significant indications. It is well known, for example, that Deschamps sent a number of his poems to Chaucer by Sir Lewis Clifford. One might argue, however, that a French writer would hardly think that an English poet would be interested in poems largely of purely local interest; but one should then be ignoring the fact (to mention only one illustration) that *The Complaint of his Empty Purse,* itself certainly of purely local political interest, resembles "in thought and structure"[18] Deschamps' begging poem written to Charles VI in 1381. There is thus evidence that Chaucer was interested in the political writings of France and that Deschamps may therefore have included these in the poems sent to England. Now the best opportunity for this transmission occurred during the negotiations for peace in 1393, which is the only known date of an actual meeting between Deschamps and Sir Lewis, then one of Richard's commissioners in France. In recently discussing the subject, Professor Lowes has therefore singled out this occasion for the transmission of the French poems to Chaucer. As the balades related to *Stedfastnesse* appear to have been composed about 1390, it seems altogether likely that these poems were included in the group Deschamps dispatched to Chaucer, most probably in 1393.[19] So far as literary grounds may be relied on, the evidence would appear, then, to favor not an early but a late time and one might on the basis of literary grounds propose 1393 as the earliest possible date for Chaucer's composition.

But the chief argument for the later chronology must center on historical data; for I believe it is possible to show that Chaucer's criticisms apply with full appropriateness to the nineties and not to the eighties.[20] In point of fact, the remarks about those who repudiate obligations, show disrespect for plighted word, and care only for "mede" and selfish ends, as well as the injunction to Richard to "hate extorcioun!" would have special point in the late nineties. The last three years of Richard's reign, according to a recent investigation,[21] were particularly noteworthy for lavish expenditures, constant drawings upon the exchequer, and permanent defaulting of all monetary obligations. From 1396 to 1398 one of the principal sufferers from forced loans was no other personage than the once mighty John of Gaunt, Chaucer's great patron. In the first financial period from 1377 to 1389, Gaunt's losses were only £800 and the Duke's name is last on the list of complainants. But in the second term from 1389 to

1399, the amount is no less than £2000 and his name now stands second on the list. Moreover, at Gaunt's death in 1398 his properties were confiscated,[22] and there was still £1000 due the Lancaster estates. It would accordingly appear that in advising Richard to cease doing "his neighbour wrong or oppressioun" and to give up "covetyse,"[23] Chaucer has reference to predicaments similar to Gaunt's, if not indeed to the situation of the Duke himself. On both literary and historical grounds,[24] there is thus more evidence than has hitherto been suggested for assigning *Stedfastnesse* to the late nineties.

This conclusion is strikingly confirmed by Shirley's own testimony in one of the manuscripts. In MS. Trinity Coll. Camb. R.3.20, the poem is described as a "Balade Royal made by oure laureal poete of Albyon in hees laste yeeres." Now scholars have long accepted Shirley's statements,[25] first, as to Chaucer's authorship, and, secondly, that the poem was intended for King Richard. Why, then, question his testimony as to chronology? Both the indebtedness to Deschamps and the allusions[26] to current events point to a date well-advanced in the nineties. In view of the evidence, it would appear that we are bound to accept Shirley's statement that Chaucer wrote the "Balade Royal" in "hees laste yeeres."

Finally, *Stedfastnesse,* when examined on the basis of the contemporary backgrounds which inspired its authorship, should hardly be described as "a far inferior poem."[27] Instead, it is an occasional balade skilfully and diplomatically worked out, rich both in poetic and political meaning. According to the present interpretation, the royal poem was written between 1396 and 1399; its occasion was Richard's misgovernment, especially his handling of finances. In conclusion, it seems altogether probable that while in a middle period Chaucer supported Richard, in his last years he no less certainly was a partisan of the Lancasters, those generous friends of early days.[28]

NOTES

[1] The history of the whole problem may be traced in the following studies: Thomas Tyrwhitt, *The Poetical Works of Geoffrey Chaucer* (London, 1843), p. 477; F. J. Furnivall, *Trial-Forewords* (London, 1871), p. 8; Sir A. W. Ward, *Chaucer* (New York, 1880), p. 18; W. W. Skeat, *The Complete Works of Geoffrey Chaucer* (Sec. ed.) (Oxford, 1899), I, 84, 555–556; and Skeat, *Minor Poems* (Oxford, 1888), p. lxxvii; John Koch, *The Chronology of Chaucer's Writings* (Ch. Soc. Publ. 2 Ser. 27, London, 1890), pp. 76–77; and Koch, *Geoffrey Chaucers Kleinere Dichtungen* (Heidelberg,

1928), p. 35; A. W. Pollard, *Chaucer*, rev. ed. (London, 1912), pp. 128–129; and A. W. Pollard, H. F. Heath, M. H. Liddell, W. S. McCormick, *The Works of Geoffrey Chaucer* (Globe ed., London, 1907), p. xlix; E. P. Hammond, *Chaucer, A Bibliographical Manual* (New York, 1908), p. 394; H. N. MacCracken, *MLN*, XXIII (1908), 212; S. Moore, *MLN*, XXVIII (1913), 192; Helen Louise Cohen, *The Ballade* (New York, 1915), pp. 242–243; B. L. Jefferson, *Chaucer and the Consolation of Boethius* (Princeton University Press 1917), pp. 91, 105–107, 136; R. K. Root, *The Poetry of Chaucer*, (rev. ed.) (New York, 1922), pp. 75–76; Aage Brusendorff, *The Chaucer Tradition* (London, 1925), pp. 274, 487, 492; J. E. Wells, *A Manual of the Writings in Middle English* (New Haven, Conn., 1926), pp. 640–641; G. H. Cowling, *Chaucer* (London, 1927), pp. 64–65, 134–135; Emile Legouis, *Geoffrey Chaucer* (trans. L. Lailavoix) (London, 1928), pp. 15–16; R. D. French, *A Chaucer Handbook* (New York, 1929), pp. 108–109; F. N. Robinson, *Chaucer's Complete Works* (New York, 1933), pp. 615, 977–978. When hereafter referred to, these works are cited only by author or editor.

[2] Skeat (I, 84); see Pollard (p. 129), Heath (p. xlix), and Robinson (p. 615).

[3] P. 977.

[4] Skeat (I, 84) notes that Froissart was critical of Richard near the end of the King's reign. Richard held a tournament at Windsor in 1399, which was but thinly attended; "the greater part of the knights and squires of England were disgusted with the king" (see *Froissart's Chronicles*, trans. Thomas Johnes (London, 1855), vol. II, bk. IV, ch. 105, p. 681).

[5] P. 75.

[6] P. 75.

[7] P. 109.

[8] P. 977.

[9] In order to be perfectly sure, one should compare *Stedfastnesse* with the original Chaucer was following in his *Boece*; namely, the French text of Jean de Meun (MS. Fr. 1097, Bibl. Nat.). I am indebted to Dr. L. V. Dedeck-Héry for the following excerpt from the French text Chaucer used (see further Dedeck-Héry, *RR*, XXVII (1936), 110–124)–

"Ce que li mondes tourne diversement et par estable foi ses acordables muances, ce que les contraires qualitez des elemens tiennent entreus aliance pardurable, ce que li soleus par la bele presence aporte le cler jour, ce que la lune a seignorie sus les nuiz que li vespres amaine, et que la mer couvoiteuse de pourprendre la terre referme les floz par certain terme, et que les terres ne puissent trop estendre leur larges bonnes, ceste ordenance de chosez est liee par amour gouvernant les terres et la mer et commandant neis au ciel. Se ceste amour relascoit les frains, toutez les chosez qui s'entreaiment orendroit feront tantost bataille et estriveront de depecier la facon du monde, la quelle il demainent ore en acordable foy par biaus mouvemens. Ceste amour contient neis touz peuples par aliance sainte, ceste amor enlace le sacrement de mariage par chastes amours, ceste neis donne et dite leurs droiturez aus compaignons loyaus. O beneurez fust li lignages humains, se celle amour pour quoy li cielz est gouvernez gouvernast vos courages."

It should be noted that whereas Boethius talks about the variability of the sun and the moon, the earth and the sky, and explains that these and all things are brought into accord and held together by the bond of love, Chaucer in his poem cites the characteristics of his own unsteadfast times, reciting the specific weakness of extortion and implying that Richard's recklessness and covetousness are the main causes of this instability. It would appear from the evidence that *Stedfastnesse* owes little or nothing to the *Consolation*; it therefore should not be associated with such Boethian poems as *Fortune* and *The Former Age*.

[10] P. 487.

[11] *Œuvres complétes*, SATF (Paris, 1878), II, 31–32.

[12] Traditionally the envoy was eulogistic; see the envoys attached to the balades in the *puys d'amour*; those addressed to the "Prince," president of the *puy* and to *trouveres* and to judges (Helen Louise Cohen, pp. 38, 44, 46). See the complimentary envoy to Chaucer's *Venus*, etc. Rebuking envoys are less common.

[13] *Œuvres complétes*, II, 63–64.

[14] *Œuvres complétes*, SATF (Paris, 1893), VIII, 77–78.

[15] Both the *Complaint to His Empty Purse* (see Skeat, I, 562) and the *Envoy to Bukton* (see Kittredge, *MLN*, XXIV (1909), 14) reveal the influence of Deschamps, and it is with these poems, rather than with a Boethian cycle, that *Stedfastnesse* should be linked both as to source and as to chronology.

[16] The editor's notes appear only in volume one (see p. 337), but since all of the balades are related in subject-matter, it seems logical to suppose that had the editor been discussing the other three, he would have assigned them to the same chronological period.

[17] Deschamps says (I, 113–14):

Temps de doleur et de temptacion,

Aages de plour, d'envie et de tourment,
Temps de langour et de dampnacion,
Aages meneur pres du definement.
Temps plains d'orreur qui tout fait faussement,
Aages menteur, plain d'orgueil et d'envie,
Temps sanz honeur et sanz vray jugement
Aage en tristour qui abrege la vie.

Temps sanz doucour et de maleicon,

Aage en puour qui tout vice comprant'
Temps de foleur, voy ta pugnicion,
Aages flateur, saige est qui se repent;

Temps sanz cremeur, temps de perdicion,
Aages tricheur tout va desloiaument,

Temps en erreur, pres de finicion,
Aages robeur, plain de ravissement,
Temps, voy ton cuer, vien a repentement;
Aages pecheur, de tes maulx merci crie;
Temps seducteur, impetre sauvement,

Aage en tristour qui abrege la vie.
Temps, la fureur du hault juge descent,
Aage, au jugeur t'ame ne fuira mie:
Temps barateur, mue ton mouvement,
Aage en tristeur qui abrege la vie.

These strictures the editor construes as an allusion to events of the year 1389, when, according to Michelet, whom he cites, Charles VI "plunged head-long into festivals, and made rude war on his treasury, lavishing as a youth and giving as a king." The description of one festival cited as particularly noteworthy, I quote according to an English translation:

The ceremony took place at St. Denys, with incredible magnificence, and in the presence of countless numbers of the nobility ... The venerable and silent abbey, the church of tombs, had to throw open her portals to welcome these worldly pomps... and the poor monks to become the hosts of lovely ladies, for they were lodged in the very abbey itself ... The festival was kept up for three days ... The ball was a true *pervigilium Veneris* (wake of Venus). May had just begun. "Many a damsel forgot herself; many a husband suffered" ... This bacchanal revel, so close to the vaults of death, was succeeded by a strange morrow. It was not enough to disturb the dead with the noise of these festivities; they were not let off so easily ... To awaken pleasure by contrast, or to beguile the languor of dissipation, the king had a funeral show got up for him; and his hero, he, the story of whose exploits had amused his infancy, Duguesclin, who had now been ten years dead, had the sad honor of amusing by his obsequies the silly and luxurious court (see *Hist. of France*, tr. G. H. Smith [New York, 1900], II, 15–16; or Paris editions of either 1840 (IV, 43–47) or 1876 (v, 114–118)).

18 Robinson (p. 980).

19 As Brusendorff (pp. 490–491) has keenly observed, there is–in view of the fact that only one occasion is indicated–an obvious inconsistency in the assumption that Clifford twice acted as Deschamps' deputy; Brusendorff therefore seems not unreasonable in his complaint against Lowes' designating 1386 as the occasion in 1905 (*PMLA*, XX, 769) and his later preference in 1910 (*MP*, VIII, 328) for 1393. All the evidence unquestionably favors 1393, which date Lowes of course most recently proposes. Brusendorff (p. 492) would thus seem judicious in concluding that "it may now be considered comparatively certain that Deschamps used this opportunity (i.e., 1393) for making his English *confrère* acquainted with his poems."

20 French's notion (p. 109) that if composed in the nineties Chaucer's admonition would give Richard umbrage fails to consider that the rebuke would be more inappropriate in the eighties, when as a mere boy Richard's instability would be understandable and hardly a topic for criticism.

21 For the substance of the foregoing paragraph, see Anthony Steel, *Eng. Hist. Rev.*, LI (1936), 29–51; 577–597; esp. 37.

22 Sidney Armitage-Smith, *John of Gaunt* (London, 1904), pp. 203–10.

23 According to Pollard (p. 129), Chaucer alludes to the Merciless Parliament of 1388 in these lines: "Pitee exyled, no man is merciable." According to Cowling (p. 134), Chaucer refers to Richard's banishment of Mowbray. The allusion to "Pitee exyled," which these scholars seem most impressed by, is, however, similar to conventional personifications in poems describing abuses of the age. Besides the reference to "pity" in Deschamps' balade No. 1423, see verses cited by Carleton Brown, *A Reg. of M. E. Rel. and Did. Verse* (Oxford, 1920), II, 93, etc.–Moreover, other features are probably capable of a similar interpretation. For example, the question of whether the balade gave Richard umbrage is obviously linked with the

fact that Deschamps' remonstrating balades were similarly addressed to a sovereign. Since Chaucer's poem was thus not unique but was simply one of a conventional type, the admonition might easily be regarded as an occasional verse with overt personal allusion not offensive to royalty because of its similarities to a conventional literary theme then à la mode.

[24] I have recently discussed (*PQ*, XIV (1935), 368-370) a contemporary chronicler's testimony that Chaucer's friend, Sir Peter Bukton, was appointed custodian of Richard after the dethronement, and may thus have been a witness to the King's death. I also there suggested that Chaucer may accordingly have sponsored the cause of the Duke's son, Henry of Bolingbroke, a little earlier than we have hitherto supposed. The present interpretation of *Stedfastnesse* would also seem to harmonize with the view that Chaucer in the late nineties was not a partisan of King Richard; but that, like many other Englishmen of the day (John Gower, for example), was looking forward to the ascendancy of the Bolingbroke party. For in both the balade and the envoy Chaucer unmistakeably indicates dissatisfaction of one kind or another with Richard's conduct of the affairs of government, apparently his handling of finances especially. Now in the reference to finances Chaucer may be thinking of his own condition; one may recall, in this connection, the tradition that he was in serious financial difficulties during Richard's last years. But be this as it may, it nevertheless seems important that since, shortly before his forced abdication, Richard had placed the country in financial straits, Chaucer in 1399 greeted the new King Henry with the *Complaint to His Empty Purse*. In other words, having cast a vote of remonstrance against Richard in *Stedfastnesse*, Chaucer in this *Complaint* presented himself as a now fully accredited partisan of the Lancaster family, fully justified in any expectation he might have of material assistance from a royal family itself inspired to revolt by threatened poverty and extinction. He must have had reason to expect a mark of royal favor; he most certainly received one, for, on October 3, 1399, some four days after his coronation, Henry IV, besides renewing annuities, granted to Chaucer an entirely new pension of forty marks a year.

[25] See also MS. Harl. 7333. For an account of these manuscripts, see E. P. Hammond, *Anglia*, XXVII (1904), esp. 397–398; also XXVIII (1905), 1–28; but especially L. H. Holt, *JEGP*, VI (1907), 419–431.–Shirley (1366?–1456) was in all probability personally acquainted with both Thomas and Alice Chaucer (see Brusendorff, pp. 42, 460). There thus was opportunity for him to be personally informed. By examining records of the past, we have been able to check with him up to a certain point. But when he states that the balade was actually sent to King Richard (see MS. Harl. 7333; cf. Hatt. 73) Shirley would appear to speak from information now apparently inaccessible; but since in so many other ways his testimony is corroborated by good evidence, he would appear in this case also to speak as a competent contemporary observer.

[26] In the last two lines of the envoy, Chaucer charges Richard to

Dred God, do law, love trouthe and worthinesse
And wed thy folk agein to stedfastnesse.

In May, 1389, Richard declared he was old enough to govern for himself and took over the reins of government, which, according to his distinguished biographer Wallon (*Richard II* (Paris, 1864), II, 22, 41, 59), he ruled wisely and well from about 1390 to 1392. When Chaucer asks Richard to "wed thy fok *agein* to stedfastnesse," he

The Date of Chaucer's *Lak of Steadfastnesse* 63

would appear by *agein* to be referring to this earlier period. On the other hand, if the balade was composed in the eighties, the allusion could not be similarly interpreted, for Richard did not assume control until 1389 and could therefore at that date hardly look back to a previous term of office.

27 Pollard (p. 128).

28 Of all Chaucer's poems, *Stedfastnesse* contains the highest percentage of words of French origin–a strong indication, according to Dr. Mersand's recent investigation, of late chronology (*Chaucer's Romance Vocabulary*, Brooklyn, N.Y., 1937).

Reprinted from *JEGP*, XXXVI (1937), 481-490.

8

SIR LEWIS CLIFFORD'S FRENCH MISSION OF 1391

Any new information concerning Sir Lewis Clifford is likely to meet with interest from the student of English because of Clifford's friendship with Geoffrey Chaucer.[1] Accordingly, it may be noted that H. Moranville[2] has printed a French official document[3] which affords data omitted in Froissart's account of Sir Lewis Clifford's mission in 1391 to Paris.[4]

This official document, not hitherto noted in this connection, recounts in some detail the agreements drawn up by the French and English commissioners respecting the treaty for peace, and relates besides the arrangements decided upon for a personal interview between the two respective sovereigns. The conclusion reached was that Charles VI should attend on "le jour de la Nativité Saint Jehan Babtiste prochainement . . . à Bouloigne ou à Saint Omer, et le Roy d'Engleterre à Calais."[5] This statement is not without significance, since it would appear to supersede the authority of Froissart, who reports that the conference was to be at Amiens.[6]

Two formal differences, moreover, appear between this record and the account in Froissart. First, Froissart states that the English commissioners "apportoient lettres de creance au roy et au duc de Berry et au duc de Bourgoigne";[7] but the French document mentions by name only the "duc de Burbonnois." Secondly, Froissart includes Robert Bricquet as a third member of the English embassy; but the official writ refers explicitly to only two ambassadors, Thomas de Percy and "Loys" Clifford.[8]

There is also the question as to the date of the meeting, which Froissart places as "vers la Chandeleur" (February, 1391). Now, the historian Wallon, in commenting on this passage, says: "C'est un peu trop."[9] But in this case it appears that Froissart is more nearly correct; for in the document the date of the conference is fixed as February 24, 1391.

It remains to be noted that since Clifford and his associates have attached their testimonial seals to the record of deliberations, this French writ takes precedence by its official character over Froissart as a source for facts about Clifford's mission. Moreover, inasmuch as Clifford knew Deschamps,[10] information coming to light about the activities of Sir Lewis in France is not without point. In fact, Professor Lowes[11] has singled out among other occasions the year 1391 as a likely opportunity for communications through Sir Lewis between Deschamps and Chaucer.

NOTES

[1] G. L. Kittredge, "Chaucer and Some of His Friends," *MP.*, I (1903), 1-18.

[2] *Bibl. de l'École des Chartes*, L (1889), 355-67, -380.

[3] Bibl. nat., Dupuy 306, fol. 83 R°.

[4] *Œuvres de Froissart, Chroniques* (ed. Kervyn de Lettenhove), XIV, 284, 288, 335.

[5] *Bibl. de l'École des Chartes*, L, 370.

[6] *Op. cit.*, XIV, 284.

[7] *Ibid.*

[8] *Bibl. de l'École des Chartes*, L, 370.

[9] H. Wallon, *Richard II* (Paris, 1864), II, 412 f., cf. 44f.

[10] Deschamps sent some of his poems to Chaucer by the hand of Sir Lewis. See *Chaucer's Complete Works* (ed. with intro. and notes by F. N. Robinson, New York, 1933), p. xxiii.

[11] "The Prologue to the 'Legend of Good Women' . . . ," *PMLA.*, XX (1905), 769.

Reprinted from *MLN*, LII (1937), 33-34.

9

FROISSART'S ACCOUNT OF CHAUCER'S EMBASSY IN 1377

In reopening after a considerable interval the discussion of the negotiations in which Chaucer was engaged in 1377 for a marriage between Richard, the heir to the English throne, and Princess Marie of France,[1] I would explain that the substance of this communication was sent to the editor of *The Review of English Studies* in the summer of 1935, but that circumstances not subject to my control have prevented its appearance until now.

The date of Marie's death, which Professor Manly called in question in his earlier discussion (*R.E.S.*, X. 267–72), is established by such clear evidence that it needs no further argument. Froissart's own statement in the Soubise MS. of his *Chroniques* (noted also by Manly, *ibid.*, XI. 209–13) that her death occurred shortly *after* that of Edward III (June 21, 1377) is itself a sufficient commentary on the improbability of the view that she died prior to January 1377. And the payment on May 30, 1377, for her funeral pall may be taken as fixing approximately the date of her death. In fact, I should not regard it as either necessary or profitable to reopen the discussion were it not for the fact that, in striving to exclude the explicit testimony of Froissart in regard to these marriage negotiations, Manly raised general doubts as to Froissart's reliability, thereby creating the impression that his statements are not to be trusted unless they can be confirmed by outside sources. This indictment, it seems to me, does serious injustice to Froissart's authority as an historian.

For his sweeping criticism of Froissart's *Chroniques*, the only evidence which Manly offers is a series of minor discrepancies already noted by Siméon Luce. But in this matter Manly omits to quote Luce's own carefully considered verdict:

> . . . Froissart, quoiqu'il ait embrassé dans sa narration l'histoire de plusieurs pays et qu'il ait donné à son oeuvre une étendue tout à fait exceptionelle, égale néanmoins, s'il ne surpasse, au point de vue de l'exactitude, la plupart des chroniquers contemporains (I.cxxiii).

What is still more important, we have Luce's own statement as to Chaucer's connection with these marriage negotiations:

> Chaucer ne figure dans aucune des députations officielles de 1376 et de 1377; mais il n'en saurait être autrement, puisque les négociations, auxquelles le malicieux observateur des moeurs anglaises de la fin du quatorzième siècle fut mêlé, devaient rester secrètes et n'ont point laissé sans doute d'autres traces écrites que des articles de comptabilité. Nous apprenons précisément par un de ces articles qu'un payement fut fait, le 17 février, à Geoffroi Chaucer qu'Édouard III avait chargé d'une mission en Flandre (VIII. cxxxix, n.3).

Although Froissart sometimes fell into error through depending upon his informants, he used commendable diligence in seeking wherever he had opportunity to verify the details of his narrative. According to Professor Shears, Froissart showed "unparalleled conscientiousness and industry" in gathering his data: during more than fifty years "he spared neither energy nor money in his quest for information." This tribute to Froissart's industry Professor Shears illustrates by a more detailed statement:.

> Even the knight seeking adventures "near and far" could not have led a more restless existence than the zealous scribe whom we have seen travelling the roads of England, France, Scotland and the Low Countries in quest of matter for his book. When an expedition was planned we find him inspecting and recording the preparations, whether in Bordeaux or in Flanders; when a treaty was discussed we find him in the antechamber ready to interview the ambassadors; when a marriage was celebrated he was one of the guests. Wherever he went he was looked upon as the official historian, and every knight who had news to tell was anxious to have it recorded.[2]

Particularly noteworthy is the intimate knowledge which Froissart shows of contemporary events. In discussing the battle of Otterburn, the historian Burton accepts the testimony of the *Chroniques* without qualifications:

> Froissart's narrative is the authority for this account of the battle of Otterburn. It shows so accurate a knowledge of persons and places, and gives the sequence of events so distinctly, that by internal evidence it would commend itself to belief as rendered by one who had carefully questioned them and had a peculiar capacity for getting at the truth of such affairs.[3]

Indeed, Froissart's narrative throughout convinces the reader of his fairness and good faith. In an era of patronage, he was singularly free of marked bias. His independent spirit appears in his open declaration:

> Let it not be said that I have corrupted this noble history through the
> favour accorded me by Count Guy de Blois, for whom I wrote it. No,
> indeed! for I will say nothing but the truth and keep a straight course
> without favouring one side or the other; moveover, the noble Count,
> who made me write this history, would not wish me to give anything
> but the true version of events.[4]

Moreover, he was not a respecter of persons. Few of the leading characters
in the *Chroniques* entirely escape criticism—even the Black Prince,
Froissart's greatest hero, receives censure for his arrogance—and in dealing
with the French and English he is notably impartial. Unlike the author of
the *Grandes Chroniques,* who regarded the defeat at Cressy as due to divine
interposition, Froissart seeks a purely rational explanation of events; as
Buckle testifies, "He carries us into a new world, the old theological spirit
being destroyed."[5]

The episode of the Countess of Salisbury affords an excellent
illustration of Froissart's care in checking up evidence. In his notes on this
episode as it is introduced in the play *Edward III* (see the Leopold
Shakespeare), Dr. Furnivall writes:

> The story of the Episode is founded on Froissart (I. 98, ed. 1812),
> and the history of it has some interest, for as my friend Professor
> Guizot pointed out to me, Froissart (ed. Luce, MS. d'Amiens, III. 293
> (Soc. de l'Histoire de France)) first believed in Jean le Bel's story that
> Edward III had used force and violated the Countess. Then, when he
> came to England, he inquired right and left as to the truth of the
> story, and having found it, set it down (p. ci).

Froissart's fame as a writer, which rests on other grounds than
authenticity, has unquestionably tended to magnify discrepancies that
would have been passed over in a more obscure author. But, as we have
seen, the historians are unanimous as to his trustworthiness. Indeed,
Siméon Luce declares: "l'opinion contraire est passée pour ainsi dire à
l'état de légende" (I. cxxiii).

Concerning the marriage negotiations of 1377, Froissart could easily
have secured first-hand information; for these parleys, it will be
remembered, actually took place on French soil, so that he would have had
no difficulty in interviewing the French commissioners.[6] Moreover,
Froissart was closely acquainted with all three of the English
commissioners—Chaucer, Sir Richard Stury, and Sir Guichard d'Angle—and
his personal friendship with these English members would naturally have
increased his own interest in the negotiations.

Finally, Froissart's account is also consistent with our information from other sources. In the *Instructions* sent to his envoys at Boulogne in May 1377, Charles V says:

> *Item*, le Roy ne veult pas que l'en parle de mariage de par lui, mais, se les Anglois en faisoient mencion, l'en pourroit oir ce que diroient et apres rapporter au Roy (R. Delachenal, *Chron. des règnes de Jean II et de Charles V*, Soc. de l'Histoire de France, Paris, 1920, lll. 207).

The French King's expectation that the marriage proposal would be brought forward makes it evident that he had foreknowledge of the intentions of the English, most likely from some previous discussion of the marriage. Thus interpreted, the situation finds an interesting parallel in the negotiations of February 1430 for a marriage between the young prince Henry VI and the daughter of the King of Scotland. One will observe the almost identical instructions drawn up for the government of the English commissioners on this occasion, as they are explained by Sir Harris Nicolas:

> The orders given to them in case the Scots should demand what the ambassadors considered reasonable, prove clearly that the offer of the marriage originated with the King of Scotland, inasmuch as that fact was to be urged as grounds for expecting to find his ambassadors fully prepared to treat upon the point. Whatever offers might be made by the Scots, the English ambassadors were to say that they were insufficient; and that they could only take them *ad referendum* and report them to the Council (*Proceedings and Ordinances of the Privy Council*, IV. vii).[7]

In initiating the negotiations of 1430 the Scots were in the same position the English had been in the discussion of 1377. It will be remembered that according to the original interpretation the proposals for marriage came from the English side. On the other hand, the rejection of Froissart's testimony as a "confused story" and the assumption that his account is "blended" with the negotiations of 1378[8] involve an obvious chronological contradiction. For these marriage proposals of 1378 took place in June,[9] and Chaucer could not have taken part in these since in May of that year he had departed for Italy (*Life-Records*, No. 121).

The reference to the young princess as "Baby Marie" was evidently intended to belittle the seriousness of the marriage discussion of 1377. But one should remember that in 1396 Richard actually solemnized his marriage with "Baby Isabelle," who like Marie was then a child of seven.[10]

[1] See my earlier communication, "The Historical Background of the *Parlement of Foules*," *R.E.S.*, XI. 204–9.

[2] F. S. Shears, *Froissart, Chronicler and Poet*, pp. 93–4.

[3] J. H. Burton, *The History of Scotland* II. 363, n.I.

[4] As translated by Shears, *op. cit.*, p. 103.

[5] H. T. Buckle, *Miscellaneous and Posthumous Works*, I. 234.

[6] Their names appear in Froissart and in *mandement* No. 1425.

[7] This effectually disposes of the objection which has been made that the *Instructions* sent by Charles "do not recognize any arrangement for marriage or even any previous discussion of it" (*R.E.S.*, X. 270).

[8] The assumption that the marriage discussion is either "a displacement of the discussion of 1378" or that the "negotiations of 1377 and the peace and marriage negotiations of 1378 were blended" does not accord with the fact that in the redactions Froissart names Marie, not her sister, and that "in all three he asserts that marriage was discussed and that Chaucer was one of the envoys" (*R.E.S.*, XI. 211).

[9] It is true that the payment made to Chaucer on March 6, 1381 *(Life-Records, No. 143)*, specifies his services as an envoy in the time of Edward III "versus Mounstrell 'et Parys', in partibus Francie, causa tractatus pacis pendentis" and also in the time of Richard II "causa locucionis habite de maritagio." To what marriage proposals during Richard's reign could this statement have referred? A royal deputation was appointed on January 16, 1378 *(Foedera, IV, 28)*, but the commissioners appointed were d'Angle, Segrave, and Skirlawe, and there is no record whatsoever that Chaucer was included in this embassy. Now these proposals must have concerned Isabel, inasmuch as in January her younger sister Katherine was yet unborn. Moreover, this discussion must have reached an impasse, for it would necessarily have been interrupted by the death of Isabel on February 23, 1378. The only other proposals in 1378 of which we have knowledge were for a marriage with Katherine, an infant of five months. "The long letter of the papal envoys" *(cf. R.E.S., X. 13, n. 3)*, dated May 7, 1378, to which reference has been made, relates exclusively to a truce and says nothing about marriage (Kervyn's ed., XVIII. 545-57). There is an official memorandum *(ibid., XXIII. 350-52)* stating that the English and French envoys met separately at Calais and at Boulogne, respectively, and that in joint conference, on June 25, 1378, the French representatives made formal offer of a proposal whereby Katherine should marry Richard –but this was a full month after Chaucer had departed for Italy! It will be noted that the payment to Chaucer was not made until three years later, and it is possible that, in the language of the Issue Roll, the "negotiations of 1377 and the peace and marriage negotiations of 1378 were blended." But no trace of any such confusion appears in Froissart's narrative of these negotiations.

[10] Isabelle of France was born November 9, 1389; she was married to Richard II on November 1, 1396 (Vallet de Viriville, *Bibl. de l'Ecole des Chartes*,XIX.(1857), p.477).

Reprinted from *RES,* XIV (1938), 63-67.

10

CAMBYUSKAN'S FLYING HORSE AND CHARLES VI'S 'CERF VOLANT'

Although Chaucer's exact source is unknown, significant analogues of the main features of the *Squire's Tale* have from time to time[1] been discovered. In the *Arabian Nights*, the *Cléomadès*, and the *Méliacin*, for example, there are stories very similar to the tale of Cambyuskan and the 'hors of bras'.[2] And since in the text Chaucer also refers to the 'Pegasee' and the 'Grekes hors Synon', 'As men moun in thise olde geestes rede' (*v.* 211), he seems to have been familiar with more than one account of magic steeds. But whatever Chaucer learned about flying animals from 'thise olde poetries', it would be strange indeed if he did not know something as well about King Charles VI's marvellous dream of the 'cerf volant'.

It appears that shortly before invading Flanders with an army on 3 November 1382, Charles VI, King of France, stopped for a time at the town of Senlis, where one night he dreamed a curious dream. A description of this vision is found in a contemporary report by the chronicler Froissart:

> Advenu estoit, point n'avoit lonc terme, au jone roi Charle de France, entrues que il sejournoit en la citté de Senlis, que, en dormant en son lit, une vission li vint, et li estoit proprement avis que il se trouvoit en la citté d'Arras, où onques à che jour n'avoit esté, et là estoit et toute la fleur de la chevalerie de son roiaulme, et là venoit li contes de Flandres à lui, qui li aseoit sus son poing un faucon pelerin moult gent et moult biel, et li dissoit enssi: 'Monsigneur, je vous donne à bonne estrine ce faucon pour le milleur que je veïsse onques, le mieux volant, le mieux et le plus gentieument cauçant et le mieux abatant oisiaux.' De ce present avoit li rois grant joie, et disoit: 'Biaux cousins, grant merchis.' Adont estoit il avis au roi que il regardoit sus le connestable de France, qui estoit dalés li, messire Olivier de Clichon, et li disoit: 'Connestables, alons, vous et moi, as camps pour esprouver che gentil faucon que mon cousin de Flandres m'a donné.' Et li connestables respondoit: 'Sire, alons.' Adont montoient il as chevaulx entre eus deus seulement, et venoient as camps, et prendoit li connestables ce faucon de la main dou roi, et trouvoient moult bien à voler et grant fuisson de hairons. Adont dissoit li rois: 'Connestables, jettés l'oiseil, si verons comment il cachera et volera.' Et li

71

connestables le jettoit; et cils faucons montoit si haut que à paines le pooit il cuesir en l'air, et prendoit son chemin sus Flandres. Adont disoit li rois au connestable: 'Connestables, chevauchons après mon oiseil; je ne le voel pas perdre.' Et li connestables li acordoit, et chevauchoient, che estoit il vis au roi, au ferir des esperons parmi uns grans marès, et trouvoient un bois trop durement fort et drut d'espines et de ronses et de mauvais bos à chevauchier. Là dissoit li rois: 'A piet! à piet! nous ne poons passer che bos à cheval.' Adont descendoient il et se mettoient à piet; et varlet venoient, qui prendoient les chevaulx, et li rois et li connestables entroient en che bos à grant paine, et tant aloient que il venoient en une trop ample lande, et là veoient le faucon qui cachoit hairons et abatoit, et se combatoit à eulx et eulx à lui; et sambloit au roi que ses faucons i faisoit très grant fuisson d'apertisses et cachoit oisiaulx devant lui et tant que il en perdoient la veue. Adont estoit li rois trop courouchies que il ne pooit sieuir son oisel, et dissoit au connestable: 'Je perderai mon faucon, dont je averai grant anoi, ne je n'ai loire ne ordenance dont je le puisse reclamer.' En che sousi que li rois avoit, li estoit vis que uns trop biaux chers qui portoit douse (rains),[3] et à elles, apparoit à iaulx en issant hors de ce fort bois et venoit en celle lande, et s'enclinoit devant le roi; et li rois dissoit au connestable, qui regardoit ce cerf à mervelles et en avoit grant joie: 'Connestables, demorés ichi; je monterai sus che cerf qui se represente à moi, et sieurai mon faucon.' Li connestables li acordoit. Là montoit li jones rois de grant volenté sus che cerf volant, et s'en aloit à l'aventure après son faucon; et chils chers, comme bien dotrinés et avissés de faire le plaisir dou roi, le portoit par desus les grans bois et les haulx arbres. Et veoit que ses faucons abatoit oisiaux à si grant plenté que il en estoit tous esmervilliés comment il pooit ce faire, et sambloit au roi que, quant cils faucons ot asés volet et abatu de hairons et de oisiaux tant que bien devoit souffire, li rois reclama son faucon; et tantos cils faucons, comme bien duis, s'en vint assir sus le poing dou roi. Et estoit vis au roi que il reprendoit le faucon par les longnes et le metoit à son devoir, et cils cers ravaloit par desus ces bois et raportoit le roi en la propre lande là où il l'avoit encargié et où li connestables de France le atendoit, qui avoit grant joie de sa venue. Et, sitos comme li rois fu là venus et descendus, li cers s'en raloit et rentroit au bos, et ne le veoient plus; et là recordoit li rois au connestable, che li estoit vis, comment il li estoit avenu, et dou cerf comment il l'avoit doucement porté. 'Ne onques, dist li rois, je ne chevauchai plus aise.' Et li recordoit encores la bonté de son faucon, comment il avoit abatu tant d'oisiaulx que il en estoit esmervilliés, et li connestables l'ooit volentiers. Adont venoient li varlet qui les poursieuoient, qui ramenoient leurs chevaulx; si montoient sus, et trouvoient un chemin bel et ample qui les ramenoit à Arras. Adont s'esvilloit li rois, et avoit grant mervelle de celle vission, et trop bien li souvenoit de tout, et le recorda à aucuns de ceulx de sa cambre, qui le plus prochain li estoient; et tant li plaissoit li figure de che cerf que à paines en imaginations il n'en pooit partir, et fu li une des incidenses premiers, quant il descendi en Flandres combatre les Flamens, pour quoi le plus il encarga en sa devise le cerf vollant à porter.[4]

The bearing this written version of King Charles's dream has on the *Squire's Tale* is immediately apparent. For Froissart's account affords not only a parallel of Cambyuskan's flying horse, but the description of the 'faucon pelerin moult gent et moult biel' at once suggests a similarity to Chaucer's portrayal of Canacee's 'faucon peregryn':

> For ther nas nevere yet no man on lyve,
> If that I koude a faucon wel discryve,
> That herde of swich another of fairnesse,
> As wel of plumage as of gentilesse
> Of shap, of al that myghte yrekened be.
> A faucon peregryn thanne semed she
> Of fremde land.   (*vv.* 423–29.)[5]

Now the King's vision must itself have been regarded as one of the marvels of the day. Since the 'cerf volant' was adopted for the royal emblem, the story of its origin would have been familiar in court circles. Probably, therefore, at the court of France as at Cambyuskan's, 'Ne was ther swich a wondrying as was tho' (*v.* 308).

Nor can there be any question that Chaucer heard about the dream vision.[6] Froissart was his personal friend,[7] and so was Deschamps,[8] who, though he does not retell the story, writes a ballade about Charles VI and the 'cerf volant'.[9] And as for Froissart's connexion with the *Squire's Tale*, it will be recalled that *L'Espinette Amoureuse* furnished Chaucer with certain suggestions about Canacee's mirror.[10]

Of course the more enthusiastic story-tellers doubtless invented oral[11] versions of the dream, and some one of these variants reaching Chaucer may have suggested to him the composition of a plot centering on Cambyuskan and the three magic gifts. For what further hint for a romance would a medieval poet have needed than this actual dream experience of a French king, a magical 'cerf volant', and a 'faucon pelerin' of Flemish origin, the gift of the Count of Flanders? Now Chaucer's fragmentary narrative revolves about the same essential features—a mighty king who was given a magical animal, a falcon peregrine 'Of fremde land', and a dream involving Canacee's discovery of a bird 'Amydde a tree'. Chaucer of course treats each situation differently, but knowledge of this vision may have prompted him to weld these episodes together into a single plot. There is obviously a parallel between Cambyuskan and the flying horse and Charles VI and the 'cerf volant', and it should not have been difficult to substitute Canacee's dream about the falcon peregrine for the King's dream about the 'faucon pelerin'.[12] Since it seems definitely assured that Chaucer drew his materials from composite sources and may have lacked a model for unifying the incidents round a single figure, this example of a dream experience from life may accordingly have served as the inception of the *Squire's Tale*. But should Chaucer have found the unifying element in his original or originals, the significant fact would nevertheless remain that suggestions for the half-told tale of Cambyuskan are implicit in the vision of the King of France, and the dream might thus still be regarded as influencing Chaucer's decision to include this particular type of plot in the *Canterbury Tales*.[13]

NOTES

[1] Cf. my recent article, 'The Oriental Origin of Chaucer's Canacee-Falcon Episode', *M.L.R.* (January, 1936), XXXI, No. 1.

[2] See especially H.S.V. Jones, 'Some Observations upon the *Squire's Tale*', *P.M.L.A.* (1905), XX, 346–59.

[3] In *Variantes* (p. 387) Gaston Raynaud, the editor, states: 'P. 257, 1. 23: douse rains et à elles.–*Lecons des mss.* B 1, 2.–*Ms.* A 2: moult doucement ailles.–*Mss.* B 5, 7: douze elles.–*Mss.* B 12, 20: douse branches.–rains *manque aux mss.* A 1, 7.'

[4] *Chroniques de J. Froissart,* ed. by Gaston Raynaud (Paris, 1897), X, § 292, pp. 256–8. In notes to the introductory *Sommaire* (p. lxx, n. 1), M. Raynaud says: '*Le Religieux de Saint-Denis* (t. I, p. 70) raconte d'une autre facon l'origine de l'emblème adopte par Charles VI, qui aurait pris à la chasse un cerf, porteur d'un collier sur lequel étaient gravés les mots: *Caesar hoc mihi donavit.* Le récit de Froissart faisant allusion à un cerf *volant* a au moins le mérite d'expliquer toutes les particularités de l'animal cher au roi.'

[5] All quotations are from the Student's Cambridge Edition of *Chaucer*, ed. by F. N. Robinson (New York, 1933).

[6] In his travels to France and Flanders, Chaucer may of course at some time have visited the very town of Senlis.

[7] G. L. Kittredge, 'Chaucer and Froissart', *Englische Studien* (1899), XXVI, 321–36.

[8] J. L. Lowes, 'The Prologue to the *Legend of Good Women*....', *P.M.L.A.* (1905), XX, 769 ff.

[9] In No. LXVII (*Œuvres complètes* ... (S.A.T.F., Paris, 1878), ed. by Le Marquis de Queux de Saint-Hilaire, I, 164–5; see also notes on pp. 350–1). It should be further observed that Deschamps here (*vv.* 18–24) proposes to Charles the conquest of the Orient, which was at all times one of the favourite dreams of the prince, so there would have been no fundamental inappropriateness in Chaucer's associating Charles VI and Cambyuskan.

[10] As pointed out by Professor Jones, *op. cit.* pp. 356–8. Cf. the English lines (132 ff., 367 ff.) with the French verses (2583 ff., 2623 ff.–Aug. Scheler, *Œuvres* ... , Bruxelles, 1870, I, 384 especially).

[11] Or possibly written versions, for that matter. Cf. Froissart.

[12] In this connexion, it should be observed that King Charles recaptured his favourite falcon by the aide of the 'cerf volant'. Now Chaucer says that Canacee's 'faucon gat hire love ageyn / Repentant, as the storie telleth us, / By mediacion of Cambalus'. In the fragmentary text, Chaucer does not explain how the tercelet's return was effected. Perhaps Cambalus, like Charles VI, used the flying animal to make the recovery. The magic steed was readily obtainable and would have been a likely means to use in overtaking the flown bird. Moreover, this 'hors of bras', it will be recalled, helped his brother Algarsif to win 'Theodora to his wif', and was thus in a position to do a favour for Cambalus in his search for the false tercelet.

[13] According to this interpretation, the *Squire's Tale* could not have been written before November 1382, which fact affords the only positive datum we have had as to its chronology.

Reprinted from *MLR*, XXXIII (1938), 41-44.

11

THREE CHAUCER NOTES

I. SYMBOLIC COLORS

Among such decorative poetic devices as anagrams, palindromes, and acrostics,[1] mediaeval writers often sought to embellish their styles by the employment of symbolic colors. Interestingly enough, this formula was not infrequently adopted by Geoffrey Chaucer, especially in passages concerning courtly love where he describes the diverse emotional conditions of the lover. In fact, there are several important passages which seem to show that Chaucer was applying a single, unalterable pattern.

By his own statement Chaucer uses blue to indicate a lover's loyalty or fidelity, for in the Squire's Tale (644 f.) he says that 'veluettes blewe' are the 'signe of trouthe that is in wommen sene.'[2] Moreover, in *Anelida and Arcite* (330 ff.) when 'clad in asure,' the beloved proves 'For to be trewe.' Further, in *Troilus and Criseyde* (III, 885 ff.) the 'blewe ryng' sent to Troilus assures him of Criseyde's fidelity.

In addition, the colors black, red, and white appear to have the respective meanings of sorrowful, ardent, and joyful. In the *Book of the Duchess* (445, 457) Chaucer twice refers to the knight who mourns for his lately deceased mistress as garbed in black, and the company of ladies in the Knight's Tale (899) who weep for their husbands killed in the war are 'clad in clothes blake.' Finally, red for ardent may easily have been designed in the description of the Wife of Bath in the General Prologue (A 456, A 458) and of Absolon in the Miller's Tale (3317, 3319)—the Wife's 'hosen weren of fyn scarlet reed' and she was herself 'reed of hewe,' and Absolon's 'rode was reed' also and likewise 'In hoses rede he wente fetisly.' Obviously more than coincidence is suggested by the almost identical depictions of these two similarly amorous characters.

There is a passage in the rhetorical *Anelida and Arcite* which is especially interesting: here (146 f.) several colors are grouped together so that there appears white for joyful, red for ardent, and green for disloyalty ('newefangelnesse'). In stating that Arcite has seen another lady and has 'cladde him in her hewe—Wot I not whethir in white, rede, or grene?'

76

Anelida seems careful to avoid any mention of blue inasmuch as this color would imply that Arcite was loyal. White and red have already been discussed, and the symbolism of green is evident from Chaucer's statement in the Squire's Tale (646 f.) that 'the mewe is peynted grene' to depict 'all thise false fowles.' According to the color symbolism observed in Chaucer's practice, Anelida's statement may now be interpreted as meaning that her rival's 'hewe' is 'carefree (joyful), ardent, or false.'

These examples of color symbolism definitely establish that Chaucer was consistent in the meanings he attached to certain colors when describing the diverse emotional conditions of the lover. How should this treatment be accounted for?

One possibility is that the poet's knowledge derived from proverbial lore.[3] The colors black, red, and blue do have proverbially the respective meanings in their eulogistic significance of mournful, fervent, and constant; but neither the eulogistic nor the dyslogistic significance of both green (lively, hopeful, or envious, jealous) and white (triumphant, innocent, or blank, ghostly) accords with the poet's use of green for disloyal and white for carefree, joyful.

However, if proverbial meaning does not altogether explain Chaucer's practice, there remains the possibility of literary tradition. For in seeking to explain the cult of a poetic device, the weighty influence of literary tradition clearly cannot be excluded.

In this connection, it is arresting that in *Le Remede de Fortune* Guillaume de Machaut explicitly treats color symbolism according to the formula observed in Chaucer. That is, with Machaut, blue stands for loyalty, red for ardency, black for grief, white for joy, green for novelty, and yellow for falsity. The French passage reads as follows:

> Or te vueil ces couleurs aprendre,
> Comme en Amours les dois entendre:
> Saches que le pers signefie
> Loiauté qui het tricherie,
> Et le rouge amoureuse ardure
> Naissant d'amour loial et pure;
> Le noir te moustre en sa couleur
> Signefiance de douleur,
> Blanc joie, vert nouveleté,
> Et la jaune, c'est fausseté (vv. 1901-10).[4]

Now 'in view of Chaucer's fondness for Machaut,' as Professor Kittredge expresses it,[5] there is apparently nothing to disagree with the suggestion that the English poet was following the practice of Machaut.

Chaucer unquestionably knew *Le Remede* itself, because in the *Book of the Duchess* he several times[6] translates or paraphrases verses of this French poem.[7] Instead, then, of relying solely on proverbial lore as the source of his information, Chaucer gives every evidence of awareness to literary tradition in following closely the particular system of color symbolism cultivated by Machaut. Chaucer's adoption of the formula in *Le Remede* is thus at once a commentary upon the decorative style of his lyrical passages and a testimonial as to the deep infiltration into his works of mediaeval French influences.

Moreover, it seems important to observe that the identical meanings of loyalty and disloyalty attach to blue and green, respectively, in *Against Women Unconstant* where all three stanzas conclude with the same line: 'In stede of blew, thus may ye were al grene.' The appearance of this line in Machaut's *Le Voir Dit,* 'Qu'en lieu de bleu, dame, vous vestez vert,' immediately suggests that the Frenchman was again the model, especially since the general idea in the two poems is also similar.[8] And these two facts, it seems evident, constitute strong arguments together with the Chaucerian language of the text in favor of Chaucer's authorship of the balade *Against Women Unconstant.*

To sum up, since there appears no indication that the two writers were dealing independently with a body of proverbial lore, it seems reasonably safe to conclude that Machaut here as elsewhere served as Chaucer's example.[9] Finally, Chaucer's use of Machaut's formula should not be regarded lightly inasmuch as this color symbolism appears to furnish the key to at least two interesting passages. First, the statement in the *Complaint of Mars* (8) that the birds departed 'Wyth teres blewe' Professor Robinson[10] explains by reading 'blewe' as 'livid, pale,' connecting the word with *blo* (ON. *bla[r]*). Color symbolism here seems to afford a better reading of this passage, for Chaucer appears plainly to imply by blue that, in harmony with the spirit of Saint Valentine's Day, the 'foules' were faithful, loyal, and true. Secondly, in *Troilus and Criseyde* (III, 900 f.) Pandarus advises Criseyde: 'I nolde setten at his sorwe a myte, / But feffe hym with a fewe wordes white.' Professor Robinson[11] glosses white as 'specious' or 'plausible.' But it should be noted that white as joyful is very probably the correct reading, as elsewhere in *Troilus and Criseyde* (I, 640 ff.) there is a passage which seems to imply that joy is to sorrow as white is to black. Moreover, white as joyful not only makes excellent sense but appears here also intentionally contrasted with the word 'sorwe.' Chaucer, it would thus appear, may be read with no abatement of zest and with what seems more perfect understanding if the French formula for color symbolism is only remembered.

II. CEYS AND ALCIONE

In the 'Introduction' to his Tale, the Man of Law says of Chaucer that 'In youthe he made of Ceys and Alcione' (v. 57).[12] The story of Seys and Alcione is of course included in the *Book of the Duchess,* but the form of the title given by the Man of Law (Ceys, not Seys as in *Book of the Duchess*), has often been construed as evidence that Chaucer wrote an independent poem on the subject.[13] In a recent discussion of what he considers a somewhat analogous literary situation, Professor Lowes, however, would interpret this statement as a reference to the *Book of the Duchess:* he contends that in mentioning his 'trettiés amoureus de Pynotëus et de Neptisphele' or his *'livret* de Pynotëus et de Neptisphele,' Froissart is not alluding to an independent work on this theme but only to a single episode in the *Prison Amoureuse* where these citations occur. But Professor Lowes seems to draw entirely the wrong inference, for Froissart is clearly not identifying the *livret* with the whole *livre.* Instead, at the conclusion of his long work, Froissart explicitly states that all 'chils livres fust appelés la *Prison Amoureuse.'*[14] Indeed, so far as this evidence is concerned, the situation in Chaucer and Froissart is obviously not parallel.

The question as to the Man of Law's reference is further complicated by Lydgate's statement in the *Fall of Princes* that Chaucer wrote 'The pitous story of Ceix and Alcione,//And the deth eek of Blaunche the Duchesse' (vv. 303–04).[15] But now inasmuch as it seems quite unlikely that Lydgate should describe the brief incident of Ceix and Alcione on an equal basis with the central theme of the death of Blanche as an allusion to the *Book of the Duchess,* it appears altogether possible that Chaucer may have treated this episode independently. No poem answering this description seems to be extant, but Chaucer appears to have written a number of works that are now lost, as, for example, 'the book of the Leoun' mentioned in the 'retracciouns,'[16] a lost poem thought to have been a redaction of Machaut's *Dit dou Lyon.*[17]

In this connection, it may be observed that in the fourteenth century the subject of Ceys and Alcione was treated separately in a balade by Deschamps,[18] one of Chaucer's favorite French writers.[19] Chaucer's version of this theme is based principally on Ovid,[20] but it is generally believed that he may also have used a French account. In at least one passage, however, there seems to be no French parallel, for Professor Robinson notes that 'The storm and ship-wreck are described at length in Ovid (II. 480–557). Machaut does not mention them.'[21] Accordingly, it may be important that in the second stanza of Deschamps's balade the storm at sea and the subsequent shipwreck are both narrated.[22] In any

case, the 'Ceix et Alcyone' written by Deschamps is a contemporary
illustration of the independent treatment of this episode and thus affords
evidence by way of analogy that Lydgate's reference may not apply to the
Book of the Duchess but to a separate poem composed, as the Man of Law
says, in Chaucer's 'youthe.'

If *Ceys and Alcione* may now be regarded as having first existed in
separate form, it is not at all difficult to determine why Chaucer decided
to include this episode in the *Book of the Duchess.* First of all, the
account of a loving king and queen balances appropriately with the
narrative of a faithful knight and lady. More significantly, the tragedy of
Seys and Alcione (as it has now become spelled) sets the whole tone of the
elegy and foreshadows perfectly the central motif of a grief-stricken lover
(in one case Alcione, in the other the Black Knight) lamenting the decease
of one greatly beloved. Thus, although the episode is by no means
indispensable to the exposition of the main plot, it looms, most probably
as a result of revision,[23] as one of the most moving sections of Chaucer's
elegy.

III. SIR GUICHARD D'ANGLE, A POITEVINE FRIEND

The place of Guichard d'Angle of Poitou in the Chaucerian circle is
well established by Froissart's reference to him as one of Geoffrey's
associates in the embassy to France in the spring of 1377.[24] As I have
elsewhere[25] recently attempted briefly to sketch the life of Sir Guichard,
my present purpose is not so much to review these materials as it is to
assemble some further data to illustrate his connections with Chaucer and
some of the poet's friends.

First, it seems important to observe that Guichard was so highly
regarded by his compatriots that his partisanship of the Black Prince
influenced if not occasioned a Poitevine immigration to England.[26] As he
first strongly sponsored the French cause,[27] Guichard's shift in allegiance
must accordingly be traced briefly. In fact, one of the earliest records
connects him with a patriotic demonstration, for on August 17, 1346, he
figured prominently in Jean Larcheveque's company which was on parade
in Poitiers.[28] Moreover, he shortly thereafter distinguished himself by
successfully defending Niort, of which fort he was captain, against three
successive assaults by English forces under the Count of Derby. Froissart
states that there Guichard established himself, not unlike Chaucer's Knight,
as *uns très gentilz chevaliers.*[29] Exploits like this perhaps led Philippe de
Valois to appoint him in 1351 Seneschal of Saintonge, the functions of
which office he exercised until September 24, 1354.[30] His most heroic

exploit, however, appears to have occurred in 1356 at the battle of
Maupertuis where he was left for dead *aux pieds au roi Jean,* whom he had
come forward to defend.[31] In October 1360, the French King finally
commissioned Sir Guichard to surrender to the Black Prince the keys to La
Rochelle.[32]

In the years immediately following Guichard seems to have become a
partisan of the king of England, apparently largely out of admiration for
the military achievements of the Black Prince.[33] During the years
1370–1372, Charles V completed the confiscation of d'Angle's goods and
properties,[34] but he straightway began seemingly to prosper under English
sovereignty as King Edward in 1374 appointed him his personal
representative to treat with the French.[35] On September 29, 1375, King
Edward also granted him for life or until further order, in consideration of
loss of lands taken by the French, the sum of 26s. 8d. at the Exchequer,[36]
and on January 1, 1376, he was further granted, in compensation for
damages sustained in wars and for services in the king's cause, the keeping
of the manor of Caversham until the full age of the heir of the king's
kinsman, Edward le Despenser.[37] Indeed, throughout the closing years of
Edward's reign Guichard figured in prominent circles, often being provided
by the king's order along with such notables as Lord Latimer, John of
Gaunt, and the Black Prince with suitable robes for celebrating festive
occasions.[38] It was only natural that he should be favorably regarded by
the new sovereign since the Black Prince in 1376 had appointed him
guardian of the youthful Richard.[39] Accordingly, on December 10, 1378,
King Richard II made an allowance of £1,000 yearly to 'Guychard Dangle,'
Earl of Huntingdon, having on July 16 already advanced him to this
earldom.[40] On the death of d'Angle in 1380, two of Chaucer's intimate
friends, Sir Lewis Clifford and Sir John Clanvowe, officiated as executors
of Sir Guichard's will.[41]

Finally, it remains to be noted that Guichard's unusual role in politics
enabled him to associate with more than one literary figure of the time.
For example, he became acquainted in 1360 with the Marshall Boucicault
at La Rochelle.[42] Boucicault, as Professor Kittredge has shown,[43] was a
friend of the Clifford family, and thus Chaucer may have heard of the
valiant Boucicault[44] from either Sir Lewis Clifford or Sir Guichard. At La
Rochelle, d'Angle also first met Sir John Chandos, for it was in December
1360 that he was obliged to surrender this city into the custody of
Chandos.[45] Nine years later he was to become the compatriot of Sir John
Chandos, under whose command he served at Montauban.[46] The Herald of
Chandos, moreover, gives in his narrative poem a graphic account of

d'Angle's part in the Spanish campaign.[47] Since Sir Guichard also knew Froissart,[48] Oton de Graunson,[49] Ayala,[50] and Enguerrand de Coucy,[51] his literary acquaintance was fairly extensive. These brief biographical notations thus serve to show how numerous and how significantly interwoven were the connections of the friends within Chaucer's circle.

NOTES

[1] *See* examples noted by A. Brusendorff, *The Chaucer Tradition* (Oxford, 1925), p. 48.

[2] Unless otherwise observed, all quotations are from *The Complete Works of Geoffrey Chaucer,* ed. F. N. Robinson (Boston, 1933).

[3] On the proverbial meaning of these colors, *see* Walter Sargent, *The Enjoyment and Use of Color* (New York, 1924), pp. 50–59.

[4] *SATF* (Paris, 1911), II, 68–69.–There seems to be no allusion to this passage in Robinson's edition, and although *Le Remede* is mentioned by Skeat, he does not quote these verses nor attempt to show that Chaucer followed Machaut's scheme; see *The Works of Geoffrey Chaucer,* 2d ed. (Oxford, 1899), I, 565.

[5] *MP,* VII (1910), 472.

[6] *See* Robinson's notes, esp. pp. 885–886.

[7] L. Cipriani, *PMLA,* XXII (1907), 554; *see* esp. Kittredge, *PMLA,* XXX (1915), 4–23.

[8] The French balade containing the above-mentioned refrain is a part of *Le Voir Dit (Société des Bibliophiles François* (Paris, 1875), p. 309, vv. 7544–7664; this line also occurs separately on p. 213, v. 4929), itself a collection of letters and replies, balades, lays, and rondeaux (G. Hanf, *Uber Guillaume de Machauts "Voir Dit"* [Halle, 1898], p. I); but the balade may also have circulated in another form as it appears to be a song and is included among Machaut's musical compositions (F. Ludwig, *Guillaume de Machaut, Musikalische Werke* [Leipzig, 1926], No. 36, pp. 44–45); thus the verse may have enjoyed popularity equivalent to that of a proverb.

[9] For a recent interesting discussion of and bibliographical references to color symbolism, *see* Don Cameron Allen, *PQ,* XV (1936), 81–92.

[10] Page 972.

[11] Page 937.

[12] Robinson, *op. cit.,* p. 74.

[13] *See* esp. F. J. Furnivall, *Trail-Forewords* (London, 1871), p. 115; and W. W. Skeat, ed., *The Works of Geoffrey Chaucer* (Oxford, 1894, 1900), I, 63; V, 105; but cf. J. M. Manly, ed., *Canterbury Tales* (New York, 1928), p. 564.

[14] J. L. Lowes, *PMLA,* XX (1905), 769 ff., esp. 826, n. 3. For the quotations, *see* Aug. Scheler, ed., *Œuvres de Froissart* (Brussels, 1870), I, 211–347, esp. 343.

[15] *Falls of Princes,* ed. by Henry Bergen, Carnegie Institute (Washington, 1923).

[16] Robinson, *op. cit.*, p. 314.

[17] *Ibid.*, p. 881; F. M. Dear, *Medium Ævum*, VII (1938), 105, suggests that Chaucer's *Book of the Lion* was an occasional piece for Lionel, Duke of Clarence, whom Froissart called "monseigneur Lion."

[18] Le Marquis de Saint-Hilaire, ed., *Œuvres complètes...*, *SATF* (Paris, 1878), No. XXXV, I, 118–119.

[19] J. L. Lowes, *op. cit.*

[20] F. J. Miller, ed., *Ovid's Metamorphoses*, Loeb Classical Library (London, 1916), II, 384 ff.

[21] Robinson, *op. cit.*, p. 882.

[22] There seem to be no verbal agreements between Deschamps's account and the version of Chaucer as it appears in the *Book of the Duchess*.

[23] According to Skeat (I, 63): "The original 'Ceys and Alcion' evidently ended at 1. 220; where it began, we cannot say, for the poem was doubtless revised and somewhat altered. Ll. 215, 216 hint that a part of it was suppressed."

[24] *Chroniques de J. Froissart*, ed. S. Luce (Paris, 1888), VIII, 225–226.

[25] *Three Chaucer Studies* (Oxford, 1932), No. II, pp. 34 ff.

[26] J. H. Gaillard, *Le Moyen Age*, XLII (1932), 135 f.

[27] H. Beauchet-Filleau, *Dictionnaire Historiques et Généalogique des Familles du Poitou* (Poitiers, 1891), I, 79–80.

[28] *Ibid.*

[29] *Op. cit.*, IV, 13.

[30] Paul Guérin, *Recueil des Documents concernant le Poitou* (Oudin, 1886), XVII, 258.

[31] Beauchet-Filleau, *op. cit.*

[32] Paul Guérin, *op. cit.*

[33] G.F. Beltz, *Memorials of the Order of the Garter* (London, 1841), pp. 182 ff.

[34] Paul Guérin, *op. cit.*

[35] Beauchet-Filleau, *op. cit.*

[36] *Calendar of the Patent Rolls*, 1374–77, p. 177.

[37] *Ibid.*, pp. 206, 214, 442.

[38] Sir Harris Nicholas, *History of the Orders of Knighthood of the British Empire* (London, 1842), II, xx–xxi.

[39] *Chroniques de J. Froissart*, ed. S. Luce (Paris, 1888), VIII, cxxxviii.

[40] *Cal. Pat. Rolls*, 1377–81, p. 314.

[41] Sir Harris Nicholas, *Testamenta Vetusta* (London, 1826), I, 109.

[42] R. Delachenal, *Histoire de Charles V* (Paris, 1909), II, 332.

[43] *MP*, I (1903), I ff.

[44] Cf. Édouard Guillon, *La Nouvelle Revue*, XXXVI (1918), 243 ff.

[45] Beauchet-Filleau, *op. cit.*

[46] Paul Guérin, *op. cit.*, XIX, 90.

[47] *The Life of the Black Prince*, ed. M. K. Pope and E. C. Lodge (Oxford, 1910), vv. 3239 ff., 4197 ff.

[48] G. L. Kittredge, *Englische Studien*, XXVI (1899), 321 ff.

[49] *See* my article *SP,* XXXV (1938), 515 ff.

[50] *See* my article, *PMLA,* L (1935), 69 ff.

[51] On whose connections with the Chaucerian circle, *see* H. L. Savage's brilliant paper, *Speculum,* XIV (1939), 423 ff.

Reprinted from *Essays and Studies in Honor of Carleton Brown*, N.Y.U. Press (1940).

12

THE GENRE OF CHAUCER'S *SQUIRE'S TALE*

Spenser,[1] Milton,[2] and John Lane[3] had long ago written of Chaucer's *Squire's Tale* when in 1855 Browning, referring to an idealized future, stated that "Then one shall propose . . . / To end now our half-told tale of Cambuscan."[4] In the meantime, although no poet has arisen to complete the fragmentary story, research has fortunately cast new light on the Oriental origin of Chaucer's materials and the direction certain episodes of his plot were apparently to take. These source materials may therefore be briefly cited as aids in interpreting the poet's plan. There are also fortunately some hints in the incomplete text itself as to the genre of the *Squire's Tale*.

For example, Part One (346 ll.) sets the stage for the narrative which follows, linking the story in time and place: olden days at Sarray—introduces the main characters, naming both the strange knight who brings the gifts and the members of a family group: Cambyuskan and his Queen Elpheta, their two sons Algarsif and Cambalo, and their daughter Canacee—and describes the special properties of the magical gifts, listing as machinery: the flying horse, the magic mirror, ring, and sword. All these elements are paralleled, sometimes with striking closeness, in literary source materials whose origins trace from the East: notably in the legends of *Prester John,* in the *Cléomadès* of Adenès li Rois, and in the celebrated *Arabian Nights.*[5] And, as apparently in Chaucer, these narrative elements compose a setting which is succeeded by an elaborate plot.

Part Two (325 ll.) begins to unfold the narrative action with the recital of the adventures of Canacee, who after a dream experience goes into her garden and is cautioned by a female hawk found there to beware of men. The situation wherein a dream experience involving a forsaken bird leads a princess to suspect men is not uncommon in Oriental literature. In 1936 I discussed the parallels between the Canacee-Falcon episode and its closest known analogue, the tale from the *Arabian Nights* of Tāj al-Mulūk and Princess Dunyā, so that now only a brief quotation may serve to identify Chaucer's type of story—

For this episode, as for others in the Chaucerian fragment, the *Arabian Nights* affords a close parallel. The Arabian story represents a definite type of tale in which the subsequent behaviour of a princess is motivated by a dream experience. In this dream, animals are usually represented as birds are in the *Squire's Tale,* and the vision serves to warn the princess that men are unfaithful. It is thus interpreted as picturing in the plight of a forsaken bird or beast what might occur to the princess if she accepted at face value the promises of a suitor. This simple plot, using an animal fable to foreshadow an identical situation in human affairs, is obviously folklore material. That the plot was popular in Oriental fiction appears certain on the basis of the *Arabian Nights* alone, in which collection this conventional machinery is employed no less than three times.[6]

The *Arabian Nights,* it will be observed, thus proves helpful in analyzing the source materials of both Parts One and Two of the *Squire's Tale.*

The text of Part Two may now be examined in the light of its Oriental analogues. First, it should be recalled that Canacee is to draw a moral from the bird's tale of woe since the falcon declares that her purpose is

> . . . for noon hope for to fare the bet,
> But for to obeye unto your herte free,
> And for to maken othere be war by me (II. 488—90).[7]

Secondly, the reader is allowed no doubt whatever as to wherein Canacee must "be war" inasmuch as the hawk warns her that "alle thyng, repeirynge to his kynde, /Gladeth hymself" (ll. 608—09), and that in finding a new love, "So ferde this terclet" (l. 621). Thirdly, it is evident that Canacee is not permitted to think that birds alone are fickle, for the falcon explicitly says: "Man loven of propre kynde newefangelnesse / As briddes doon that men in cages fede" (ll. 610-11). Finally, it seems perfectly clear that the fable of birds was to carry over to the affairs of Canacee, because what occasioned the dream leading to the discovery of the hawk was the magic mirror, which possessed the special power that

> . . . if any lady bright
> Hath set hire herte on any maner wight,
> If he be fals, she shal his tresoun see,
> His newe love, and al his subtiltee,
> So openly that there shal no thyng hyde (ll. 137—41).

The next question is whether or not Canacee was convinced, as was her Oriental prototype Princess Dunyā, that men are fickle creatures. Chaucer leads one to infer that in her deportment Canacee was "ful mesurable" when he states that in the midst of the revels "of hir fader hadde she take leve, / To goon to reste soone after it was eve" (ll. 363–64); and he further implies that Canacee and her ladies were deeply moved by the bird's misfortune when he says that 'Greet was the sorwe for the haukes harm" (l. 632). Surely, then Canacee's dutiful, kind nature would incline one to believe that she listened approvingly to the falcon's warning about men.[8] There is happily one piece of evidence which seems to remove any doubt as to Canacee's sentiments. I refer to a passage which illustrates Chaucer's use of symbolic colors.[9] It will be recalled that in the garden the falcon peregrine tells the princess that "Men loven of propre kynde newefangelnesse" (l. 610). By the time Canacee reaches home she appears to have become convinced that the bird fable applies also to human beings, for it should be noted that she builds a cage covered on the inside with blue velvet to signify that women are true and painted on the outside green to show that male birds are false.

> And by hire beddes heed she made a mewe,
> And covered it with veluettes blewe,
> In signe of trouthe that is in wommen sene.
> And al withoute, the mewe is peynted grene,
> In which were peynted alle thise false fowles (ll. 643–47).

One concludes that the moral about infidelity among birds is intended to be attached to men and women. As a final point, it is deeply significant that Edmund Spenser, who was intimate with Chaucer's *Squire's Tale* and who imitated his color symbolism,[10] seems from reading the Chaucerian text alone to have arrived at an identical conclusion with regard to Princess Canacee's aversion to men:

> *Cambelloes* sister was fayre *Canacee*, . . .
> She modest was in all her deedes and words,
> And wondrous chast of life, yet lou'd of Knights and Lords.
> Full many Lords, and many knights her loued,
> Yet she to none of them her liking lent . . .
> So much the more as she refused to love
> So much the more she loued was and sought (F.Q., IV, ii, 35–37).

At this juncture—that is, immediately following the description of the "mewe"—Chaucer breaks off with the statement:

> Thus lete I Canacee hir hauk kepyng;
> I wol namoore as now speke of hir ryng,
> Til it come eft to purpos for to seyn

How that this faucon gat hire love ageyn
Repentant, as the storie telleth us,
By mediacion of Cambalus,
The Kynges sone, of which that I yow tolde.
But hennesforth I wol my proces holde
To speken of aventures and of batailles,
That nevere yet was herd so grete mervailles (ll. 651–60).

Before returning to Canacee ("Til it come eft . . ."), Chaucer next proceeds with a promise to relate three main episodes: (1) how Cambyuskan won many cities, (2) how Algarsif won Theodora for his wife, and (3) how Cambalo won Canacee. But this is all he does say, for the *Squire's Tale* is incomplete after the succeeding couplet, which begins Part Three. Barren as the outline is, one may yet perceive not a few traces of the narrative content of these three episodes. Since these faint hints are all the text affords, they should be scrutinized most carefully. For instance, the passage just quoted contains an important datum on Chaucer's narrative procedure: we see that the foregoing three episodes are to be told before he returns to Canacee; he postpones telling her adventures until later, saying that from this point forward ("But hennesforth I wol my proces holde") he will speak of great battles and so go on to tell (1) how Cambyuskan won many cities, . . .

What technique involving postponements and overlappings in the narrative development does Chaucer seem to be proposing?

Let us consider a few facts. Since the *Squire's Tale* (1) has an Eastern atmosphere, (2) deals with source materials originating in the East, and (3) would contain (as projected) several different episodes, an Oriental style admittedly would be most appropriate. And there is an Oriental device which satisfies the foregoing requirements; namely, the well-known framing tale, of which there are two chief types.[11] One type opens with a situation returned to by the narrator as often as tributary incidents are finished; and this is well illustrated by the *Arabian Nights,* where Scheherazade each evening postpones her own death by entertaining the Sultan with her recitals. The other type begins with a principal story for the frame and is followed by several intercalary incidents before the framing tale is resumed and closed; and this is fully exemplified by the Persian *Thousand and One Days,* where Princess Farruknaz has conceived an aversion to men because of the influence of a dream involving a gentle doe deserted by a faithless stag.

Now the appearance in the Persian *Thousand and One Days* of an animal fable being carried over to the affairs of human beings affords an obvious parallel to the situation in the Canacee-Falcon episode. Thus we clearly have one point of contact between the *Squire's Tale* and the *second type* of Oriental framing device. Moreover, the technique of beginning with a frame story which is interrupted for the inclusion of a series of episodes also seems to match Chaucer's method of postponement in the account of Canacee. A further examination of the Persian framing story would therefore appear to be suggested, not only for its connection with the Canacee-Falcon episode, but also for its possible bearing on Chaucer's whole plan. For this reason, the Oriental plot may be briefly summarized—

> Togrulbey, King of Casmire, had besides one son a beautiful daughter, Farruknaz, whose hand was sought in marriage by ambassadors from all the courts of Asia. But before these ambassadors reached the King's court, all men had become odious to the Princess because she had dreamed of a faithless stag abandoning a gentle doe. After conferring with the King, Farruknaz's nurse for a thousand and one days told the Princess stories of faithful lovers, but the Princess remained unconvinced until she saw in scenes created on a wall the very opposite of her dream, at which time she then declared: "Ah, I am doubtless mistaken in my estimate of men." And becoming thus assured of man's fidelity, she is led to accept her most loyal suitor, who had privately arranged the scenes she saw.[12]

Of course neither the *Arabian Nights* nor the *Persian Tales* were known to Europe in Chaucer's day,[13] but, as we have already seen, the plot in which a princess is influenced to suspect men because of a dream experience involving animals was popular in Eastern literature from earliest times. In fact, the motif occurs in the seventh-century Hindu romance, *Vāsavadattā*, by Subandhu.[14] It is also significant to note that *Vāsavadattā* is likewise a framing story of the *second type*, that it mentions a magic horse named Manōjava, and that the animal episode serves here, as in the Persian *Thousand and One Days*, to introduce the frame itself. Thus, although no one of the known Oriental framing accounts has been proved to be a direct source, there seems clear indication that Chaucer was using a model.

That Chaucer was following an original is suggested indeed by statements in the fragmentary text; for example, Professor Robinson[15] calls attention to a few passages implying that Chaucer "was following an original." In the note on ll. 29 ff. (which describe Elpheta, Algarsif, Cambalo, and Canacee) Robinson says that "Probably all four names come from an undiscovered source, or sources, of the *Squire's Tale.*" Professor Manly contends that "Chaucer possibly took the name 'Elpheta' from some list of the principal stars";[16] but I may note in support of Robinson a further literary use of the name *Elphita* in an early fifteenth-century chanson by the Catalan Andreu Febrer.[17] Moreover, there is some internal evidence favoring the theory of an original in the description of Cambyuskan's "feeste":

> And eek it nedeth nat for to devyse
> At every cours the ordre of hire servyse.
> I wot nat tellen of hir strange sewes,
> Ne of hir swannes, ne of hire heronsewes.
> Eek in that lond, as tellen knyghtes olde . . . (ll. 65–69).

Still more important is Chaucer's own testimony that he will tell how the falcon got her love again "Repentant, as the storie telleth us" (l. 655).

In short, there appears good evidence that Chaucer was not inventing the *Squire's Tale* and that in the Canacee-Falcon episode he was following a definite Oriental motif. We also have the further datum that this particular literary motif (wherein an animal fable carries over to human affairs) was used in the Persian *Thousand and One Days* as the frame of the *second type* of Eastern framing story. This last fact thus leads one logically to inquire whether the Canacee-Falcon episode, like its Oriental analogues, was not similarly employed as the frame for a series of shorter narratives.

In making the inquiry, I may again cite Chaucer's own words, for the Chaucerian text would seem itself to offer internal evidence in support of this interpretation. Immediately before Canacee finds the forsaken falcon, Chaucer expressly states:

> The knotte why that every tale is toold,
> If it be taried til that lust be coold
> Of hem that han it after herkned yoore,
> The savour passeth ever lenger the moore,
> For fulsomnesse of his prolixitee;
> And by the same resoun, thynketh me,
> I sholde to the knotte condescende,
> And maken of hir walkyng soone an ende (ll. 401–09).

Chaucer's declaration clearly appears to mean that Canacee's experience in the garden is to be the "knotte" of the *Squire's Tale*. In fact, over fifty years ago, the eminent Dr. Alois Brandl, although he mistakenly interpreted the bird fable as an allegory of an actual human drama in Chaucer's time, recognized the bearing of these lines on the poet's whole plot when he regarded the falcon episode as the "knotte" of the entire story as projected.[18] In view, then, of its Eastern analogues and of Chaucer's own words, the Canacee-Falcon episode appears to be the "knotte why that" the *Squire's Tale* "is toold."

It will be recalled, first, that the *second type* of Oriental framing tale opens with the frame story; secondly, that the frame is followed by intercalary incidents; and thirdly, that the frame is then returned to at the close. We have already seen that Canacee's experience with the hawk fulfills the first part of the definition in opening the narrative or introducing the "knotte." The next question is, then, whether or not intercalary incidents follow after the frame, as would be expected in the *second type* of framing device. We have already observed too, that Chaucer postpones completing the report on Canacee until he shall have related the three episodes featuring (1) Cambyuskan, (2) Algarsif and Theodora, and (3) Cambalo and Canacee. Indeed he quits the narration of Canacee's adventures at almost precisely the same point in the development of the plot that the story is interrupted for adding intercalary materials in both the accounts of Princess Dunyā and Princess Farruknaz, for the narrative of Princess Dunyā is also a framing story. The first part of the tale of Princess Dunyā is followed by the episode about Azīz and his beloved Azizah; that of Princess Farruknaz, by recitals covering a thousand and one days. Chaucer's proposed plan thus far appears to match the style of the *second type* of framing tale. We may therefore pass next to the final requirement, according to which the frame is resumed and closed. That the recital of Canacee's fortunes will be resumed is indicated by both Chaucer's "Til it come eft to purpos for to seyn" (l. 653) and his concluding statement in Part Two: "And ther I lefte I wol ayeyn bigynne" (1.670). Furthermore, that the tale featuring the Princess is to close the whole plot appears from the fact that the last episode mentioned in Chaucer's outline has to do with Canacee. Accordingly, from the standpoint of the three essential requirements, Chaucer's Canacee-Falcon episode would appear designed, not as one of the intercalary incidents, but as the framing tale itself.

There remains, however, the puzzling problem of the three episodes. Fortunately we are not left wholly at a loss as to the probable nature of even these. As for the incident of Algarsif's winning Theodora by help of "the steede of brass" (l. 666), similar incidents have already been noted in the *Arabian Nights* and the *Cléomadès.*[19] The identity of the "strange knyght" (l. 89) is a more difficult question. Perhaps he is not really the ambassador of the "kyng of Arabe and of Inde" (l. 110), but the king's own son, as this disguise is a common literary motif. Indeed Prince Tāj

al-Mulūk, who in the Arabian collection would thus correspond to
Chaucer's "strange knyght," does not disclose to Princess Dunyā his real
identity until after she has become convinced that men are loyal and true.
But by far the most puzzling circumstance in the fragmentary *Squire's Tale*
is that Chaucer first introduces Cambalo in l. 31 as Canacee's brother (he is
called Cambalus in l. 656) only later to state that Cambalo ". . . faught in
lystes with the bretheren two / For Canacee er that he myghte hire wynne"
(ll. 668–69). Possibly a suitor named Cambalo fought the brothers
Cambalo and Algarsif. Possibly "Cambalo" in l. 667 was inserted as a
scribal error. Possibly, since the "two-brothers" motif occurs in the legends
of *Prester John,* Chaucer means merely that Cambalo rescued his sister
from two knights who were brothers. But, inasmuch as five lines
beforehand Chaucer uses *win* in the sense of espousal when stating that
Algarsif "wan Theodora to his wif" (l. 664), it seems most likely that
Chaucer means that Cambalo wedded his sister Canacee.

Without pressing the point unduly, I may note the significant
occurrence of the incest motif in the cycle of romances to which the tale
of Tāj al-Mulūk and Princess Dunyā belongs. This tale belongs to a whole
series of stories concerning a family group reminiscent of the personnel in
the *Squire's Tale;* these personages are King Omar bin al-Nu'umān, his two
sons Sharrkan and Zau al-Makān, and his daughter Nuzhat al-Zamān. The
adventures of this family comprise one hundred and one nights, in the
famous Medina Edition some four hundred pages, and compose the longest
tale in the whole Arabian collection. These adventures are excluded from
Lane's translation of the *Arabian Nights* because they depend "upon
incidents of a most objectionable nature",[20] but they are duly included by
the celebrated translator Sir Richard F. Burton. The parallels between the
Squire's Tale and this Arabian analogue are unmistakable: (1) King Omar
bin al-Nu'umān's family has the same membership as Cambyuskan's; (2)
Omar, like Cambyuskan, was celebrated for his victories; (3) the two
remarkable sons, presumably like Algarsif and Cambalo, performed many
brave deeds in their travels; and (4) it is a story of incest, for Princess
Nuzhat al-Zamān weds her brother Sharrkan.[21]

Inasmuch as there are parallels between several episodes in Chaucer
and in the *Arabian Nights,* the fact that an incest motif also occurs in this
Oriental analogue may have some bearing on the plot of the *Squire's Tale.*
We may presume that as a man Chaucer would not tolerate the idea of
incest, because as a poet he certainly speaks against it in the *Pardoner's
Tale:*

> Lo, how that dronken Looth, unkyndely,
> Lay by his doghtres two, unwityngly;
> So dronke he was he nyste what he wroghte (ll. 485–87).

Although the reference is probably to Gower's incestuous tale of "Canace," the Man of Law is speaking of Chaucer when he says:

> But certeinly no word ne writeth he
> Of thilke wikke ensample of Canacee,
> That loved hir owene brother synfully;
> (Of swiche cursed stories I sey fy) (ll. 77–80).

One might argue, then, that the reason for the abrupt termination of the *Squire's Tale* is connected with the circumstance that incest which is featured in the Arabian story was probably included in Chaucer's original.

But, if there was this unattractive theme of incest in his source, why did Chaucer begin the story at all? The concluding couplet in the extant text constitutes some argument in favor of a lost fascicule,[22] and thus Chaucer may have been already engaged on Part Three of the *Squire's Tale* when he found that his source ended with a reference to incest. In view of the excessive length of the Arabian analogue—one-eighth of the whole Arabian collection—it is certainly possible that he began to retell his original before reading to its conclusion. If this was the fact, it seems likely that the poet next sought to fit a new ending to the story to include it in the *Canterbury Tales*. That he did try to adapt his materials has been well argued by Dr. Willis Wager, who observes that ll. 63–75, containing the *occupatio* device, seem to have been added to adapt the *Squire's Tale* to the Canterbury scheme.[23] Why Chaucer failed to complete the adaptation remains uncertain, as is the case with the incomplete *Cook's Tale*.

Sir Alfred W. Pollard did not exaggerate when he stated that in the Canterbury collection "the genesis of the *Squire's Tale* has baffled investigation more than any other."[24] There are some notable instances, however, where the present evidence opens a new stream of suggestions bearing on the interpretation of Chaucer's plan. Since the text is incomplete, the theory that the Squire proposed to narrate a series of boxed incidents is obviously incapable of a practical demonstration. But there are an impressive number of facts supporting this view:—(1) the opening 346 ll. are merely introductory; (2) Chaucer outlines what his whole plot is to contain; (3) he promises to return to Canacee and her hawk; (4) he refers to the Canacee-Falcon motif as the "knotte" of his story; and (5) there are pertinent analogues of this motif used as a frame.

Finally, when the several incidents projected by Chaucer are regarded as originally designed for a framing story, the *Squire's Tale* appears more unified and certainly more understandable.

NOTES

[1] *F. Q.,* IV, II, 30 ff.; see *The Works of Edmund Spenser,* ed. R. Morris (London, 1929), pp. 239 ff.

[2] *Il Penseroso,* ll. 109–15; see *The Poetical Works of John Milton,* ed. D. Masson (London, 1929), p. 506.

[3] *Continuation of Chaucer's "Squire's Tale,"* ed. F. J. Furnivall, *Ch. Soc. Pub.* (London, 1888), 2nd. S., No. 23, pp. 1–268.

[4] *Old Pictures in Florence,* st. 35; see *The Complete Poetic and Dramatic Works of Robert Browning,* ed. H. E. Scudder (Boston, 1895), p. 178.

[5] H. S. V. Jones, "The Squire's Tale," *Sources and Analogues,* ed. W. F. Bryan and G. Dempster (Chicago, 1941), pp. 357 ff.

[6] See my article, "The Oriental Origin of the Canacee-Falcon Episode," *MLR,* XXXI (1936), 11–19.

[7] All quotations are from *The Complete Works of Geoffrey Chaucer,* ed. F. N. Robinson (New York, 1933).

[8] In *Against Women Unconstant* Chaucer says: "Al light for somer, ye woot wel what I mene" (l. 20). This allusion to light summer garments appears to imply fickleness or wantonness. Canacee was arrayed lightly (ll. 389–90), but she was taking a walk in her own park, attended by her own ladies. See *The Complete Works of Geoffrey Chaucer,* ed. W. W. Skeat (Oxford, 1894), I, 566.

[9] See my article, "Three Chaucer Notes," *Essays and Studies in Honor of Carleton Brown* (New York, 1940), pp. 91 ff.

[10] Don Cameron Allen, "Symbolic Color in the Literature of the English Renaissance," *PQ,* XV, (1936), 81–92.

[11] H. B. Hinckley, "The Framing-Tale," *MLN,* XLIX (1934), 69–80; Louis H. Gray, "Literary Studies of the Sanskrit Novel," *Wiener Zeitschrift für die Kunde des Morgenlandes,* XVIII (1904), 39–58.

[12] *The Thousand and One Days: Persian Tales,* tr. Ambrose Philips (London, 1783), pp. 7–9, 296–306; or see the edition of J. C. McCarthy (London, 1892), I, 1–6; II, 255–56.

[13] Duncan B. Macdonald, "A Bibliographical and Literary Study of the First Appearance of the 'Arabian Nights' in Europe," *Library Quarterly of the University of Chicago,* II (1932), 387–420.

[14] *Vāsavadattā by Subandhu,* tr. Louis H. Gray (New York, 1913), 1 ff.

[15] *Op. cit.,* p. 821.

[16] J. M. Manly and E. Rickert, *The Text of the Canterbury Tales* (Chicago, 1940), IV, 480.

[17] See my forthcoming article, "Chaucerian Minutiae," *MLN*.

[18] Alois Brandl, "On the Historical Personages of Chaucer's 'Squyeres Tale'," *Chaucer Soc. Publ.* (London, 1888), 2nd S., No. 29, p. 629.

[19] Jones, *op. cit.*

[20] *The Arabian Nights' Entertainments,* tr. E. W. Lane (New York, 1927), p. 1069.

[21] In December, 1935, I made brief notes on this story in the Henry E. Huntington Library, but I am now able to quote from more extensive notes sent me on February 9, 1942, by my friend Professor Arthur Dickson, who read in the Columbia University Library, Special Collections–

King Omar bin al-Nu'umān, who ruled over east and west, had an only son Sharrkan, twenty years old. A Greek concubine named Sofiyah conceived by the king and bore twins: a boy Zau al-Makān and a girl Nuzhat al–Zamān. Sharrkan knew only about the daughter's birth, for the eunuch carried tidings before waiting to discover that a son was subsequently born. For some years thereafter Sharrkan is away from home performing many prodigies of valor. His story is much like the *Cléomadès,* an analogue of the *Squire's Tale,* in which a youth rides off on a magic horse (Sharrkan's horse is real), meets a princess in a foreign land, and woos and wins her. When Sharrkan returns home, he learns that he has a brother and sister; he envies them, asks to be allowed to leave court, and is made Viceroy of Damascus. Meanwhile, Zau al-Makān and his twin sister (she in man's clothing) set out secretly on a pilgrimage to Meccah. They extend their pilgrimage to Jerusalem, where Zau falls ill. Nuzhat al-Zamān goes out to look for work and fails to return. An old Bedouin tricks her and sells her to a kindly slave dealer, who presents her to Viceroy Sharrkan, her half brother. When Sharrkan beheld her, "blood yearned to blood, though she had been parted from him in childhood and though he had never seen her" (II, 154). The story is confused, but the point is that Sharrkan buys her, frees her, and marries her. "Then Sharrkan went in unto her and took her maidenhead." Here Burton says: "This gratuitous incest in ignorance injures the tale and is as repugnant to Moslem as to Christian taste" (II, 172). One may note that Sharrkan apparently did not know who Nuzhat was; but she must have known who he was since she lived fourteen years at her father's court, and at one place in the story a merchant speaks to her of Viceroy Sharrkan and Sharrkan's father King Omar. One does not see why she did not make herself known. Perhaps this indicates a reworking of older material? In any event, when Sharrkan shows his wife a letter from their father, they discover the incestuous relationship to their horror. Nuzhat is hurriedly married to the Chamberlain and later rejoins her brother Zau. Burton says: "Here ends the wearisome tale of the brother and sister" (II, 190).–See *The Book of the Thousand Nights and a Night,* tr. Richard F. Burton (Burton Club. n.p., n.d.), II, 77–333; III, 1–145.

[22] Carleton Brown, "*Shul* and *Shal* in the Chaucer Manuscripts," *PMLA*, XXVI (1911), esp. 28 ff.

[23] Willis Wager, "The So-Called Prologue to the *Knight's Tale*," *MLN*, L (1935), 306–07.

[24] *The Squire's Tale,* ed. A. W. Pollard (London, 1926), p. vii.

Reprinted from *JEGP*, XLI (1942), 279-290.

13

CHAUCERIAN MINUTIAE

The following brief notes, here assembled after the fashion of a diminutive Gordian knot, might with appropriateness be entitled "Chaucerian Puzzles" since each has to do with either a disputed passage or some intricate detail reflecting a disputed larger issue about which it seems impossible to draw now any final authoritative conclusions. Nonetheless I believe that in at least a few instances fresh data are offered which lead to the solution of, or which suggest a new approach to, several significant problems in Chaucer.

1. *Perkyn*

The discovery[1] of an *Indenture of Apprenticeship,* dated 1396 (between John Hyndlee of Northampton, Brazier, and Thomas Edward, son of Gilbert Edward of Wyndesore), suggests immediately a comparison with the incomplete *Cook's Tale,* which enumerates little more than the defections of the apprentice Perkyn Revelour. This *Indenture*—one of the oldest and most detailed extant—contains among others three important stipulations. First, the apprentice shall not absent himself illegally from his aforesaid service: "A servicio suo praedicto seipsum illicite non absentabit." Secondly, the goods and chattels of the said master John he shall lend to no one without permission: "Bona et catalla dicti Johannis magistri sui absque ejus licencia nulli accommodabit."[2] Finally, he shall not visit taverns, prostitutes, dice, and other similar games to the loss of time of his master: "Tabernam, scortum, talos, aleas, et joca similia non frequentabit, in dispendium magistri sui praedicti."

In turning now to the *Cook's Tale,* it is arresting to observe that Perkyn violated all of the three foregoing agreements. First, he absented himself from duties without permit: "Out of the shoppe thider wolde he lepe ... he wolde nat come ayeyn" (vv. 4378-80). Secondly, this "joly prentys" freely expended his master's substance: "and thereto he was free / Of his dispense, in place of pryvetee / That fond his maister wel in

96

his chaffare" (vv. 4387-89). Finally, "He loved bet the taverne than the shoppe" (v. 4376), for certainly he was "a prentys revelour / That haunteth dys, riot, or paramour" (vv. 4391-92). There is thus no lack of evidence that Perkyn broke the covenant with his master.

Accordingly, after he had "his papir soghte" (v. 4404), the master in the *Cook's Tale* gave acquitance to Perkyn, who was "ny out of his prentishood" (the term is seven years in the *Indenture*). Now Professor Robinson glosses "his papir" as "perhaps his account book."[3] But the allusion seems to be to the indenture, or deed of mutual covenant, between the two parties, which two copies in early days (the first dates from c. 1304) were written on one piece of parchment or paper cut asunder in a serrated line so that when brought together the two edges fitted and showed they were parts of one original document.[4]

It remains to note that although Perkyn was almost criminally negligent, the penalty for infractions of the rules was distinctly not always permanent expulsion. This of course may have been the reading in the aforesaid "papir"; but in the Indenture of 1396 it is only stated:

> And if the said Thomas shall fail to carry out any of his agreement, or in any prescribed article, he shall make satisfactory amends to his master John according to the kind and enormity of his crime, or else the aforementioned term of his apprenticeship will be doubled, duplicating his set term of service.[5]

Moreover the master-craftsman was himself bound to the covenant and was largely responsible, as is well known, for the moral upbringing of his charge. In any case, the agreement between the descriptions in the *Cook's Tale* and this contemporary historical record attests to Chaucer's superb realism.[6] If in the completed narrative Perkyn was returned to his apprenticeship, it is significant that the plot would appear to involve the "expulsion and return" motif of the *Tale of Gamelyn*, which in a number of MSS follows the Cook's fragment.

2. *A Crowned 'A'*

On the gold brooch of the Prioresse (*Gen. Prol.*, vv. 161-62) "there was first write a crowned A, / And after *Amor vincit omnia.*" As noted by Professor Lowes,[7] a crowned letter as a contemporary royal emblem was hardly unconventional; e.g., Edward III wore a crowned E̽ and his Phillippa a similarly crowned P̽. Among the badges and devices on the Parliament Robes of Richard II and his Anne in the effigies in Westminster Abbey appear both the crowned $\overset{*}{R}$ and $\overset{*}{A}$.[8] But these instances are inapplicable to the Prioresse: she was not of royal lineage and besides "she was cleped madame Eglentyne."

In the first line of Lydgate's *Complaint for My Lady of Gloucester* in Shirley MS Trinity College Cambridge R. 3.20, Miss Hammond[9] interpreted the lettering as a sort of compound capital of a fused M, A, and R topped by a crown, and in 1904 she regarded this as possibly an anagrammatic M*ari*a. Further study of Shirley MS Ashmole 59 (Bodleian), and consideration that in the Trinity MS the letter stands where an A is expected, led her in 1907 to declare in favor of a crowned $\overset{*}{A}$, or a fusion of the lettering in Am*or*.[10] But it is not at all certain that John Shirley meant either M*ari*a or A*mor*, for the questioned letter in Ashmole appears on verso of the flyleaf as follows: "A + JOYE + $\overset{*}{A}$ + SHIRLEY + +."

Significantly enough, this same phraseology appears in the Mostyn MS (Bodleian) of the Herald of Chandos' poetical narrative on the Black Prince, and the first owner of this MS was no other than the scribe Shirley. On recto of the first flyleaf occurs the identical large lettering noticed above: "MA + JOYE + $\overset{*}{A}$ + SHIRLEY + +." This decorative capitalizing seems nothing more than John Shirley's abbreviated inscription of MS ownership[11]—"Ma joye; a Shirley"; i.e., "My joy; it belongs to Shirley."[12]

3. *Elpheta*

The personages in the *Squire's Tale* Chaucer describes as the Tartar King Cambyuskan, his wife Elpheta, their two sons Algarsyf and Cambalo, and the daughter Canacee. The name Cambyuskan has been tentatively identified with that of Genghis Khan (1162-1227), founder of the Mongol Empire. All the other names are unexplained. The celebrated Kublai Khan had a grandson called Kambala, which closely approximates Cambalo. Canacee occurs in the tale told by Ovid and Gower and condemned in the Man of Law's *Prologue* (II, 77 ff.). Professor Robinson suggests that Elpheta and Algarsyf look like Oriental forms, and he comments that they are unlikely to have been invented by Chaucer.[13]

As for Elpheta, Professor H. B. Hinckley[14] observed in 1908 that *Elfeta* (the peculiar spelling[15] of the Hengwrt MS) is the name given a star in certain star-lists in Skeat's edition of Chaucer's *Astrolabe*.[16] In 1928 Professor J. M. Manly announced that "My own view is that Chaucer found the name in some list of the principal stars";[17] and in 1940 Manly made a final statement: "Chaucer possibly took the name 'Elpheta' from some list of the principal stars; it occurs in several such lists, e.g. in 'Liber

Astronomicus qui dicitur Albion,' ascribed to Richard de Wallingford, abbot of St. Albans c. 1326 (MS Harley 80, f. 51a)."[18]

The possibility of literary, not astronomical, origin must be favorably considered inasmuch as Chaucer expressly states that he will proceed "as the storie telleth us" (v. 655). This statement has support from the suggestive analogues now known to exist for all episodes in the fragmentary narrative.[19] There thus seems good reasoning behind Professor Robinson's[20] recent summation: "Probably all four names (Elpheta, Algarsyf, Cambalo, and Canacee) come from an undiscovered source, or sources, of the *Squire's Tale.*" But for at least Elpheta no occurrence in medieval literature except in Chaucer has been thus far discovered.

I may observe in this connection a second literary reference to Elphita, although the name is employed by a poet writing some fifty years after Chaucer's death. In a stanza of an untitled fifteenth-century *chanson* the Catalan Andreu Febrer[21] alludes to an Elphita as follows--

> *Altra n i say en qui natur a mesa*
> (There is not there any other in whom nature has put)
> *Gentils fayços e morosa peruença:*
> (Gentle manners and lofty inclination:)
> *Don Yolant que b gaya captenença,*
> (Don Yolant, who with gay countenance)
> *Ab dolç squart mostra sa gran noblesa.*
> (And pleasing gaze, shows her great nobleness.)
> *Na Beatriz d Anglesola a avança*
> (Lady Beatriz d'Anglesola advances)
> *Lossanament lost stranys aculhir;*
> (Graciously to receive the strangers;)
> *E Johana Pineda qui felhir*
> (And Johana Pineda, who is not inferior to any one)
> *No sab, ne nquer Elphita la de Franca.*
> (Not even to Elphita, the one from France.)

Repeated efforts have not enabled me to identify the Elphita here eulogized or to disclose a likely source for Febrer's information. However, Professor Orgel del Río, whose translation is quoted above, suggests the following answer to my appeal made through Professor R. S. Loomis: "As to the identity of the persons mentioned, I think that they are ladies of the court of Aragon and Naples in the XVth century. That of Johana Pineda is found in other 'courtier' poems of the same epoch."

If in the early fifteenth century Elphita was already used as a proper name, it is altogether possible that this nomenclature was current in Spanish literary tradition at a period contemporary with Chaucer. To suggest a connection between Chaucer and Catalonia is by no means far-fetched since the poet's interest in Spanish affairs is well-known from the Monk's inclusion of *Petro-Rege Ispannie* among the tragical "Modern Instances"; and, inasmuch as the friend Oton de Graunson complimented in the *Complaint of Venus* was for some years imprisoned in Catalonia, Chaucer would have ready access to knowledge of Spanish culture from an experienced informant.[22] It may be recalled that the Catalan Map of 1375 mentions the Sea of Sarra[23] (Sarray is Cambyuskan's capitol) and that for the episode of the flying horse in the *Squire's Tale* the common source of the related *Cléomadès* and *Méliacin* appears to be a Spanish version.[24] Finally, as for Eastern influence in medieval Europe, Moorish invasions of Spain would also seem best to explain the Oriental form of the name Elpheta.

NOTES

[1] C. S. G., "Indenture of Apprenticeship, Temp. Ric. II," *Archaeological Journal* (London, 1872), XXIX, 184-85.

[2] One early record states that the apprentice is not to steal his master's goods by sixpence in the year; see E. Lipson, *An Introduction to the Economic History of England* (London, 1920), p. 281.

[3] F. N. Robinson (ed.), *The Complete Works of Geoffrey Chaucer* (Boston, 1933), p. 792.

[4] *NED.*

[5] "Et, si praedictus Thomas de aliqua convencione sua vel articulo praescripto defecerit, tunc idem Thomas juxta modum et quantitatem delicti sui praefato Johanni magistro suo satisfaciet emendam aut terminum apprenticiatus sui praedicti dupplicabit, iterando servicium suum praefixum."

[6] For further evidence that Chaucer was fictionizing contemporary persons and events, see Earl D. Lyon, "The Cook's Tale," in W. F. Bryan and G. Dempster (eds.), *Sources and Analogues* (Chicago, 1941), pp. 148-54.

[7] *PMLA* (1908), XXIII, 285 ff.

[8] Mary G. Houston, *Medieval Costume in England and France* (London, 1939), pp. 134-35.

[9] *Anglia* (1904), XXVII, 393.

[10] *Anglia* (1907), XXX, 320.

[11] It is thus interpreted by Sir Israel Gollancz in his unpaginated pamphlet on the Black Prince: *"Ich Diene,"* London, 1921.

[12] In Chaucer's age lovers sometimes wore a crowned initial or abbreviation of the name of a beloved; but the Prioresse probably had no *amie.*

[13] F. N. Robinson (ed.), *The Complete Works of Geoffrey Chaucer* (Boston, 1933), p. 822.

[14] *The Academy,* I, 866.

[15] For variant spellings, see J. M. Manly and E. Rickert, *The Text of the Canterbury Tales* (Chicago, 1940), IV, 5.

[16] *Chaucer Society Publications* (London, 1872), pp. xxxii ff.

[17] *The Canterbury Tales,* p. 598.

[18] Manly and Rickert, *op. cit.,* IV, 480.

[19] H. S. V. Jones, "The Squire's Tale," in W. F. Bryan and G. Dempster (eds.), *Sources and Analogues of Chaucer's Canterbury Tales* (Chicago, 1941), pp. 357 ff.; my article, "The Genre of *Chaucer's Squire's Tale," JEGP,* XLI (1942), 279-90.

[20] *Loc. cit.*

[21] No. VII, as printed by Manuel de Montoliu, "Las poesías líricas de Andreu Febrer," *Revue hispanique,* LVII (1923), 52-53.

[22] See my article, "The Two Petros in the 'Monkes Tale,'" *PMLA,* L (1935), 69 ff.

[23] J. M. Manly, "Marco Polo and the 'Squire's Tale,'", *PMLA,* XI (1897), 351.

[24] H. S. V. Jones, *op. cit.,* pp. 365-66.

Reprinted from *MLN,* LVIII (1943), 18-23.

14

CHAUCER'S WANDERING HERMIT

The mysterious old man in the *Pardoner's Tale* (II, 711-767) has long been recognized as at once one of Chaucer's most impressive and yet puzzling figures. There is nothing arresting in Chaucer's depiction of an aged wanderer endowed with such typical attributes of advanced age as a decrepit body and a staff supporting it, but in the fifty lines of his description Chaucer individualizes this mysterious character further by connecting him with death, by locating his home in the earth (upon which he knocks for admittance), and by suggesting that he is a restless caitiff fated to wander. The closest prototype for Chaucer's creation is doubtless the immortal Wandering Jew, although scholars have found many parallels of important features in the literature of the Orient and Europe. Thus in some accounts the part of the old man is taken by no less a personage than Buddha himself. However, so far as I know, no one has linked Chaucer's character with the New World.

As for an American analogue, the report of Cabeza de Vaca's experiences among the Indians in the American Southwest affords a similar narrative of an old wanderer whom the natives called Bad Thing.[1] When the Spaniards first came to the Southwest, more than one Indian tribe reported that some fifteen or sixteen years before Cabeza de Vaca's arrival a strange being had wandered about the country, occasionally visiting the natives with death or injury. Bad Thing was an old man of small stature who wore a beard. He was altogether mysterious, and no one ever could see his features clearly enough to describe them accurately. Although Bad Thing performed many exploits (such as healing wounds he had caused himself and destroying Indian lodges by throwing them in the air) which apparently have no connection with Chaucer, there does remain yet another important circumstance to recall the *Pardoner's Tale.* Like Chaucer's aged hermit, Bad Thing, when asked whence he came, pointed to a rent in the earth and said that his home was down below.

The addition of this American analogue to the number already known to exist in many languages of the Orient and Europe illustrates anew that folklore resides in no one clime and at no one date. We alone can limit peregrinating truth in regarding Chaucer's old man as removes from either the Oriental Buddha or the American Bad Thing.

NOTES

[1] See Cleve Hallenbeck, *Journey and Route of Cabeza de Vaca* (Glendale, California, Arthur H. Clark Co., 1940).

Reprinted from *Calif. Folklore Quart.,* IV (1945), 82-83.

15

THE COOK'S MORMAL AND ITS CURE

In the description of the Cook in the "General Prologue" (line 386) Chaucer states "That on his shyne a mormal hadde he."[1] When Professor Skeat commented on this passage, he seemed to believe that the Cook was suffering from a serious affliction, inasmuch as in his discussion he preferred the definition of "a cancer or gangrene."[2] The later editors of the Globe Edition of Chaucer merely glossed the word as "gangrene,"[3] thus omitting reference to the more nearly incurable disease of cancer. In a yet later and more thorough examination of Chaucer's knowledge of the medieval sciences, Professor Curry concluded that the mormal "must not be confused with cancer or gangrene" but is "a species of ulcerated, dry-scabbed apostema produced by corruption in the blood of natural melancholia or sometimes of melancholia combined with *salsum phlegma*."[4] This definition is clearly not in disagreement with the idea of "a sore" included in some of the medieval glosses discussed by Skeat.[5] Indeed Curry's interpretation today everywhere commands esteem: in notes to his recent edition Professor Robinson also emphasizes the "dry" mormal in calling it "a species of dry-scabbed ulcer" and in glossing it as a "sore, gangrene."[6]

Mormal, however, is defined in the *New English Dictionary* simply, without reference to dryness or wetness, as "an inflamed sore, especially on the leg"; and the same source affords an early citation of the word: "c. 1400 *Lanfranc's Cirurg*. 178. the blood letyng of this veyne is good . . . for cancrena that ben in the hipis and for a mormal."[7] Now the usage of the two words in Chaucer would appear to approximate closely the conception of a cancer in the hips and a sore on the leg; for in the *Parson's Tale* (line 427) Chaucer speaks of "cancre" on "the hynde part of hir buttokes,"[8] whereas the Cook's mormal seems to be not a cancer but an old leg sore. On the basis of the scant description in the *Canterbury Tales*, it may appear an impossibility to seek an accurate or detailed analysis of the Cook's malady; yet Chaucer does say mormal, not cancer, and does locate the sore on the Cook's leg.

Fortunately, too, there is yet a fuller delineation of a mormal in the *Treatises*[9] by the contemporary layman-surgeon, John Arderne (*fl.* 1370).[10] The relationship which Arderne's explanation of an unnamed canon's mormal has to the Chaucerian meaning of this word was first observed by Professor Cook, who cited from the surgeon's *Treatises* an account of "a large wounde" in the leg: "And about the ankles three or four smalle woundes to the brede of one halfpeny"; that is, a "wet" mormal where "wex pusceles brovnysch and clayisch."[11] It remains to note that Professor Cook omitted some 235 words of Arderne's description, presumably because most of these relate to the treatment. There is thus one passage in the *Treatises* not hitherto quoted in connection with Chaucer; and, what is still more important, it approximates the depiction of the mormal on the Cook's "shyne" as nearly as the foregoing reference to the unnamed canon's wounds "about the ankles." This passage does not refer to the canon's ailment as cited by Professor Cook but concerns a hypothetical instance of a mormal "aboue the schyn-bone" which Arderne treated as follows:

> If the mormale be euen aboue the schyn-bone, that it be more sikerly and more sone cured it is profitable to cutte the dede flesch and putte it away if the pacient consent. And if it be cutte, alsone after the cuttyng is to be putte in a cloute wette in whyte of ane ay al a nyght.[12]

These directions, it will be observed, not only supplement the present diagnosis of the mormal as a "wet" old sore or "wounde" where "wex pusceles brovnysch and clayisch" but also explain the subsequent therapy. In point of fact, the application of the white of an egg for curing an old sore was presumably well known in the Middle Ages, this remedy being included among others in an Old French manuscript:

> For an old sore, take goat dung and old grease and make a plaster of them and put on the sore. If the scab is too hard, open it; if it is too raw, then close it, or make a paste of barley flour and white of an egg, and put it on the sore; thus is it cured.[13]

In summary, the evidence from medieval sources appears to substantiate the theory that the mormal on the Cook's "shyne"[14] was an ulcer or a sore, not a cancer. The evidence, moreover, seems to favor not a "dry" but a "running" sore; and interpreted as "wet or running," there seems special point in Chaucer's following the description of the mormal with the immediate statement (line 387): "For blankmanger, that made he with the beste." Finally, as for the mormal, Chaucer gives no assurance of a cure; but when the Cook later appears as a Canterbury story-teller, there is no further mention of his ailment.

NOTES

[1] F. N. Robinson, ed., *The Complete Works of Geoffrey Chaucer* (Boston, 1933), p. 23.

[2] W. W. Skeat, ed., *The Complete Works of Geoffrey Chaucer,* 2nd ed. (Oxford, 1900), V, 37-38.

[3] A. W. Pollard, H. F. Heath, M. H. Liddell, and W. S. McCormick, eds., *The Works of Geoffrey Chaucer* (London, 1923), p. 760.

[4] W. C. Curry, *Chaucer and the Mediaeval Sciences* (New York, 1926), p. 48.

[5] Skeat *(op. cit.,* V, 38) notes the mormal as a sore in Lydgate, Skelton, Palsgrave, *et al.*

[6] *Op. cit.,* pp. 762, 1089, respectively.

[7] *NED* (Oxford, 1908), VI, 665.

[8] Robinson, *op. cit.,* p. 286.

[9] *Treatises of Fistula in Ano,* by John Arderne, E.E.T.S., No. 139 (London, 1910), pp. 52-55.

[10] *DNB,*I, 548-49.

[11] A. S. Cook, "Correspondence-Miscellaneous Notes," *MLN,* XXXIII (1918), 379; "Chaucerian Papers," *Trans. Conn. Acad.,* XXIII (1919), 27-29.

[12] Arderne, *loc. cit.*

[13] L. Wiese, "Recettes médicales en français," *Mélanges offerts à M. Alfred Jeanroy* (Paris, 1928), p. 668.

[14] Professor D.D. Griffith has kindly called my attention to the reading "chynne" in *CX*[1] and Ii (see J. M. Manly and E. Rickert, *The Text of the Canterbury Tales* [Chicago, 1940], V, 33).

Reprinted from *MLQ,* VII (1946), 265-267.

16

CHAUCER AND DAME ALICE PERRERS

The relatively numerous appearances of Chaucer's name in official records[1] during the reign of Edward III conclusively testify that he enjoyed at the English court generous patronage. In not a few instances Chaucer's good fortune was due to the King's second son, the renowned John of Gaunt,[2] but a yet larger number of the rewards for excellent services came from the Exchequer of the King, and thus arrived by intercession of Edward III or through his royal influence.[3] Now, it must be borne in mind that in his declining years King Edward III, as is well known, was dominated in private and official life by his ambitious mistress, Dame Alice Perrers.[4] Indeed her influence became so extensive that in 1376 the Good Parliament took action against her for interference in the bestowal of the King's favor, banishing her thereafter from court.[5] It is therefore not without interest that in 1888 the eminent French historian, M.Siméon Luce, when commenting on Froissart's statement about Chaucer in 1377, should refer to the English poet as 'le protégé de la favorite Alice Perrers.'[6]

Unfortunately Luce does not cite authority for his statement, and so the connection he observes between Chaucer and Dame Alice may well be no more than an inference--though it is possible that he depended upon some document which he fails to mention. The suggestion that Chaucer owed allegiance to the King's mistress, clearly not unsupported at least by what is known about Alice's close affinity with the throne, would without question explain plausibly some of the most confusing problems respecting patronage to Chaucer in Edward's last years. There are thus strong reasons for searching anew[7] to determine if data exist to link the King's mistress with the fortunes of Geoffrey Chaucer.

In this undertaking one of the first points of relationship is that, almost without exception,[8] members of Dame Alice's clique prove to be either Chaucer's associates at court or else his own personal friends. Sir Philip la Vache, whom Chaucer has immortalized in *Truth* as 'Thou Vache,'[9] was in 1375 associated with Sir Philip de Countenay, admiral of the fleet towards the West, in the 'gift and sale' of the marriage of a ward to 'Dame Alice Perrers.'[10] Sir Lewis Clifford, Chaucer's great friend,[11] and

Sir Guichard d'Angle, in 1377 the poet's fellow ambassador to France,[12] were two of the seven mainpernors on August 20, 1376, who obtained the release of Alice's husband 'William de Wyndesore from the tower prison.'[13] One of Alice's main supporters was Sir Richard Stury, who was with Chaucer on several missions both at home and abroad.[14] An anonymous contemporary chronicler asserts that Stury, Lord Latimer (also known to Chaucer),[15] and that 'shameless woman & wanton harlott, called Ales Peres' were all intimates of Edward III, 'That att there beck the Kynge permitted all matters of the realms to be disposed, & commyted also the government of hym selfe.'[16]

In the rental and disposal of properties and other matters involving lands Dame Alice appears in the records along with personages also well acquainted with Chaucer. In 1368 John de Cobeham, with whom in 1386 Chaucer served on a commission of peace, conveyed the lease of the manor of Ardyngton, co. Berks (which he had held as the King's gift) to Alice Perrers for life.[17] In later years Thomas Chaucer was the King's Escheator in Berks and owned several properties there.[18] Sir Robert Ashton, who in 1386 was, with Chaucer, a member of the King's household,[19] gave certain lands in Dorset to be held for her use, while *sole,* at some time before her marriage to Windsor.[20] Although obliged by Parliament in 1377 to forfeit her properties (including the new hostel lately constructed on the bank of the Thames and all the new London houses which she had built)——some of which were claimed by John of Gaunt and others by that John de Holand [21] whom the scribe John Shirley associates with the *Complaint of Mars*[22]--Alice Perrers at the apogee of her influence had accumulated no inconsiderable wealth. It appears that she possessed the manor of Gaines (or Gaynes) in Essex (in Edward's time annexed to Hertfordshire)[23] by the King's gift, in which shire Richard de Perers, believed to be her father, was several times Sheriff.[24] In 1367 she held in custody the lands of Robert de Tiloil.[25] On June 30, 1368, Alice Perriers and heirs were granted a plot of land called 'Manylawes,' co. Northumberland, in the King's hand as escheat.[26]

Controlling valuable properties in the several counties, as well as in London, Alice had opportunity to favor many famous persons. The writs may not always fully disclose her negotiations with middle class gentry; on the other hand, the nobility in seeking her aid adopted open means: the redoubtable John of Gaunt,[27] the worshipful William of Wykeham,[28] and even the Pope turned to her.[29] Thus her assistance, although doubtless sometimes proceeding as if granted by Edward alone, was unquestionably sought by personages both small and great. It has been noted already that she owned houses and lands in London. It now may be observed further that her husband,[30] William de Windsor, the King's Lord Lieutenant of Ireland, owned besides other properties a home in Southwark.[31] Is it possible that before the decease of Edward III (June 21, 1377)[32] Alice Perrers may have helped Chaucer to gain deeds to property? In this period the only deed of land known to have been granted to Chaucer is the lease of Aldgate (Algate, Alegate). The deed is quite important and must be examined carefully, for among Comptrollers of the Custom Chaucer alone enjoyed this free rental.[33]

On May 10, 1374, Chaucer obtained, from the Mayor, Aldermen, and Commonalty of the City of London, a lease to the 'mansion' above the gate of Aldgate 'for the whole life of him, the said Geoffrey.'[34] Important stipulations of this deed are, first, that it shall endure unto 'the decease of the same Geoffrey' and, secondly, that, inasmuch as no payment is mentioned, Chaucer was entitled to free rental. Moreover, occupancy of the lodgings at Aldgate would enhance considerably the social position of Geoffrey and his wife, Philippa Chaucer, since it appears that 'mansions' of this type were usually named 'Inns' after the owners, as 'Scrope's Inn,' 'Grosvenor's Inn,'[35] and thus perhaps 'Chaucer's Inn.' These 'Inns,' it appears further, were posted with signs displaying the arms of the occupants, so that during his residence Chaucer may have placed outside an emblematic signboard of his address similar to the 'nouell signe' he in 1386 testified that he saw one time 'en Friday- strete' in London.[36] Living in Aldgate, home of earlier mediaeval notables, Geoffrey and Philippa Chaucer would be as well situated as any other rich and influential London burgher family.

In the environs of Aldgate, it should be recalled, Chaucer's father and mother, John and Agnes Chaucer, once owned property which the latter had inherited from Hamo de Copton, uncle of Agnes, so that in now removing to lodgings at Aldgate Geoffrey Chaucer, in effect, was coming home again. There are among the *Life Records* some nine writs (dating from 1354 to 1367) which have to do with the tenements of John and Agnes Chaucer without Aldgate. Four of these writs concern tenements, including a brewhouse, houses, shops, gardens, etc., located in the parish of St. Botolph without Aldgate,[37] the Church of St. Botolph being itself at the junction of Aldgate Street and Houndsditch.[38] Three more writs describe other properties at Aldgate. Two remaining writs (both dated in 1367) refer to Aldgate tenements in St. Botolph's deeded to others by Bartholomew atte Chapel and Agnes his wife, 'formerly wife of John Chaucier, late citizen and vintner.'[39] These official documents show, then, that at least from 1354 to 1367 the Chaucers owned Aldgate properties, principally tenements in the parish of St. Botolph, immediately outside the wall. Were it not for the all-important concession involved in the free rental, there would be no difficulty whatever in explaining why Chaucer returned to Aldgate. But at the only other time (1372) in Edward's reign that Aldgate was leased, John Lucas (the tenant) paid a yearly rental of 13s.4d.[40] The import of the free deed, therefore, is unmistakable. Chaucer did not work for the City of London. His labors were for the glory of the realm, in the interest of increasing the prestige of notables at court. Although unquestionably deserving, Chaucer needed at that time, even as men sometimes do today, a friend to aid him in negotiatiating the hurdles of court intrigue.

One suggestion is that Chaucer owed the lease to John of Gaunt, who made this payment because of the love he bore either Chaucer[41] or, in a different sense,[42] his wife Philippa. But there is no evidence that Gaunt at this time possessed lands at Aldgate or was in any way responsible for their disposal. In March, 1377, Gaunt secured from the King deeds of confirmation to the manors of Gryngeley and Wheteley, which he bestowed upon his mistress, Katherine Swynford;[43] however, since no similar deeds appear for Aldgate, the situation with respect to the Chaucers and to Katherine Swynford is not parallel. A more likely hypothesis is that the lease was due to Edward III: it is known, for example, that in 1382 Aldersgate was granted at the King's request to John Beauchamp who had asked for it. Compensation for the expenses of Chaucer's mission to Genoa was long overdue; hence the King may have felt that Chaucer deserved something for this mission other than the pitcherful of wine daily,[44] although of course the 'old King was now in dishonored dotage.'[45] If the King in 1374 was inactive, his mistress certainly was not: instead, as court favorite, she was the center of political intrigue about which fortune seekers oscillated.[46] In fact, although he deserted her cause during her banishment, Gaunt was himself among the notables who earlier curried favor with her; thus it may have been Gaunt who besought her to have the King take due notice of Chaucer's good services. Now, most of Alice's own properties, it is also worth noting, were held either rent free or as the King's gift. It is therefore perfectly clear that she was skilled in negotiating the type of free lease enjoyed by Chaucer. Fortunately, the whole question of Aldgate seems finally resolved by the circumstance that Dame Alice once had at her disposal certain of the properties now in discussion. This piece of information is afforded by the will of William Burford, proved February 12, 1390, which states that he is to be buried in the Church of St. Botolph without Aldgate and that he bequeaths a tenement in the parish of St. Botolph without Aldgate to his son Robert, which property he had 'acquired from Alice Pereris.'[47] Certainly, inasmuch as Alice's own lands were confiscated in 1376, her holdings in Aldgate belong to a period contemporary with the date of Chaucer's lease. It thus would have been possible for Dame Alice as an Aldgate land-owner to speak with authority in recommending that Chaucer be granted a free lease. There is no reason to believe that Gaunt would not support the proposal with eagerness.

Yet more interesting, there is strong evidence that from earliest times Chaucer and Alice Perrers were in close association. Both she and Chaucer were members of the King's Household in 1359.[48] Robes for Christmas, 1368, were provided for Geoffrey and Philippa Chaucer and for Alice's husband, William de Wyndesore.[49] For mourning at the funeral of Queen Philippa, Chaucer on September 1, 1369, received 3 ells of black cloth, short, and both Phelippe Chaucere and Aliceon Perrers were given 6 ells of the same, long.[50] On May 1, 1373, both Alice Pirers and Philippe Chancy received presents at the Savoy as the gift of John of Gaunt.[51] Payments for wine pensions to Chaucer and Alicie Perers were made for the dates from November 25, 1376, to July 26, 1377.[52] All of the evidence tends to demonstrate that at the King's court Dame Alice and Chaucer were frequently associated. In point of fact, if Alice's ancestry were better known, it might be possible to connect one of her early relatives with Chaucer's grandfather Robert. For it was no other than Elias Pier (Peres, Piores, Pieres, etc.) who on September 14, 1309, succeeded Robert Chaucer (appointed November 15, 1308) as Deputy to the King's Butler in the City and Port of London.[53] Moreover, on August 2, 1310, Robert le Chaucer and this same Elias Perr' (Perrers) were appointed, jointly or severally, to collect at the port of the City of London the custom on wines brought by merchant vintners from the Duchy of Aquitaine.[54]

Whatever be the details about Alice's reputation, Richard Perrers, probably her father, was himself a prominent figure in being several times Sheriff of the counties of Essex and Hertfordshire. In 1324 the Earl of Richmond had letters of protection on going abroad for three envoys, including 'Ricardus de Pereres, milites.'[55] Her husband, as also has been noted, was twice Lord Lieutenant of Ireland. Dame Alice had two daughters, Jane and Joan. The wife of Robert Skern, a man of rank in Surrey, was Joan, reported the 'daughter of the notorious Alice Perrers.'[56] After the decease on September 15, 1384, of William de Windsor, heavily in debt to the Crown, the fortunes of Dame Alice experienced the final eclipse. Plagued by debts and the lawsuits of her husband's nephew, Alice suffered a decline more serious than her banishment in 1376.[57] It is also worthy of note that whereas before her husband's death she was always regarded as 'our beloved Alice,' thereafter she appears to have lost favor with Richard. It is interesting that Chaucer's loss of the deed to Aldgate in 1386[58] should coincide so strikingly with Alice's own waning prosperity.

Conceivably it could be argued that only a series of coincidences account for (1) the granting of a free lease to Chaucer during Alice's ascendancy, (2) her own landownings in this very ward of Aldgate, and (3) Chaucer's loss of the lease during her decline. But this attenuated reasoning would encounter yet another series of arresting circumstances. For, it must be remembered, in 1374, the date of the Aldgate lease, Chaucer also received the appointment as Comptroller of the Custom. And here once more Dame Alice appears to have figured. In 1371 she took part, by leave of the King, in controlling the customs and subsidies.[59] John of Gaunt doubtless favored the appointment, too – he, Richard Stury, and several others being in 1372 and 1374 represented in a commission enforcing the payment of the customs on shipments of wool.[60] Thus the personage familiar with the office and in the best position to recommend the appointment of Chaucer to the Comptrollership was no other individual than Alice. Again as before, in 1386 Chaucer lost not only his home in Aldgate but also the Comptrollership. By 1386 Gaunt had returned to favor with Richard II, so that Chaucer's misfortune could hardly be traced to Duke John. The situation with respect to Alice was precisely the opposite: in 1386 she was many times removed from the throne, helpless to regain even her own lost prestige. Chaucer's sudden loss of Aldgate and the Comptrollership – hitherto unsatisfactorily explained – may perhaps most reasonably be explained as a result of Alice's own political eclipse.

What remains of the story of the King's favorite is death preceded by decay and perhaps memories of earlier grandeur. Gone were the bright days at court – and forever – for that young Maid of Honour whom the royal writs once identify by the affectionate diminutive of her name: Aliceon. No more would she ride, as in 1375, from the Tower to the tourneys at Smithfield dressed as the Lady of the Sun.[61] This woman had not been the toast of the poets, but neither had she passed unnoticed. In *Miroir de l'Homme* John Gower has an uncomplimentary allusion to her.[62] The author of *Piers Ploughman* appears to refer to her disparagingly as Lady Meed[63] and to pun on her name (Perr') in speaking 'of the preciousest perre.' On the other hand, Chaucer, although seeming to allude in the *House of Fame* to his residence at Aldgate,[64] nowhere appears to refer to Alice's reputation or to mention her name.[65] Dame Alice died in 1400, the same year as Chaucer. If she be that one in 1397 mentioned at

Monmouth – 'Item quod Jankyn ap Gwillum fornicatur cum Alicia Parrer'[66] – her end was sorry indeed.

The least which can be said,[67] at last, is that Geoffrey Chaucer, his wife Philippa, and their friends and associates were at the zenith of her influence all well acquainted with 'la favorite Alice Perrers.' More than any other high personage at court, she appears likely to have assisted in granting the free Aldgate lease to Chaucer on the basis of both her own landlordship there and her recognized supremacy over Edward. Her recommendations to the King would also account for Chaucer's appointment as Comptroller. Her loss of influence after the decease of her husband would, in turn, best explain Chaucer's surrender in 1386 of the deed to Aldgate and the end of his Comptrollership. The name of Dame Alice Perrers should henceforth assume a not unimportant place in the biography of the poet Geoffrey Chaucer. The more one learns about him, the more Chaucer appears a prosperous man of the world – a trusted burgher in his time intimately acquainted with many of the most stirring historical events and certainly some of the most colorful mediaeval figures. No one personage was alone responsible for Chaucer's prosperity. His success in later years as a competent, loyal follower of Richard II is fully foreshadowed in the early recognition accorded his services by John of Gaunt, Edward III, and the old King's mistress – Dame Alice Perrers.

NOTES

[1] R. E. G. Kirk (ed.), *Life Records of Chaucer* (Ch. Soc., Sec. Ser., 1900), pp. 139 ff.

[2] Sydney Armitage-Smith, *John of Gaunt's Register* (London, 1911), index.

[3] E. P. Kuhl, 'Index to the Life-Records of Chaucer,' *MP* (1913), X, 527-552.

[4] C. L. K., 'Alice Perrers,' *DNB*.

[5] *Rotuli Parlimentorum* (n.p., n.d.), II, 329; V. H. Galbraith (ed.), *Anonimalle Chronicle* (London, 1927), pp. 87-91.

[6] S. Luce (ed.), *Chroniques de J. Froissart* (Paris, 1888), VIII, cxxxix, n. 3.

[7] I first referred to Alice Perrers and Chaucer in *Three Chaucer Studies* (New York, 1932), No. II, p. 41.

[8] Georg Felbrigg, who testified against Alice in Parliament, is said to have been one of the jury in 1377 who found her guilty of maintenance; see J. R. Hulbert, *Chaucer's Offical Life* (Chicago, 1912), p. 35.

[9] Edith Rickert, "Thou Vache,' *MP* (1913), XI, 209 ff.

[10] *Cal. Pat. Rolls*, p. 280.

[11] G. L. Kittredge, 'Chaucer and Some of His Friends,' *MP* (1903), I, 1-18.

[12] See my paper, 'Three Chaucer Notes,' *Essays and Studies in Honor of Carleton Brown* (New York, 1940), p. 97.

[13] *Cal. Close Rolls*, p. 443.

[14] *Life Records*, Nos. 34, 53, 102, 109, 217.

[15] *Ibid.*, No. 53

[16] T. Amyot (ed.), 'An Historical Relation ...' *Archaeologia* (1829), XXII, 233; see also V. H. Galbraith (ed.), *Anonimalle Chronicle* (London, 1927), pp.87-92, 106.

[17] A. A. Kern, *The Ancestry of Chaucer* (Baltimore, 1906), p. 161.

[18] A. C. Baugh, 'Kirk's Life Records of Thomas Chaucer,' *PMLA* (1932), XLVII, 461 ff.

[19] *Life Records*, No. 53.

[20] *Cal. Close Rolls* (1381-1385), pp. 354, 376.

[21] *N & Q*, 7 S., VIII, 449.

[22] See my paper, 'Chaucer and Graunson: The Valentine Tradition,' *PMLA* (1939), LIV, 363.

[23] John Norden, *Speculi Britanniae Pars* (London, 1840), p. 12.

[24] Philip Morant, *History and Antiquities of Essex* (London, 1768), I, 107.

[25] *N & Q*, 7 S., VII, 148, 215, 449.

[26] *Cal. Pat. Rolls*, p. 146.

[27] Sydney Armitage-Smith, *John of Gaunt* (London, 1904), p. 184.

[28] C. L. K., 'Alice Perrers,' *DNB*.

[29] *Papal Letters*, IV, 96.

[30] The marriage, apparently secret, seems to have occurred prior to 1376, possibly following Windsor's first return from Ireland in 1373.

[31] M. V. Clarke, *Fourteenth Century Studies* (Oxford, 1937), pp. 149, 159, n. 2; and Sir J. Ayloffe, *Calendar of the Ancient Charters* (London, 1774), p. 447.

[32] Thomas Walsingham, *Historia Anglicana* (London, 1863), I, 329.

[33] E. P. Kuhl, "Chaucer and Aldgate,' *PMLA* (1924), XXXIX, 109.

[34] *Life Records*, No. 80.

[35] Charles Pendrill, *Old Parish Life in London* (Oxford, 1937), p. 207.

[36] *Life Records*, No. 193.

[37] *Life Records*, Nos. 31-32, 37-38.

[38] Sir Walter Besant, *Survey of London* (London, 1910), VIII, 171.

[39] *Life Records*, Nos. 36, 40-41, 44-45.

[40] R. R. Sharpe (ed.), *Calendar of Letter Books* (London, 1904), p. 81.

[41] Kuhl, *op. cit.*, p. 112.

[42] Russell Krauss, *Three Chaucer Studies* (New York, 1932), No. 1, pp. 131 ff.

[43] T. Rymer, *Faedera* (London, 1821), VII, 140.

[44] *Life Records,* No. 79.

[45] Kuhl, *op. cit.,* p. 111.

[46] M. V. Clarke, *op. cit.,* pp. 149 ff.

[47] R. R. Sharpe (ed.), *Calendar of Wills of the Court of Husting* (London, 1889), II, 301.

[48] *Life Records,* p. 155, n. 1.

[49] *Life Records,* No. 53.

[50] *Life Records,* No. 58.

[51] Sydney Armitage-Smith, *John of Gaunt's Register* (London, 1911), p. 194.

[52] *Life Records,* No. 109.

[53] *Life Records,* No. 2; *Cal. Pat. Rolls,* p. 65.

[54] *Life Records,* No. 4.

[55] G. P. Cuttino, *English Diplomatic Administration* (Oxford, 1940), p. 111.

[56] Major Alfred Heales, 'Early History of Kingston-Upon-Thomas, Surrey,' *Surrey Arch. Soc.* (1883), VIII, 13-156; J. Lewis André, 'Female Head-Dresses Exemplified by Surrey Brasses,' *Surrey Arch. Soc.* (1891), XVI, 35-54.

[57] T. R. Gambier-Parry, 'Alice Perrers and her Husband's Relatives,' *English Hist. Rev.* (1932), XLVII, 272-276.

[58] *Life Records,* No. 192.

[59] *N & Q,* 7 S., VII, 30, 449. *Cal. Pat. Rolls,* p. 50.

[60] *Cal. Pat. Rolls* (1370-74), p. 197; (1374-77), pp. 5, 62.

[61] C. L. K., 'Alice Perrers,' *DNB.*

[62] G. L. Kittredge, *The Date of Chaucer's Troilus and Other Chaucer Matters* (Ch. Soc., Sec. Ser., 1909), pp. 79-80.

[63] Oscar Cargill, 'The Date of the A-Text of Piers Ploughman,' *PMLA* (1932), XLVII, 354 ff.

[64] Kuhl, *op. cit.,* p.110.

[65] In connection with Canacee's magic ring in the *Squire's Tale* Professor Kittredge has observed that at the trial of Alice Perrers in 1376 mention is made of magic rings; see F. N. Robinson (ed.), *The Complete Works of Geoffrey Chaucer* (Boston, 1933), p. 823.

[66] Rev. Canon A. T. Bannister, 'Visitation Returns of the Diocese of Hereford in 1397,' *English Hist. Rev.* (1929), XLIV, 445.

[67] Some further words need to be said about Alice Perrers, and some day I hope to say them.

Reprinted from *Speculum,* XXI (1946), 222-228.

17

TWO CHAUCER NOTES

1. Chaucer On Murder: *De Petro Rege de Cipro*

The "worthy Petro, kyng of Cipre" $(1.B^2 3581)^1$ was not a fictitious nor a legendary character like most of the personages in the *Monk's Tale;* instead, he was a celebrated contemporary historical figure who had visited England on at least two notable occasions and whose father, Hughes IV, Chaucer himself may have seen in 1358 at the banquet given by King Edward III[2]. At all events, the historically authentic facts as to the circumstances of his death were matters of common knowledge in Chaucer's day--(1) Pierre (Petro) of Cyprus was assassinated by a group of his subjects whom he had ill-treated; (2) he was attacked when "upright and outside his bed" (*"debout et hors de son lit"*) "in the adjoining apartment" (*"en pièce voisine");* and (3) he died at midnight of January 17-18, 1369.[3] These are substantially, then, the salient, correct, and known details of the tragic end of Pierre of Cyprus.[4]

Now, as to the foregoing well-documented facts, precisely nothing is said in the *Monk's Tale*; for in his account of this King, Chaucer, as elsewhere noted, follows the inaccurate statements in *La Prise d' Alexandrie* by Guillaume de Machaut, his favorite French poet. Both Chaucer and Machaut report (1) that Pierre was treacherously killed by his own disloyal subjects, (2) that "They in thy bedde han slayn thee" $(1.B^2 3586)$, and (3) that he was killed early in the morning.[5] Accordingly, the tragedy of Pierre of Cyprus is unique among all the tragedies in the *Monk's Tale* in being an unhistorical account, based as it is on the fiction of Machaut.

Inasmuch as the historically accurate details of Pierre's death were well known, why did Chaucer elect to transcribe an inaccurate report? Not simply, one believes, to pay respect to Machaut or to practice translating French into English! In seeking to explain Chaucer's procedure in the *Monk's Tale,* it is important to recall that in the three other contemporary tragedies, or Modern Instances *(De Petro Rege Ispannie; De Barnabo de Lumbardia;* and *De Hugelino, Comite de Pize),* each person was brutally slain; so that in describing Pierre it would have been introducing a discordant element to report the truth--namely, that the King of Cyprus, who had been sleeping, not with his wife, but with his mistress,[6] was killed by his own outraged subjects while he was in a position to defend himself, being then upright and outside his bed in an adjoining apartment. Thus, instead of reporting the true story, Chaucer chose to disregard history by saying that the king was slain in his bed early in the morning.

In making this statement, it is significant to observe, Chaucer patently states that Pierre, like the other personages in the Modern Instances, was nothing less than treacherously murdered. For the circumstances as explained by Chaucer are in medieval law tantamount to murder. According to the thirteenth-century legal compilation entitled *Les Etablissements de Saint Louis,* "Murder is when [*sic*] a man or woman is killed in their [*sic*] bed, or in any manner for which they are [*sic*] not *en mêllée.*"[7] The only other occurrence of bed-slaying in Chaucer makes it clear that he meant murder, for in the *Knight's Tale* he refers to "The tresoun of mordrynge in the bedde" (1.2001).[8] Chaucer, who was familiar with the legal code through wide experience at court and who indeed may once have been a student at the Inner Temple,[9] thus would appear to have consciously depicted Pierre as the victim of murder when stating "They in thy bedde han slayn thee" (1.B^{2}3586).

It is thus perfectly clear that in *De Petro Rege de Cipro* Chaucer chose to ignore the well-established data of popular contemporary history; also that when he selected Machaut's version for his source, he was altogether cognizant of the fact that he was as erroneously picturing King Pierre as the victim of what today might be termed first-degree murder. Did Chaucer merely mean to show that in his own day crimes were becoming increasingly violent, or did he intend reference to some high personage precariously situated at the English court by thus revising true history in order to emphasize murder as the horrendous motive to the so-called Modern Instances?

2. CHAUCER'S "BRETHEREN TWO" AND "THILKE WIKKE ENSAMPLE OF CANACEE."

In the *Squire's Tale* Chaucer names five members of a family group: Cambyuskan and his queen Elpheta, their sons Algarsif and Cambalo, and their daughter Canacee. All these personages are clearly identified except Cambalo, who is first named Cambalo (1.31), then Cambalus (1.656), and then again Cambalo (1.667). Although the name is spelled in these two different ways, there seems no reason to doubt that reference is to one person. Chaucer last mentions him as follows: "And after wol I speke of Cambalo/That faught in lystes with the bretheren two/For Canacee er that he myghte hire wynne" (11.667-69).[10] Now, it has sometimes been suggested that Cambalo was here inserted erroneously by a scribe, since it would appear unconventional for the brother Cambalo to win his sister Canacee, especially if *win* is employed here, as it is five lines beforehand, in the sense of espouse.[11] On the other hand, the explanation that the 'bretheren two' are Algarsif and Cambalo--and that the Cambalo who is to win Canacee is a different personage with the same name--appears distinctly improbable. First, as for the two spellings of the name, the other brother is once designated as Algarsyf (1.31) and then later as Algarsif (1.663); so that the variant spelling 'Cambalus' for Cambalo has no special significance (compare Arcita for Arcite, Pandarus for Pandare). Moreover, as earlier noted by Professor Lowes,[12] the occurrence of the 'two brothers motive' is not uncommon. What remains, then, as most probable is that Canacee's own brother Cambalo fought two other brothers, although no similar situation ever has been cited.

In this connection, it seems significant to observe that in the contemporary *Anonimalle Chronicle*[13] there appears an arresting episode involving two brothers opposed to one man--

> Mesme celle an mille CCCLXXVII deux freres iermayns et twynlynges de Inde queux furount Ethiops viendrent al roy Despaigne encontre la ley et foy de seint esglise dissauntz qe Dieu ne prist my chare ne saunk en la virgine Marie et ceo vodroient prover par bataille; et le custome de lour pais fuist et est qe deux twynlynges deveroient combatre en lieu de une homme, ovesqe une homme. . . . En celle temps furount enprisone del roy Despaigne vi chivalers et xvi esquiers Dengleterre, queux furount pris ovesqe le count de Penbrok . . . et au darrein une chivaler Dengleterre, monsire Johan de Harppenden nomme. . . prist la bataille. . . le dit chivaler occist le ayne frere et puis le pusne. . .[14]

The reference to "deux freres iermayns et twynlynges de Inde" is of high importance since it affords the first close parallel of Chaucer's allusion to the "bretheren two." Moreover, the strange knight visiting Cambyuskan's court, it will be recalled, was a representative of "The Kyng of Arabe and of Inde" (1.110). It is not at all unlikely, therefore, that Cambalo fought against two brothers who followed this King of India. The Western custom in tournaments traditionally pitted one knight against another; and thus the Eastern practice of two knights against only one adversary Chaucer may have consciously added from some such source as this to deepen the Oriental atmosphere of the *Squire's Tale*.

As for Chaucer's knowledge of the incident, perhaps he was acquainted with a manuscript version of the contemporary *Anonimalle Chronicle*. Or, since his two friends Guichard d'Angle and Oton de Graunson (referred to in *The Complaint of Venus*, 1.82) were among the English captives imprisoned in Spain,[15] it is altogether possible that he heard the story from them on their return to England in 1374. The story as told in the *Anonimalle Chronicle*, whether historically authentic or otherwise,[16] would accordingly be easily accessible to Chaucer.

There is yet another datum bearing on the "bretheren two." Chaucer's Canacee-Falcon episode has for its closest analogue the Arabian tale of Tāj al-Mulūk and Princess Dunyā. In point of fact, this famous story from the *Arabian Nights*, elsewhere discussed more fully,[17] concerns a family group strikingly similar to the one in the *Squire's Tale;* that is, Omar bin al-Nu'umān (Cambyuskan), his two sons Zau al-Makān (Algarsif) and Sharrkan (Cambalo), and his daughter Nuzhat al-Zamān (Canacee). What is still more important, the long narrative of the adventures of this Oriental family involves an incident which seems to parallel the situation in the *Squire's Tale:* namely, the fact that after a long separation which has rendered them unknown to each other Sharrkan unwittingly weds his sister Nuzhat al-Zamān.[18]

In thus entertaining the hypothesis that under similar circumstances Cambalo weds Canacee, one is obliged to consider Chaucer's remarks in the *Pardoner's Tale:* "Lo, how that dronken Looth unkyndely/Lay by his doghtres two, unwityngly;/So dronke he was he nyste what he wroghte" (11.485-87). Further, although the reference (unless it has more than one application) is to Gower's incestuous story of Canacee in *Confessio Amantis*, the Man of Law is speaking of Chaucer when he says:

> But certeinly no word ne writeth he
> Of thilke wikke ensample of Canacee,
> That loved her owene brother synfully;
> (Of swiche cursed stories I sey fy) [11.77-80].

Both these statements might be construed to show that Chaucer would have avoided the selection of incest as a motive in the *Canterbury Tales* were it not for the arresting occurrence of a pertinent passage on the marriage of cousins in the account of Hypermnestra in *The Legend of Good Women:*

To Danao and Egistes also–
Althogh so be that they were brethren two,
For thilke tyme was spared no lynage--
It lykede hem to make a maryage
Bytwixen Ypermystre and hym Lyno (11.2600-04).

Concerning this important statement that no degree of consanguinity
was a bar to marriage, Professor Robinson remarks: "Chaucer seems to have
had no authority for saying that the union was within the prohibited
degrees."[19]

But as for the interpretation that Cambalo was to wed Canacee,
Chaucer of course had for precedent the authority of the "storie" (1.655)
similar to the Arabian analogue. The story of incest in the *Arabian Nights*
is both long and involved; and it is possible that Chaucer began his
narrative before completing the account he was reading and accordingly
determined to leave the *Squire's Tale* incomplete when he encountered the
incest motive in the material he was studying. Whatever the circumstances,
he appears to have retained as a reference to Oriental practice the
significant detail about two brothers fighting as one man against one man.
The least which can be said, therefore, is that the *Anonimalle Chronicle*,
although it does not afford an instance of "thilke wikke ensample of
Canacee," strengthens the hypothesis of Chaucer's use of the incest motive
found in the Arabian analogue. In mentioning two brothers from India, this
contemporary chronicle also unequivocally suggests that Canacee's own
brother Cambalo was obliged to combat two brothers from India.

NOTES

[1] F. N. Robinson (ed.), *The Complete Works of Geoffrey Chaucer* (Boston,
1933), p. 231.

[2] See my paper, "The Two Petros in the 'Monkes Tale,' " *PMLA* (1935), L,
77-80.

[3] L. de Mas-Latrie, "Guillaume de Machaut et *La Prise d'Alexandrie*,"
Bibliothèque de l'École des Chartes (1876), xxxvii, 445-63.

[4] See may paper, *loc. cit.*

[5] *Ibid.*

[6] L. de Mas-Latrie, *loc. cit.*

[7] J. W. Jeudwine, *Tort, Crime, and Police in Medieval Britain* (London, 1917), p.33.

[8] Compare the *Nun's Priest's Tale* (ll. 3004ff.); see Robinson (ed.), *op. cit.*, p. 240.

[9] J. M. Manly, *Some New Light on Chaucer* (New York, 1926), pp.8, 10-12, 30.

[10] F. N. Robinson (ed.), *The Complete Works of Geoffrey Chaucer* (Boston, 1933), p. 162.

[11] Algarsif "wan Theodora to his wif" (l. 664).

[12] J. L. Lowes, "The *Squire's Tale* and the Land of Prester John," *Washington University Studies* (St. Louis, 1913), I, ii, 17.

[13] V. H. Galbraith (ed.), *The Anonimalle Chronicle* (London, 1927), pp. 115-16.

[14] *Loc cit.*—Mr. Richard Strawn, formerly one of my graduate students, translates from French into English:

In that same year 1377 two brothers-german, twinlings from India, who were Ethiops, came to the King of Spain, opposing the law and faith of the holy church, saying that God took no flesh nor blood from the Virgin Mary, which they would prove in battle; and the custom of their country was and is that the twins should fight in place of one man, against one man... At this time there were imprisoned by the King of Spain six knights and sixteen squires of England, who were captured with the Count of Pembroke... and finally a knight from England, Sir John of Harpedon by name... accepted the challenge... the aforesaid knight killed the elder brother and then the younger.

[15] See my paper, "The Two Petros in the 'Monkes Tale,'" *PMLA* (1935), L, 77.

[16] On Chaucer's use of contemporary historical material, spurious or authentic, see my paper, "Cambyuskan's Flying Horse and Charles VI's 'Cerf Volant,'" *MLR* (1938), XXXIII, 41 ff.

[17] See my paper, "The Genre of Chaucer's *Squire's Tale*," *JEGP*(1942), XLI, 287 ff.

[18] *Ibid.*

[19] Robinson (ed.), *op. cit.*, p. 969.

Reprinted from *MLN*, LXII (1947), 173-179.

18

CHAUCER'S PHILIPPA, DAUGHTER OF PANNETO

The fragmentary household accounts of Elizabeth of Ulster for the years 1357-1359 mention gifts to and expenses of Chaucer and of, among others, a lady designated as Philippa Pan'.[1] Her name appears in the records four times, in each instance being spelled in unexpanded form as Ph Pan.[2] The first name, written as Ph, unquestionably stands for *Philippa;* however, some real uncertainty has existed as to how the second name should be expanded. The early explanation in 1886 of Edward A. Bond is that Pan was "probably the contracted form of the word Panetaria--mistress of the pantry."[3] The more recent opinion in 1926 of the late Professor John M. Manly is that Pan represented a family name and that as such it appears "in many forms: Panetaria, de la Panetrie, Pentry, Panter, and the like."[4] In this connection, one may point out that the will of Johis de Salkeld, proved January 20, 1358/9, includes another variant of this family name in mentioning a man called Thome de Paniteri.[5] But the contracted form of Pan may well represent some wholly different name; in fact, Manly himself cites a wealthy family in fourteenth-century England named Pantolf and says that "the abbreviation may as well stand for this name as for *panetaria,* and may well be a family name and not an official designation."[6]

To pursue a further possible identification of the name, the "mysterious lady who is designated as Philippa Pan"[7] may not be at all mysterious. Indeed, she may be no other person than Chaucer's wife Philippa, daughter of Paon, a knight from Roet, a small town in Hainaut. Early in the century, her father was rewarded for services in England, Kervyn de Lettenhove calling attention to the fact that "En 1332, un comte de la maison de la reine d'Angleterre mentionne un don fait 'a Panneto de Roed, de Hannonia."[8] The appearance in this record of the word Panneto (sometimes elsewhere spelled Paonnet or Paunet) suggests immediately the full form of the name abbreviated in the household accounts as Pan. In other words, Philippa Pan' and Philippa, daughter of Panneto, obviously may be one and the same person. This is both a natural and a satisfactory identification of Philippa Pan'; thus Manly, apparently unaware of the spelling Panneto, had insufficient evidence for claiming that the "mysterious lady" was a person different from "that Philippa who at some time before 1366 became the poet's wife."[9]

NOTES

[1] Edward A. Bond, *Life-Records of Chaucer* (Sec. Ser., 1886), XXI, 98-99.

[2] R. E. G. Kirk, *Life-Records of Chaucer* (Sec. Ser., 1900), XXXII, 152-153.

[3] Bond, *op. cit.,* p.98.

[4] John M. Manly, *Some New Light on Chaucer* (New York, 1926), p. 62; see also Walter Rye, *London Athenaeum* (January 29, 1881), pp. 166 ff.

[5] R. S. Ferguson, *Testamenta Karleolensia* (1353-1386) (London, 1893), No. XIX.

[6] Manly, *op. cit.,* p. 62.

[7] *Ibid.*

[8] Kervyn de Lettenhove, *Œuvres de Froissart* (Brussels, 1877), XXIII, 28.

[9] Manly, *op. cit.,* p. 57; see also p. 63.

Reprinted from *MLN*, LXIV (1949), 342-343.

19

CHAUCER'S DON PEDRO AND THE PURPOSE OF THE *MONK'S TALE*

Henry Savage's theories regarding the occasion of Chaucer's tragedy of King Pedro in the *Monk's Tale* call for a re-examination of the poem and the facts behind it.[1] For one thing, Chaucer, so far as is known, had neither a reading nor a speaking knowledge of the Spanish tongue, so that it is highly improbable that he consulted a Spaniard about the king's death. For another, Mr. Savage fails to explain the peculiar English slant on the enemy French which appears in Chaucer's second stanza, where the tone of its criticism suggests that the informant was, not a Spaniard, but a patriotic Englishman.

If fact, the brutal assassination in March, 1369, of King Pedro of Spain by his illegitimate brother Henry, described by Chaucer in the *Monk's Tale* (VII, 2375ff.), was contemporary tragedy of special interest to the English court. Pedro's cause long had been supported by the English, whereas the claims of Henry, in a later version stigmatized by Chaucer as "bastard brother,"were upheld by the French. Shortly after the death of Pedro, John of Gaunt made a claim to the Spanish throne by wedding the dead king's eldest daughter, Constance of Castile.

References to the murder occurred in the ballads of that day, Sir Walter Scott's poem, "The Death of Peter the Cruel," being a nineteenth-century translation of an early Spanish ballad on the theme. On the other hand, since no literary source for the Monk's two stanzas on Pedro is known, Chaucer probably depended for his information upon gossip which was then current in England.

Chaucer might easily have learned, as I suggested in 1935,[2] all about the assassination from some one of his friends who had been partisans of the Spanish king. A number of these friends, I may add now from the eyewitness report of the Herald Chandos, fought for the king's cause at the battle of Nájera in 1367--such noblemen, for example as Thomas Percy, William Beauchamp, John Devereaux, and Guichard d'Angle.[3] But this is not all. I may cite now, on the authority of the chronicler Froissart, that two English soldiers-of-fortune, James Roland and Ralph Holmes, were killed in the same tent with Pedro.

This happened when they sought, from motives of chivalry or in an attempt to protect the king for later ransom, to defend his royal person from an unfair attack.[4] The murder of these two Englishmen in the affray made the whole episode doubly topical among patriots at the English court. There was no mystery whatsoever surrounding Pedro's death, and thus one need not look beyond the immediate range of Chaucer's circle of friends for a likely informant--say, Guichard d'Angle, who was a man well known to Chaucer and his sometime associate on missions abroad.

Chaucer's account contains two definite statements: that Henry committed the murder and that Mauny set the trap. There is also in the Monk's second stanza an indirect allusion to the heraldic armor of another French general, Bertrand du Guesclin. The fact that Henry did the killing was of course common knowledge, but the further statements belittling the two Frenchmen are a somewhat different matter. If Chaucer talked over the affair with Guichard d'Angle, he was doubtless here echoing the feelings of his friend. Sir Guichard had good cause for hating both Bertrand du Guesclin and Oliver de Mauny. It was these French generals who attacked Guichard d'Angle's castle during his absence and who on that occasion were unchivalrous in their behavior towards his unprotected wife. Although the works of Chaucer rarely criticize the French, his sympathies were unquestionably with the English; and his markedly critical attitude in the *Monk's Tale* respecting Du Guesclin and Mauny may well reflect the personal sentiments of Sir Guichard d'Angle.

As for the role of Constance of Castile in the historical background of the *Monk's Tale,* it was Sir Guichard who suggested to Gaunt the policy of his betrothal to this eldest daughter of the lately deceased Pedro. Guichard d'Angle both arranged the marriage and attended the wedding ceremonies. For this reason, he qualifies as the person best acquainted with the various aspects of the whole affair of the murder in Spain and the resulting question of who should be the successor to the Spanish crown. Clearly, it was unnecessary for Chaucer to get at the facts by seeking out a Spaniard in the retinue of this new Duchess of Lancaster, as recently suggested by Mr. Savage. The language of the Monk's stanzas does not reveal any detectable flavor of the Spanish idiom nor contain any particular information dependent on a Spanish literary source. There appears, then, no reason for dismissing Guichard d'Angle as, in the circumstances, Chaucer's most probable informant.

Henry Savage, however, pursues yet another hypothesis. In his new theory about Don Pedro, which interprets the Monk's stanzas as an occasional poem composed for Pedro's daughter Constance of Castile, he states: "It can be seen, then, that there is every possibility that the story of 'Petro, glorie of Spayne' was written at the time that a second Duchess of Lancaster appeared at the English Court."[5] This is an astonishing construction to place on Chaucer's lines, which report only that Pedro was slain by his bastard brother and that the Frenchman Mauny set the trap for the murder. If the stanzas were written to celebrate the marriage of Duke John and Constance of Castile, one would expect that Chaucer should at least mention her or the fact that she was now an English duchess. But he does neither. On the other hand, in the *Book of the Duchess,* an occasional poem, Chaucer makes unmistakable punning references to both the Duke of Lancaster and his deceased wife Blanche. In the Monk's stanzas, which Mr. Savage says were composed to welcome the second Duchess to England, there is not the slightest indication of any such personal allegory.

Like those on the three other contemporary worthies, Peter of Cyprus, Barnabo of Lombardy, and Ugolino of Pisa, the stanzas on Don Pedro were written with "tragedy" in mind. In writing these four so-called "Modern Instances," Chaucer was collecting biographies for a Falls of Princes brought up to his own time. It might be possible to construe them as a warning to a reigning sovereign, in this instance King Edward III, to beware of assassins inasmuch as the "Modern Instances" all concern noblemen who met their end through treachery. Chaucer does not say so explicitly, although he does say, at the beginning of his poem, that it is his purpose to bewail in the manner of tragedy the misfortune of those who once stood in high estate and urges that his readers "Be war by thise ensamples trewe and olde" (VII, 1998).[6]

But certainly there is nothing in the Monk's stanzas on Pedro about either his daughter or her marriage to John of Gaunt. The *Monk's Tale* should be studied for what it is: a magnificent collection of tragedies from various sources--literary, bibical, oral--and from materials of earliest times right up to his own day. The stanzas on Pedro do not contain a sequel to the *Book of the Duchess* and are not a new poem celebrating the wedding of the recently bereaved Gaunt to a second Duchess of Lancaster. The Monk seems to know nothing of this marriage and has his eye only on tragedy, which is the avowed theme of his entire collection.

NOTES

[1] Henry Savage, "Chaucer and the 'Pitous Deeth' of 'Petro, Glorie of Spayne,' " *Speculum*, XXIV (1949), 357-75.

[2] "The Two Petros in the *Monkes Tale* " *PMLA*, L (1935), 69-80; *Chaucer and the French Poet Graunson* (Baton Rouge, La., 1947), p. 51.

[3] Edith Rickert, ed., *Chaucer's World* (New York, 1948), pp. 325-29. For this reference and other suggestions about this paper, I am indebted to Professor D. D. Griffith.

[4] Thomas Johnes, tr., *Sir John Froissart's Chronicles* (London, 1806), III, 359.

[5] Savage, *loc. cit.*, p. 371.

[6] F. N. Robinson, ed., *Complete Works of Geoffrey Chaucer* (Boston, 1933), p. 226.

Reprinted from *MLQ*, XIII (1952), 3-5.

20

CHAUCER'S COMIC VALENTINE

If *The Parlement of Foules* pictured the birds assembling on Saint Valentine's Day for the sole purpose of chirruping about the mating season, it would be a literary exercise interesting only to ornithologists and bird fanciers. The poem is given universal interest when Chaucer has the birds speak like men and act like them. Some readers have even viewed it as a serious treatise, seeing in its convocation either a weighty discussion of true and false felicity[1] or a scholastic disagreement between realists and idealists,[2] although this would hardly be Chaucer's usual practice in a treatise, as in his *Boethius,* which is a direct translation of a philosophical classic and in no sense the settlement of a debate between two systems of thought. Since the assembly of birds is obviously comparable to a parliament of men, Mr. Gardiner Stillwell has rightly analyzed the poet's plan in recently stating that "Chaucer's poem is comic."[3] There is always patent comedy in any situation describing human behavior by animal representation, as in the comparison made in the Parliament of 1371, where the clergy were likened to the owl who "had lost her feathers,"[4] so that Chaucer's assembly of birds, when viewed in the light of the Good Parliamant of 1376,[5] is seen to be unmistakably humorous in its basic framework.

The only time Mr. Stillwell's interpretation is strained occurs when he argues that Chaucer's purpose is ironic rather than simply humorous. No one could possibly cavil with Mr. Stillwell's statement: "Goose, duck, cuckoo, turtle-dove, tercels, formel, merlin--they are all comic figures."[6] But it is significant that they are all given their own natural characters and are not made ironic caricatures. For example, the foolish cuckoo is not endowed with the wisdom of an owl, nor the awkward goose with the sedateness of a swan. The fowls of ravine, on whom the plot centers, are described with equal realism. Inasmuch as the formel is a sovereign lady, it may appear contradictory that the three tercels are permitted to do the choosing, until one recalls that this was the condition prescribed by Dame Nature: "By my statut and thorgh my governaunce,/Ye come for to cheese" (387-388). The situation, it is clear, would not be ironic, as Mr.

Stillwell asserts, unless the circumstances were reversed, with the formel, contrary to Dame Nature's rule, making all the proposals herself. Since Chaucer presents no such burlesque of Nature's law, Mr. Stillwell appears wrong in stating that "The poet's humor touches even the fowls of ravine, and does so in such ironic fashion as to make one skeptical of the view that Chaucer's intention was the paying of a courtly compliment to actual persons whose marriage was in process of being negotiated when the poem was written."[7]

The foregoing statement of Mr. Stillwell, a reference to the bethrothal of Prince Richard and Princess Marie--in the negotiations for which Chaucer played an official part--is objectionable upon an historical basis. He seems to believe that the poet would not include a courtly compliment in a comic poem. If he is right, then the obvious agreement between the *Parlement* and this contemporary event of 1377 is a meaningless coincidence.

In considering this problem, a short review of Chaucer's procedure in a number of other occasional poems should prove instructive. The balade *Truth,* which was written to cheer his friend Sir Philip la Vache, contains in its "Envoy" a humorous reference to him as "thou Vache." Moreover, Chaucer's *Complaint of Venus* refers with good-natured humor to the "curiosite" of his friend Sir Oton de Graunson's versification at the same time that it compliments him as "flour of hem that make in Fraunce." Furthermore, that the poet regarded a comic poem as a fit setting for a courtly compliment is established by the occasion of *The Complaint of Chaucer to his Purse.* Of this poem, which is addressed to King Henry IV, Professor Robinson says: "Chaucer's complaint, with its humorous adaptation of the language of a lover's appeal to his mistress, is certainly one of the happiest variations on the well-known theme."[8] From this evidence, it is perfectly clear that the poet, instead of being averse to the device, was actually prone to use compliments in a humorous setting. As a great humorist, Chaucer evidently recognized that the effectiveness of the compliment would be thus enhanced.

Indeed, now that the *Parlement* has been placed in the realm of comedy, one may well wonder if it did not have the same purpose as the comic *Complaint of Chaucer to his Purse.* Henry IV, whom the poet compliments as "conquerour of Brutes Albyon," was crowned king on September 30, 1399; about a fortnight later, on October 13, he promptly rewarded Chaucer for faithful service with a pension of forty marks. In the *Parlement* the poet says that he hopes to "mete som thyng for to fare/The bet"; on April 11, 1377, he received, as a reward for his services in negotiating the betrothal of Richard and Marie in February, a "special gift" of forty pounds. In accord with these circumstances, the unity of the *Parlement,* with its complimentary allusion to this betrothal, is nowhere more apparent than at its end, where the birds sing a roundel whose "note," Chaucer says, "imaked was in France" (677).

NOTES

[1] R. M. Lumiansky, "Chaucer's *Parlement of Foules:* a Philosophical Interpretation," *RES,* 24 (1948), 81-89.

[2] B. H. Bronson, "In Appreciation of Chaucer's *Parlement of Foules,"* *Univ. of Calif. Pub. in Eng.,* Vol. 3 (1935), No. 5, pp. 193-224.

[3] G. Stillwell, "Unity and Comedy in Chaucer's *Parlement of Foules,"* *JEGP,* 49 (1950), 470-495.

[4] H. Braddy, *Chaucer and the French Poet Graunson* (Baton Rouge, Louisiana State University Press, 1947), p. 84.

[5] *Ibid.*

[6] Stillwell, *op. cit.,* p. 487.

[7] *Ibid.,* p. 471.

[8] F. N. Robinson (ed.), *The Complete Works of Geoffrey Chaucer* (New York, 1933), p.981.

Reprinted from *MLN,* LXVIII (1953), 232-234.

21

CHAUCER'S BAWDY TONGUE

Linguistically speaking, the most sensational aspect of Chaucer's works is his folk realism, nowhere more graphically displayed than in the bawdy vocabulary which he employs to describe situations of a ribald or scatological nature. In the General Prologue he says that "The wordes moote be cosyn to the dede" (1.742).[1] This passage, often accepted as an enunciation of his artistic creed, does not fully explain what happens in Chaucer's poetry. There the speech always fits the speaker. For example, a type of incest becomes the basis of uncle Pandarus's relationship with his niece Criseyde. Chaucer unmistakably communicates the idea of their unwholesome alliance, but he does so, not by coarse vulgarisms that match their unnatural "dede," but by inoffensive verses that conform to both the social status of his characters and the tastes of his courtly audience.

> With that his arm al sodeynly he thriste
> Under hire nekke, and at the laste hire kyste.
>
> I passe al that which chargeth nought to seye.
> What! God foryaf his deth, and she al so
> Foryaf, and with here uncle gan to pleye,
> For other cause was ther noon than so.
> But of this thing right to the effect to go,
> Whan tyme was, hom to here hous she wente,
> And Pandarus hath fully his entente (III, 1574-82).

Later on Chaucer, who sometimes praised one thing and portrayed another, spoke directly against incest in the *Pardoner's Tale*.

> Lo, how that dronken Looth, unkyndely,
> Lay by his doghtres two, unwityngly;
> So dronke he was, he nyste what he wroghte (ll. 485–87.)

For a second instance, the Man of Law's Introduction appears to disparage Gower, who wrote an incestuous tale about Canace. Then the text pronounces an anathema, perhaps in part jocosely, on such stories.

But certeinly no word ne writeth he
Of thilke wikke ensample of Canacee,
That loved hir owene brother synfully;
(Of swich cursed stories I sey fy!) (11. 77-80).

On the basis of these two passages, I long ago proposed that Chaucer abruptly terminates the *Squire's Tale* to avoid the brother-sister incest motif featured in its lengthy Arabian analogue, a basic theme also probably included in the "storie" (1.655) that he was following.[2]

Chaucer foregoes similar restraint when he deals with a bawdy situation involving humbler characters. The notable examples are of course the incidents recited by the Miller and the Reeve, where the folk element looms large in both the homely plot and the rustic vocabulary. As Dr. Joseph Mersand remarks, "the stories told by these two men of the countryside have a smaller Romance content than Chaucer's works in his Court period."[3] From this fact, Mersand discounts a French analogue and reasons "that these two tales were probably based on native English originals, in which the Anglo-Saxon element was exceptionally large."[4] The total vocabulary of Chaucer has been estimated at 8,430 words.[5] Since his bawdy terms number only 119[6], he hardly may be regarded seriously as a foul-mouthed poet plagued with an obscene mind.[7]

The small proportion, in number and frequency, of Chaucer's vulgarisms is more than compensated for by their unreserved frankness and stark honesty. Conservative translators of earlier times, mindful of high school students and college undergraduates, found his simple directness altogether unmanageable. The original verse in the *Miller's Tale* about Absolon's being "somdeel squaymous/Of fartyng, and of speche daungerous" (11.3337-38) Dr. Tatlock rendered as "he was somewhat dainty, and bashful of his speech."[8] Dr. Lumiansky, a more recent translator, comes closer to the true meaning when he modernizes these harmless lines as "he was rather squeamish about breaking wind and a bit fastidious in his speech."[9]

In the original Middle English, the sensitive reader will find that the ribald passages reveal Chaucer's expert insight into the uninhibited lives of the folk rather than his unhealthy concern with pornography and coprophilia. In general, Chaucer shies away from the abnormal; his Pardoner, depicted in the General Prologue as "a geldyng or a mare" (1.691), but who claims in his Prologue to "have a joly wenche in every toun" (1.453), is hardly equivalent to a sex pervert. Surely it is a sign of preoccupation with degeneracy when a present-day critic speculates that Chaucer wrote the *Tale of Sir Thopas* to ridicule King Richard II's alleged homosexuality.[10] Dr. George Williams cites as his only grounds for the imputation Shakespeare's fictional passages in Richard II (III, i). The charge is historically baseless, as has everywhere been recognized by Shakespearean scholars.[11] Equally strained is the same critic's recent conjecture that *Troilus and Criseyde* records an erotic intrigue in the Lancastrian household. To fulfill these conditions, the poet himself allegorically represents Pandarus, takes the opportunity as middleman to fornicate with his niece Criseyde (Chaucer's sister-in-law Katherine Swynford), and in this way betrays Troilus (Chaucer's patron Lancaster).[12] Chaucer throughout his works is bold and manly, seldom given to dwelling on aberrant sexual behavior. What one meets with in the tales is a rugged, direct presentation of lusty simple folk, not hidden allegory about his own concupiscence or the sexual derelictions of royal members of his circle. He presents lechery and flatulence heartily, robustly--always without the leer of the abnormally prurient or the snigger of the hypocritically pious.

Chaucer intrepidly joins sex with scatology in the *Miller's Tale,* in which two clerks cuckold a carpenter. First "hende" Nicholas prevails upon the wife Alisoun to grant him her body.

> And prively he caughte hire by the queynte (1.3276).
> And heeld hire harde by the haunchebones (1.3279).
> And thakked hire about the lendes well (1.3304)

Later the parish clerk Absolon has his own singular experience upon bestowing on Alisoun's posterior his unforgettable kiss.

> And Absolon hath kist her nether ye (1.3852).

After this misdirected buss, Alisoun articulates one tiny ejaculation of glee. She says, "Tehee!" (1.3740), certainly as suggestive a giggle as ever heroine emitted. In this tale Chaucer remains invariably candid when describing parts of the human body, for he meticulously proceeds to identify pudendum, buttocks, anus, and pubic hair.[13] He does so in a language harmonizing with the sportiveness of the participants. Absolon was a squeamish fellow, but Nicholas, with a better developed carminative faculty, "anon leet fle a fart,/As greet as it had been a thonder-dent" (11.3806 f.).

Chaucer waxes somewhat more restrained with the Wife of Bath and the Merchant, both a notch or so higher in social status than the country Miller. The Wife, who already had enjoyed five husbands, defends their multiplicity by citing Don Solomon in heartfelt admiration of his sexual prowess.

God woot, this noble kyng, as to my wit,
The first nyght had many a myrie fit
With ech of hem, so well was hym on lyve.
Yblessed be God that I have wedded fyve! (11. 41-44).

She then deduces irrefutably the reasons for the creation of the organs of generation.

Glose whoso wole, and seye bothe up and doun,
That they were maked for purgacioun
Of uryne, and oure bothe thynges smale
Were eek to knowe a femele from a male,
And for noon oother cause,—say ye no?
The experience woot wel it is noght so (11. 119-124).

In her Prologue the Wife begins to use some of Chaucer's many euphemisms for the genitals in words like "harneys" (1.136), "membres" (1.116), and "sely instrument" (1.132). Then she refers to them again in successive phrases that flash with verbal wizardry.

Is it for ye wolde have my queynte allone? (1.444).
For if I wolde selle my *bele chose* (1.447).
A likerous mouth moste han a likerous tayl (1.466).

I hadde the beste *quoniam* myghte be (1.608).

That made me I koude noght withdrawe
My chambre of Venus from a good felawe (11.617-18).

For sexual intercourse, her diction becomes more conventional and less forthright than that of either the Miller or the Reeve. She terms coition "the experience" (1.124), "swynke" (1.202), "meschaunce" (1.407), and simply "daliance" (1.565); but eroticism preys on her mind, as may be shown by a few of her many references to it.

I sette hem so a-werke, by my fey (1.215)
Thus seistow, lorel, whan thow goost to bedde (1.273)
Be maister of my body and of my good (1.314)
Ye shul have queynte right ynogh at eve (1.332)
Thanne wolde I suffre hym do his nycetee (1.412)
And lete hir lecchour dighte hire al the nyght (1.767)

The husband January's procedure with his bride, though ultimately involving a somewhat individual routine, also utilizes almost hackneyed amative terminology, particularly so at the start.

> This Januarie is ravysshed in a traunce
> At every tyme he looked on hir face;
> But in his herte he gan hire to manace
> That he that nyght in armes wolde hire streyne
> Harder than evere Parys dide Eleyne (11. 1750-54).

Then, stimulated by aphrodisiacs, January hints that his sexual behavior may not be entirely regular, because he avers that "A man may do no synne with his wyf" (1.1839). His intentions are soon made clear.

> Anon he preyde hire strepen hire al naked;
> He wolde of hire, he seyde, han some plesaunce,
> And seyde hir clothes dide hym encombraunce,
> And she obeyeth, be hire lief or looth.
> But lest that precious folk be with me wrooth,
> How that he wroghte, I dar nat to yow telle;
> Or wheither hire thoughte it paradys or helle
>   (11. 1958-64).

As in most of the Wife of Bath's less colorful references to the sexual act, Chaucer with the Merchant falls back on a stylistic device in keeping with the morality of January's bourgeois caste. Flush at the climax, the author refuses the opportunity to become ribald and turns lamely to the insipid euphemism of "I dar nat to yow telle" (1.1963).

By contrast, the vocabulary of the folk characters is unreservedly earthy. The conquests of Malyne by Aleyn in the *Reeve's Tale* and of Alisoun by Nicholas in the *Miller's* veer sharply from the pattern of courtly love. The possible satirical intent is clear enough when the Reeve bawdily narrates what befalls both a miller's wife and his daughter before the dawn. The clerk John puts the husband to shame in the Reeve's account of how the wife enjoys the sexual prowess of the clerk more than that of her spouse: "So myrie a fit ne hadde she nat ful yoore" (1.4230). The daughter in her turn also passed a merry night. The clerk Aleyn declares that "I have thries in this shorte nyght/Swyved the milleres doghter bolt upright" (11. 4265-66). Chaucer spares little of ribaldry in the *Reeve's Tale* when utilizing such graphic metaphors as "he leith on soore" (1.4229) and "He priketh harde and depe as he were mad" (1.4231).[14]

Chaucer spares equally little of scatology when the Host, Harry Bailly, replies to the Pardoner's offer of saints' relics to kiss. The offer inspires Harry with perhaps the most amazing concentration of profanity and rural crudity in the *Canterbury Tales*.

"Nay, nay!" quod he, "thanne have I Cristes curs!
"Lat be," quod he, "it shal not be, so theech!
Thou woldest make me kisse thyn olde breech,
And swere it were a relyk of a seint,
Though it were with thy fundement depeint!
But, by the croys which that Seint Eleyne fond,
I wolde I hadde thy coillons in myn hond
In stide of relikes or of seintuarie.
Lat kutte hem of, I wol thee helpe hem carie;
They shul be shryned in an hogges toord!" (11. 946-55).

Evidently the London author knew and relished the hearty and robust aspect of folk humor. His own *Tale of Sir Thopas* was stopped in its tracks when host Harry interrupted the narrator with the cry, "Thy drasty rymyng is nat worth a toord!" (1.930).

Chaucer's most prominent scatological theme is flatulence, this being the subject that he at least found most amusing. There occur only a few scattered references in the *Canterbury Tales* to elimination in words like "toord," "pisse," and "shiten."[15] In phrases expressing anger, the references more often occur as "dung," "gong," and "jurdones."[16]

The Summoner recites the one story in the collection devoted exclusively to the carminative faculty. It opens in a bland style, with a begging friar endeavoring to secure gifts. But an early indication of the offensiveness to transpire comes in the narrator's play on the literal meaning of *eructare,* to belch, in the statement, "Lo, 'buf!' they seye, '*cor meum eructavit!*'" (1. 1934). A few lines further on a pun on the pronunciation of "ferything" suggests not a belch, but a flautus: "What is a ferything worth parted in twelve?" (1.1967). That Chaucer intended to vary the pronunciation emerges in two subsequent locutions: "an odious meschief" (1.2190) and "ars-metrike" (L.2222).

The *Summoner's Tale* then continues with a caption that abandons innuendo for grossness.

The wordes of the lordes squier and his kervere for
departynge of the fart on twelve.

The "squier" thereupon explains that a cartwheel with twelve spokes must be brought into the hall for twelve friars to stick their respective noses in at "every spokes ende" (1.2263). Then a "cherl" will place himself at the nave of the wheel and "lete a fart" (1.2270).

And ye shul seen, up peril of my lyf,
By preeve which that is demonstratif,

> That equally the soun of it wol wende,
> And eke the stynk, unto the spokes ende (1. 2271-74).

With these lines Chaucer probably shocked the sensibilities of his audience. At the same time he had intelligence enough to foresee their reaction. He therefore sought to explain in the General Prologue his creed as a writer.

> But first I pray yow, of youre curteisye,
> That ye n'arrete it nat my vileynye,
> Thogh that I pleynly speke in this mateere,
> To telle yow hir wordes and hir cheere,
> Ne thogh I speke hir wordes proprely.
> For this ye knowen al so wel as I,
> Whoso shal telle a tale after a man,
> He moot reherce as ny as evere he kan
> Everich a word, if it be in his charge,
> Al speke he never so rudeliche and large,
> Or ellis he moot telle his tale untrewe,
> Or feyne thyng, or fynde wordes newe (1. 725-36).

The Miller's Prologue also contains a fervent bid for lenience or under-standing.

> For Goddes love, demeth nat that I seye
> Of yvel entente, but for I moot reherce
> Hir tales alle, be they bettre or werse,
> Or elles falsen som of my mateere (11. 3172-75).

Finally, at the end of the *Parson's Tale,* which closes the whole collection, the poet advises his hearers that "if ther be any thyng that displese hem, I preye hem also that they arrette it to the defaute of myn unkonnynge, and nat to my wyl, that wolde ful fayn have seyd bettre if I hadde had konnynge" (11. 1082 ff.).

Chaucer's bawdy tongue is inescapably a part of the *Canterbury Tales*[17] and, what is more important, of the man himself. His folk lexicon, though containing words of both foreign and native origin, did not bulk large in his total vocabulary. That lexicon contained entries of chiefly Anglo-Saxon derivation. Their pungency is effective and always fitting to the most naturalistic occasion. What sets Chaucer apart from such great contemporaries as Gower and the author of *Sir Gawain and the Green Knight,* each of whom also wrote of illicit love, is Chaucer's unparalleled artistry with country language and its crude but basic humor. He achieved this unique place in Middle English poetry through his cognizance that folklore provides grist for the literary mill and by his intimation that rustic laughter is basic and lasting. Usually we feel superior to humble characters in their homely dilemmas; but we never become too refined to misunderstand their idiom. The homely expressions in the *Canterbury Tales* remain almost unchanged over the centuries; they are often the easiest ones to read in the East Midland dialect of Chaucer; and they continue today to draw inquisitive readers to the works of the father of modern English.

NOTES

[1] For all quotations from the poet's text, see F. N. Robinson (ed.), *The Works of Geoffrey Chaucer* (Boston, 2nd ed., 1957).

[2] "The Genre of Chaucer's *Squire's Tale*," *JEGP*, XL (July, 1942), 279-90.

[3] *Chaucer's Romance Vocabulary* (New York, 1937), p. 109.

[4] *Ibid.*, p. 123. For a French analogue, see Robinson, *op. cit.*, p.687; or W. F. Bryan and Germaine Dempster (eds.), *Sources and Analogues of Chaucer's Canterbury Tales* (Chicago, Ill., 1941), pp. 124-147.

[5] *Ibid.*, p. 46.

[6] This is the number appearing in the Glossary by Howard L. McCord, *Chaucer's Bawdry: A Study of Ribald Words and Situations in the "Canterbury Tales"* (unpublished M. A. thesis, the University of Utah, Salt Lake City, 1958), pp. 35-54.

[7] Lord Byron regarded Chaucer's bawdry as "obscene and contemptible"; see Caroline Spurgeon, *Five Hundred Years of Chaucer Criticism and Allusion* (Cambridge, 1925), ii, 29.

[8] John S. P. Tatlock and Percy MacKaye (trs.), *The Complete Poetical Works of Geoffrey Chaucer* (New York, 1936), p. 55.

[9] R. M. Lumiansky (tr.), *The Canterbury Tales* (New York, 1948), p. 58.

[10] George Williams, *A New View of Chaucer* (Durham, N.C., 1965), pp. 147 n. 151.

[11] Hardin Craig (ed.), *Shakespeare* (New York, 1931), p. 495 n. Shakespeare's fictional account of Richard's effeminacy may have been influenced by Marlowe's portrayal of the homosexual King in *Edward II*. The unwarranted allegation about King Richard finds no place in the definitive biographies by H. Wallon, *Richard II*, 2 vols. (Paris, 1864); and Anthony Steel, *Richard II* (Cambridge, 1962).

[12] Williams, *op. cit.*, pp. 71, 73, 75, and especially 77-78.

[13] McCord, *op. cit.*, p. 24.

[14] For further references to bawdry in the *Man of Law's Tale* and elsewhere in Chaucer, see McCord, *op. cit.*

[15] *Pardoner's Tale,* 1. 955: *Wife of Bath's Tale,* 1. 729; and General Prologue, 1. 504, respectively.

[16] *Nun's Priest's Tale,* 11. 3048-49; *Parson's Tale,* 1. 884; and *Pardoner's Tale,* 1. 305, respectively.

[17] In his Retractation Chaucer says that he also wrote "many a leccherous lay" (1. 1086), but his Court poetry now extant appears remarkably free of the bawdy element discussed here.

Reprinted from *SFQ,* XXX (1966), 214-222.

22

CHAUCER'S BILINGUAL IDIOM

In his courtly poetry Chaucer wrote mainly for a London audience of noblemen and ladies who spoke native English but who also knew and fancied refinements of the French tongue.[1] On the way to Canterbury, however, the versatile poet featured speakers of a language at times learned but more often provincial, or at least plain-spoken. As Controller of Customs, he had the opportunity to learn the speech of even rogues. In *The Cook's Tale* the wastrel Perkyn Revelour squanders his time and steals from his master. The words "lowke," "sowke," and "brybe" (CkT 4415-17) have to do with thieves' cant and mean respectively "confederate," "cheater," and "robber."[2] In *The Miller's Tale* the words "cherl" and "gnof" (MillT 3182, 3188) represent slang of Germanic origin referring to coarse or rough fellows. The Host interrupts *The Tale of Sir Thopas* with "Thy drasty rymyng is nat worth a toord!" (930), where the last word reeks of eliminative functions in keeping with the Anglo-Saxon prototype of the adjective "draestig," which means filthy.

More neutral examples of the folksy ring involve the idiomatic phrase "come off," which Chaucer used often. Alison cautions her lover Absolon to "com of, and speed the faste,/Lest that oure neighebores thee espie" (MillT 3728-29). When the Summoner is browbeating the old woman to pay him, he exclaims, "Com of, and lat me ryden hastily" (FrT 1602). After John loses his horse, he urges his companion Aleyn to "Step on thy feet! Com of, man, al atanes!" (RvT 4074). Equally simple and direct are the mild swearwords and dialectical exhortations in *The Reeves's Tale*, "for Goddes banes" (4073) and "Ga whistle thou" (4102). A number of simple figures of speech have a like tone.

> Thereto she koude skippe and make game,
> As any kyde or calf folwynge his dame (MillT 3259-60).
> His rode was reed, his eyen greye as goos (MillT 3317).
> So was hir joly whistle wel ywet (RvT 4155).

The Wife of Bath speaks in zesty vernacular. She characterizes one husband as "olde barel-ful of lyes!" (WBT 302) and tells of her fourth husband that, when he tried to make her jealous, "in his owene grece I made him frye" (WBT 487).

The North Midland dialect of the two scholars in *The Reeve's Tale* revels in the folk flavor of native English. In spite of its provocative analogue in French, the tale owes little of its style to *la langue française*. Instances of the Cambridge students' linguistic peculiarities are "boes" for "behooves" (4027), and "swa" for "so" (4030), "waat" for "knows" (4086), "lathe" for "barn" (4088), "fonne" for "fool" (4089), "ymel" for "among" (4171), and the like. In fact, the Reeve himself hails from Norfolk and says "ik" for "I" (3867). Chaucer, when his poetic diction permitted him, used major characteristics of North Midland speech; namely, *a* for *o*, *k* for *ch*, *s* for *sh*, and distinctive inflections.[3] The adoption of this dialect furnished opportunity for playing on shades of meaning. Thus a pun may occur in the collegian John's solicitation to the Miller: "I pray yow spede us heythen that ye may" (4033), because "heythen" could stand for either "hence" or "heathen." If John means to style himself and his companion as "heathen," this double-entendre would sharpen Aleyn's otherwise harmless inquiring of the Miller, "Hou fares thy faire doghter and thy wyf?" (4023). This semantic shading would escape a rustic miller but not Chaucer's sophisticated audience. It is also quite possible that John's excited cry, "for Goddes banes" (4073), would fall on ears attuned to the Mercian dialect ("banas" for "murderers"), not as an insipid "by God's bones," but as the darker curse "by God's slayers."

Ribald terms[4] of course figure naturally in a discussion of bourgeois vocabulary. Alice of Bath has "a coltes tooth" (WBT 602); so did the Norfolkian Reeve: "And yet ik have alwey a coltes tooth" (RvT 3888). An equivalent of this Middle English locution exists in the modern phrase, "sweet tooth," when carrying erotic connotation. When the Merchant describes the old cuckold in his yarn simply as "al coltissh" (MerchT 1847), the expression has an identical modern counterpart. In middle-aged concupiscence, Alice prefers young men over old. She asserts that "in bacon hadde I nevere delit" (WBT 418), evidently rating bacon as cured or old meat. Since she brags about being "a lusty oon" (WBT 605), Alice appears to be dilating on her sexual prowess when she vaunts that "Gat-tothed I was" (WBT 603; GenProl 468). The entirety of Wife Alice's amative lexicon may be described as multilingual, with morphological entries that smack of French, Latin, and Anglo-Saxon. "*Bele chose*" (WBT 510) is patently French; "chambre of Venus" (618), mythological Latin; and "sely instrument" (132), adjectivally Anglo-Saxon ("saelig").

Chaucerian oaths and imprecations vary considerably in their tone.[5] Two ubiquitous Frenchified oaths, "parfay" (MillT 3681) and "pardee"

(MillT 3158), are wholly inoffensive, as indeed is the bilingual Prioress' "by Seinte Loy" (GenProl 120). When one remembers that the poet apparently wrote under no such censorship as did Shakespeare, Chaucer manifested marked restraint in his numerous other recurring Anglicisms. He resorted to such bland language as "for Christes peyne" (RvT 4084), "by Goddes herte" (RvT 4087), "by God" (RvT 4089), "For Christes saule" (RvT 4263), "By Goddes corpus" (MillT 3743), "God it woot" (MillT 3769), "Goddes armes two" (WBT 833), and "Goddes mooder" (SumT 2202). Of similar kidney are a few imprecations like "God his bones corse" (MerchT 1308); "Pees! with myschance and with mysaventure!" (FrT 1334), and "Unto the devel . . ./ Yeve I thy body and my panne also!" (FrT 1622-23). For slight variation, he has "By seinte [sic] Note" (MillT 3771), "for Cristes sweete tree" (3767), and "Cristes foo" (3782), meaning either "Christ's foot" or "Christ's foe" (i.e., the Devil); and Chaucer also respected the convention of the Latinate *"benedicitee!"* (3768).

The introduction of tales of venery obliged Chaucer to refer to chambering, which he did in a copious display of racy diction. Commonplace terms include "pleye" (MillT 3686; RvT 4198), "aton" (RvT 4197), "myrthe" (WBT 399), "daliance" (565), and "bisynesse" (933). Somewhat less familiar locutions are "rafte hire maydenhed" (WBT 888), "lust abedde" (927), and "pricketh harde and depe" (RvT 4231). The respectable word "swonken" (RvT 4235), meaning "labored," is a hoary term for coition. The amative signification of "hende" (MillT 3397), evocative of erotic "laying on of hands," should be known to Americans as it is preserved inferentially in the musical strain from *Yankee Doodle:* "and with the girls be handy." Among words more heavily charged with eroticisms, Chaucer fancied the expression "dighte." This homely verb, always glossed euphemistically ("lie with"), should be recognized for the vulgar vernacular, "dick." A famous instance occurs in Alice's Prologue about wives who have slain their husbands in their beds "And let hir lecchour dighte hire al the nyght, / Whan that the corps lay in the floor upright" (WBT 767-68).

Two passages in the General Prologue, it must be noted, convey a like flavor. First, speaking of the Summoner, Chaucer said that "a fynch eek koude he pulle" (GenProl 652). Here the phrase may signify that the Summoner could "pluck a pigeon" in the sense of swindle a gullible person. It seems more plausible, however, since "pigeon" is familiar cant for an attractive female, that Chaucer meant that the Summoner knew how to pull a young girl aside for his purposes. Second, speaking of the Pardoner, Chaucer said: "Ful loude he soong 'Com hider, love, to me!' / This Somonour bar to hym a stif burdoun" (GenProl 672-73). Here the text appears to mean only that the ardent Summoner endorses the theme of the song by joining the Pardoner in a loud refrain. One finds it impossible to construe these lines as implying a homosexual relationship between these two pilgrims, the Summoner and the Pardoner.[6] While on this amorous theme, one may turn now to the wifely widow Alice, who remarks that after the death of her fourth husband she "was purveyed of a make" (WBT 591). Usually glossed as "match" or "mate," the Chaucerian noun sounds more like such Modern English erotica as "to be put on the make" or "to make" a sex partner.

No reason exists for arguing or debating about the earthy ingredients in Chaucer's diction. When he said "ers" (SumT 1690), he meant "ass." He exhibited no qualms in using the word and seemingly relished a play on it in the compound "ars-metrike" (SumT 2222). Neither did he balk at saying "tayl" (RvT 4164); in fact, he toyed with such echoes of "tayle" as "talys" (WBT 319) and "taille" (ShipT 416). Absalon is "squaymous / Of fartyng" (MillT 3337-38); not so Chaucer of "telling," "tallying," or "tailing." "Tale" for story introduces the lusty pun that concludes the Shipman's fabliau:

> This endeth now my tale, and God us sende
> Taillynge ynough unto oure lyves ende. Amen.
> (ShipT 433-34)

In bicultural England Chaucer's homely vocabulary features words of both French and Anglo-Saxon origination. Many of the Romance terms were already so much a part of contemporary London speech[7] that they should be regarded as the native vernacular in current usage by the folk. In this group one may classify French-derived "queynte" (WBT 444), "jurdones" (PardT 305), "coillons" (PardT 952), and several others. In a second group belongs the English locution "burel folk" (SumT 1872), from Anglo-Saxon *būr*, a bower, one fit for a lady's chamber; hence strong or agile folk rather than bumpkins or the laity.[8] Here also should go "Jakke" (MillT 3708), which Alison calls Absalon; the appellation is usually glossed as lout but obviously represents the label for a man highly endowed sexually. But "Malkyn" (MLT 30), meaning "wanton woman," partakes of French *mal* (wicked) and the diminutive suffix "kyn" (German *chen*). Household and countryside jargon further illustrate the homely folk character of Chaucer's down-to-earth language. Some particularly vivid examples include "a pulled hen" (GenProl 177), "pissemyre" (SumT 1825), "piggesnye" (MillT 3268), "the value of a flye" (ShipT 171), "make a clerkes berd" (RvT 4096: WBT 361), and "Nat worth an oystre" (GenProl 182).

There has been a tendency recently to extend the role of French influence from Chaucer's courtly poetry over into the mother wit of *The Canterbury Tales*. The diction of the tales by the plebeian Miller and Reeve has been analyzed as adopted largely from the clichés of *amour courtois* in the Old French fabliaux.[9] One author has gone so far as to claim that these two stories represent examples of the best narrative art of the Middle Ages because they were composed in the French style and contained *"idées importées de France."*[10] From what has already been set forth, the present writer must raise the voice of dissent. I would appraise Chaucer's artistry in terms, not of his tawdry plots, but of his naturalistic choice of words. It can be maintained that this plainspoken element is an indispensable part of Chaucer's genius. His earthy tales reproduce faithfully the speech of fourteenth-century England, an unforgettably idiomatic speech boldly enlivened with bicultural native expressions largely then in everyday use in that land.

NOTES

[1] The present article is based on a paper read at the meeting of the South-Central Modern Language Association, Austin, Texas, November 11, 1966.

[2] All textual references are to F. N. Robinson (ed.), *The Works of Geoffrey Chaucer* (Boston, 1957).

[3] Martin M. Crow, *"The Reeve's Tale* in the Hands of a North Midland Scribe," University of Texas *Studies in English* (1938), pp. 14-24.

[4] Haldeen Braddy, "Chaucer's Bawdy Tongue," *SFQ*, XXX (1966), 214-22; see further Howard L. McCord, *Chaucer's Bawdry* (Unpublished M. A. thesis, Univ. of Utah, Salt Lake City, 1958).

[5] Chaucerian imprecations display some variety but little obscenity. Herbert W. Starr, "Oaths in Chaucer's Poems," *West Virginia University Bulletin: Philological Studies,* IV (1943), 44-63; see also references cited by Beatrice Daw Brown, Eleanor K. Heningham, and Francis Lee Utley, *A Manual of the Writings in Middle English, Ninth Supplement* (New Haven, Conn., 1951), p. 1925.

[6] An anonymous reader for *PMLA* once made this suggestion in an editorial note, but see Braddy, *op. cit.,* p. 216.

[7] In a review of Joseph Mersand's *Chaucer's Romance Vocabulary* (1937), James R. Hulbert (*PQ*, XXVI (1947), 306) correctly observed that Chaucer did not introduce into Middle English any considerable number of French words not previously in use in the London speech of his day.

[8] Robinson, *op. cit.*, p. 707.

[9] Gardiner Stillwell, "The Language of Love in Chaucer's Miller's and Reeve's Tales and in the Old French Fabliaux," *JEGP*, LIV (1955), 693-99.

[10] Per Nykrog, *Les Fabliaux* (Copenhagen, 1957), p. 262.

Reprinted from *SFQ*, XXXII (1968), 1-6.

23

CHAUCER – – REALISM OR OBSCENITY?

Chaucer was a multivoiced writer of both poetry and prose.[1] His interests ran to astronomy and politics, to countryside and city, and to war and love. He employs human characters in *Troilus and Criseyde* and *The Legend of Good Women*, beasts or birds in *The Nun's Priest's Tale* and *The Parliament of Fowls*. His lyre resounds with many strains: the tragic, the pathetic, the sentimental, and more often the comic. Let me say at once that I would not characterize his entire poetic output, much less his rarer pieces in prose, as characteristically obscene. What I plan to do, instead, is to analyze the poet's point of view towards man and nature as fundamentally realistic. I further question if his descriptions of men and women, his choice of words, and his selection of subject matter are not in many subordinate but important passages evidence of Chaucer's rather extraordinary knowledge of the obscene. After that, we must judge for ourselves if Chaucer joyed in dirt for dirt's sake, if he had a moral or immoral purpose, or if his usage of smut was artistically intended.

It must be perfectly clear that I do not wish to leave the false impression that the poet Chaucer was always either realistic or obscene, or a blend of the two. I do nonetheless hold it true that his greatest art was realistic and that this transcendent realism at times utilizes secondary elements of the obscene when true-to-life portraiture, or verisimilitude, demanded. The Wife of Bath, accordingly, speaks pointedly of her erotic relations with her numerous husbands, five so far, in her *Prologue*. She has no inhibitions when she there refers to her private part, or her "play-pretty," as "my *bele chose*" (447). This epic boast of hers is hardly offensive and probably no overblown exaggeration, either. She comes nearer the sensational when she tells of wives who slew their husbands in their beds and let their lovers "shag" them all night long (WBT 767–68). Now Chaucer does not say "shag"; he says "dighte." Most editors gloss "dighte" in its amorous meaning as "lie with," but obviously "dicked," a homely word in which *gh* has evolved into *ck*, speaks more directly.

In the passages just mentioned Chaucer presents both realism and obscenity. His technique seems to fit the subject, namely the Wife of

Bath's confession of consecutive nuptial blisses with her five spouses. What I want to stress now is the fact that Chaucer often introduces obscenity as only an element, albeit an important one, in a tale predominantly romantic, or idealistic, or supernatural. One must not be misled by externals or false appearances in studying Chaucer.

One of the greatest stories of the Middle Ages was in most of its features highly romantic, but Chaucer assigned his realistic variation of it to earthy Alice, the Wife of Bath. I refer to the floater which could be called "What Women Most Desire in the World." Its setting involves the ancient court of fabled King Arthur. A young knight is overcome in battle or suffers some other mishap; and to save his life or requite his sin, the circumstances require that he discover what it is that women most yearn for. The question of course poses difficulties, and he is given a year in which to complete his research. At this point in my Chaucer class, I often ask my students to write on a piece of paper their own answers. These I read aloud before turning to Chaucer's solution. Typical student replies, and very sensible ones I must say, include "money," "security," "love and children," "stocks and bonds," and the like. Then I tell them that Chaucer went to the heart of the husband-wife relationship when he predicted that what women most desire is to rule or govern their mates. The psychological basis of Chaucer's idea is encompassed in the old folksay that women desire to wear the trousers in the family. To speak truthfully, women want sovereignty and usually get it.

The Chaucerian twist, to return now to the timeworn plot, comes out a little differently. In Alice of Bath's version, the heroine as "wyf" presents a choice to her husband. He may have her either faithful but ugly, or beautiful but faithless. Having found it perilous to ask college students to answer this one, I pass on promptly to the Chaucerian answer, which is that the young knight yields up his sovereignty by replying that his wife may choose for herself because he places himself in her "wise governance" (WBT 1231). At this, the heroine rejoices. Since the Knight husband has become her subject, she changes miraculously into a beautiful young lady, who remains faithful to him forever.

Chaucer, I submit, gave a realistic answer to a question posed in a romantic, supernatural tale. The idea of men and women fighting for supremacy or leadership in the family arrangement reappears often in *The Canterbury Tales*. Three aspects of the contest occur in the tale by the Clerk of the patient Griselda, in the account by the Man of Law of the ever faithful Constance, and in the recital by Melibee of the wise counseling of Dame Prudence. Of course other echoes of contending mates recur elsewhere in Chaucer.

I should like, for example, to examine next the propositions in *The Manciple's Tale*. I interpret Chaucer's plot as a recasting of the ancient and widely circulated folk idea of women's preference for inferior men. I need hardly add that in this floating legend women prefer inferior men because they are easier to rule. This takes us back to where we started, namely the idea of sovereignty. In favor of this reading, I ask you to remember that Phebus is rightly praised as worthy, brave, genteel, the very "flour of bachilrie" (125). But his wife preferred an inferior man and cuckolded her god-husband.[2] She chose, Chaucer states, "A man of litel reputacioun" (199). In realistic terms Chaucer describes how a scorning of the superior is virtually a law of nature.

> Taak any bryd, and put it in a cage,
> And do al thyn entente and thy corage
> To fostre it tenderely with mete and drynke
> Of alle deyntees that thou kanst bithynke,
> And keep it al so clenly as thou may,
> Although his cage of gold be never so gay,
> Yet hath this brid, by twenty thousand foold,
> Levere in a forest, that is rude and coold,
> Goon ete wormes and swich wrecchednesse (163–71).

Would it be any wonder if after discovering this basic law of nature Chaucer might have resorted to obscenity? Perhaps the wonder is that he did not fall to blaspheming or cursing. His writings, however, are singularly free of any large number of oaths of any kind. In aggregate, Chaucerian oaths sound mild and harmless; they compare with the hollow blasphemy of Shakespeare's "zooks" and "zounds." But in his character portrayals Chaucer did introduce into his art a galaxy of hearty folk reciting a constellation of lusty tales couched in diction that is sometimes euphemistic and sometimes down-to-earth, but in either case most often basically erotic.

Among sturdy folk in the General Prologue, none is more vital than Wife Alice, with her fine scarlet hose (GenP 456). Make no mistake about her health: she was an apple-cheeked widow. She may have had lovers in her youth before the five husbands: or, as I think, she confined her love-making legally to the marriage bed. "Withouten" more likely means "without" than "not excepting" in the following verses.

> Boold was hir face, and fair, and reed of hewe,
> She was a worthy womman al hir lyve:

> Housbondes at chirche dore she hadde fyve,
> Withouten oother campaignye in youthe (458–67).

Love challenged Alice as an art, and Chaucer remarks that "she koude of that art the olde daunce" (476).

A hardly less fervent devotee of the art of love is the Squire. When I was a student, one of my distinguished professors consistently glossed "hoote" as the insipid cliché "ardently." But in "So hoote he lovede that by nyghtertale / He sleep namoore than doothe a nyghtyngale" (97–98), I hold that realist Chaucer means the more erotic adverb "hotly."

The General Prologue also gives realistic portraits of a few clerical figures. The Friar was wanton and merry. He knew the gestures and vocabulary associated with sex; no person in the four holy orders understood "So muchel of daliaunce and fair langage" (211) as this beggar Huberd. The Summoner was another slave of love, a most unattractive one: "As hoot he was and lecherous as a sparwe" (626). Folklore holds the sparrow to be the most promiscuous and vulgar of birds. Often drunk, the Summoner at times cried out as though he were insane. When inebriated, he spoke nothing but Latin. Evidently he preferred wine above all else, since he would remit a full year's sin with a concubine for a quart of wine. "Ful prively a fynch eek koude he pulle" (652) probably refers to his prowess with what today one calls "a chick" or, better, "a bird." The Summoner, who later tells the most repulsive episode in the entire collection, was, in "Mod" diction, a "bird watcher." Chaucer's vignette of the Pardoner is also repellent, the Pardoner being one with the Summoner.

Some critics interpret these two characters as yoked in a homosexual relationship, but this perhaps overplays it. Since the Pardoner had little or no beard, Chaucer regards him as a "geldyng or mare" (691), a description which betokens both emasculation and feminization; but Chaucer's further delineation of the Pardoner as having a voice as small as a goat's links this ecclesiastic with an animal that symbolizes the virility of a male. When Chaucer says that the Summoner "bar to hym a stif burdoun" (673), the poet emphasizes that the Summoner endorsed the Pardoner's idea of having his love to come hither to him. Chaucer means that the Summoner bore down on the chorus with a strong refrain.[3] Finally, the convivial Pardoner was, not a part-time "homo," but a veteran bird catcher. In his own prologue, he declares that "I wol drynke licour of the vyne, / And have a joly wench in every toun" (452–53).

In *The Canterbury Tales* the Summoner's scatological contribution on flatulence ranks as Chaucer's most offensive writing. Passages like these qualify him as a writer of the obscene—at least of the offensive. Of similar quality, yet much less objectionable, the amorous exploits detailed in the fabliaux by the Miller and the Reeve rate as the most celebrated examples of the obscene element in the Canterbury gatherum. Here Chaucer depicts his lowly characters as uninhibited in their sex drives and promiscuous in their erotic behavior. The Miller tells how the studious Nicholas successfully arranges to make love with a reeve's wife named Alisoun. This bawdy tale features the incident of the misdirected kiss, a rival coming in the night to buss Alisoun's face kisses Nicholas' rear instead. In narrative counterblast, the Reeve degrades the Miller by telling how two Cambridge students go to bed with both a miller's wife and his daughter. Of the wife, Chaucer reports that "So myrie a fit ne hadde she nat ful yoore" (RvT 4230). But Malyne suffered no neglect, student Aleyn declaring that "I have thries in this shorte nyght/ Swyved the milleres doghter bolt upright" (4265–66). Touches like these in delineations of the folk as "he leith on soore" (4229) and "He priketh harde and depe as he were mad" (4231) illustrate what the general reader usually means by Chaucerian ribaldry.

In dealing with higher social classes like the bourgeois and the nobility, Chaucer waxes less frank and yet broad enough. The Merchant's Tale has to do with an old husband and his young wife. Merchant January leads the reader on with his suspenseful statement that "A man may do no synne with his wyf" (1839). Plying himself with stimulating aphrodisiacs, January soon makes his intentions clear.

> Anon he preyde hire strepen hire al naked;
> He wolde of hire, he seyde, han some plesaunce,
> And seyde hir clothes dide hym encombraunce,
> And she obeyeth, be hire lief or looth (1958–61).

Immediately after this, an aroused reader may feel only frustration. For Chaucer, who matches diction with character rather than with deed (GenP 742), falls back on euphemisms of style which harmonize with the prudery of January's bourgeois caste. Flush at the climax, erstwhile plainspoken Chaucer spurns the opportunity to become ribald, turning lamely to the insipidity of "I dar nat to yow telle" (MerchT 1963).

> But lest that precious folk be with me wrooth,
> How that he wroghte, I dar nat to yow telle;
> Or wheither hire thoughte it paradys or helle (1962–64).

The evidence goes to show that sex symbolism also occurs in royal romances commonly thought to idealize lords and ladies. The Canterbury anthology opens with a tale of courtly love and chivalry by the Knight. It was he who never spoke any villainy in all his life to any kind of person (GenP 70-71). The Knight's romantic love-epic Chaucer follows with the Miller's smutty short-story. A cornerstone of modern criticism is that in these two tales Chaucer contracts the decorous nature of courtly love with the animal behavior of students and rustics. But this implied contrast does not actually exist, because Chaucer introduces the sexual act in both tales. There has never been any doubt about the Miller's meaning. Nor can there be any doubt about the Knight's, once the reader understands the realism, or verisimilitude, involved in Chaucer's matching euphemistic diction with courtly situation.

In praying to the Goddess Venus, Palamon promises to war against Emelye's chastity and aspires to die in her service. Here Chaucer evidently uses the verb to "dye" (KnT 2243) in the Shakespearean sense of "to have sexual intercourse." Moreover, in the three prayers of Emelye, Palamon, and his rival Arcite, an image of fire predominates. All three personages call love a fire; all three vow to consecrate fires to the appropriate deity. At Diana's altar the fires represent the prayers of both Palamon and Arcite. Then Chaucer spotlights Emelye and what befell her.

> But sodeynly she saugh a sighte queynte,
> For right anon oon of the fyres queynte,
> And quyked agayn, and after that anon
> That oother fyr was queynt and al agon;
> And as it queynte it made a whistelynge (2333–37).

Chaucer here returns to "*bele chose*" imagery again. It has been correctly asserted that "With four 'queynts' and a whistle in five lines, Chaucer leaves no doubt where the fire is."[4]

I believe that one meaning of a dramatic scene in *Troilus and Criseyde* says much the same thing. A key word is dance for the sex rite. Wife Alice, you will recall, knew "the olde daunce" (GenP 476); Pandarus tells Criseyde that they must observe May and "daunce" (II, 111–12). Yet other euphemisms for sex appear in descriptions of the erotic adventures of Prince Troilus and widow Criseyde. In 1966 I interpreted afresh an original passage in the *Troilus*—that is, one not found in Chaucer's acknowledged source, Boccaccio's *Il Filostrato*—as erotically intended, when I equated "death" with "sexual orgasm."[5] Shakespeare has "I will live in thy heart, die in thy lap . . ." (*Much Ado*, V, ii, 104) and "I will die bravely, like a smug bridegroom" (*Lear*, IV, vi, 202).[6] Chaucer's scene finds uncle Pandarus comforting his niece Criseyde the morning after her nocturnal tryst with Troilus. She has remained in her uncle's bedroom. At first the niece covers her face with the sheet, whereupon "Pandarus gan under for to prie" (III, 15) before he proffers his sword and invites Criseyde to take vengeance on him. Upon her evident refusal of the offer, the intimate scene continues.

> With that his arm al sodeynly he thriste
> Under hire nekke, and at the laste hire kyste.
>
> I passe al that which chargeth nought to seye.
> What! God foryaf his deth, and she al so
> Foryaf, and with here uncle gan to pleye,
> For other cause was ther noon than so.
> But of this thing right to the effect to go,
> Whan tyme was, hom to here hous she wente,
> And Pandarus hath fully his entente (III, 1574–82).

By "God foryaf his deth, and she al so/Foryaf . . . ," I see Chaucer meaning that God forgave Pandarus' death; that is, his coition with Criseyde. In Spanish the phrase is "sweet death" (*dulce muerte*). In D. H. Lawrence's modern poem, "Love on the Farm," a woman says

> . . . and a flood
> Of sweet fire sweeps across me, so I drown
> Against him, die, and find death good.[7]

An earlier speech in *Troilus* (II, 1637–38) bears likewise on this imagery. I refer to the words of Pandarus "ibrought have I thi beere!" The new gloss here implies that Troilus is to have Criseyde as his *bier* to die on (sexually).[8]

What these interpretations enable one to perceive is that Chaucer did not restrict his sexual references to two or three Frenchified fabliaux. In Chaucer eroticism as realism bulks larger, or hovers more omnipresently, than critics generally suppose. Chaucer's art reveals its depth and magnitude if one comes to understand that his total portrayal of love embodies sources other than French, techniques beyond the romantic, and ideas distinct from the obscene. When introducing his tale, the Man of Law mentions Chaucer, citing him as an authority on love stories.

> And if he have noght seyd hem, leve brother,
> In o book, he hath seyd hem in another.
> For he hath toold of loveris up and doun
> Mo than Ovide made of mencioun (51-54).

Clearly, one might make a strong case for regarding Chaucer as a medieval D.H. Lawrence.

Much of Chaucer's reputation as an off-color writer derives from his pungency and suggestiveness. Synonyms of the Wife for coition include "the experience" (124), "swynke" (202), "Meschaunce" (407), and simply "daliance" (565). Her synonyms for sex organs include *"Bele chose"* (510), "sely instrument" (132), "harneys" (136), and "chambre of Venus" (618). The Miller's descriptions of "hende Nicholas" (3742) and of how he quickly would seize Alisoun ("hire hente anon,"[3347]) evoke the practice of erotic "laying on of hands." The practice should be known to Americans as it is preserved inferentially in the musical strain from *Yankee Doodle*: "and with the girls be handy." The only way one could escape Chaucer's directness would be to cover one's ears. When he said "ers" (SumP 1690), he meant "ass." He hardly balked at the synonym "tayl" (RvT 4164); in fact, he toyed with such echoes of "tayle" as "talys" (WBT 319) and "taille" (ShipT 416). Absalon, reportedly, was "squaymous/Of fartyng" (MillT 3337–38); but Chaucer was not squeamish about "telling," "tallying," or "tailing." A lusty pun closes the Shipman's narrative (433–34).

> Thus endeth now my tale, and God us sende
> Taillynge ynough unto oure lyves ende. Amen.

Now, Chaucer's raciness stands virtually unique among the masterpieces of early English. Certainly nothing corresponds to it in such sturdy but pious elders as Aelfric, Alfred, Bede, Caedmon, Cynewulf, or the *Beowulf*-poet. Nor do counterparts occur in his major contemporaries, Gower, Langland, Wyclif, or the *Pearl*-poet. Perhaps the nearest echo in the Middle Ages stems from the lyric "Sumer Is Icumen In," where the "bucke verteth" (8). It is a mistake, I think, to characterize the Latin songs of the medieval *Carmina Burana* as obscene. This goliardic effervescence represents something much lighter, its predominant mood being merely rollicking and frolicsome.

Chaucer was clearly a pioneer in early English literature when he delved into intimate lore on the human organs of elimination and procreation. Indeed, he may be more concerned with the body of love than the soul of love. As already seen, he steered away from homosexuality. For a fact, he manifested little, or no, interest in any aspect of aberrant sex, in what one might call sick love. Exhibitionism did not engage him. He mentions nudity in *The Merchant's Tale* but pays no abnormal attention to it. He did not, however, establish a precedent for the ultramodern theater of today. His freest license did not anticipate the passionate nude love scene in Zeffirelli's 1968 screen revamping of Shakespeare's *Romeo and Juliet*. The mass exhibitionism now on stage of *Hair* goes leagues beyond Chaucer's scant allusions. He stinted even more on such fads of avant garde letters as sadism, masochism, sapphism, pederasty, and zoophilpsychosis. Londoner Chaucer is no poet, plier, or prophet of sick sex.

Sooner or later devotees of Chaucer must face the question of to what degree the father of Modern English was either realistic or obscene. At times when I have been reading some of the statements in the Wife of Bath's prologue a third answer to the question has occurred to me. It is to accept the jarring conviction that this English writer of French name and descent must be plainly pronounced neither a realist nor a pornographer but often rather something of both. Would it not be accurate to categorize Alice's prologue as realistically obscene? To my ear, Chaucerian "purple passages" vary much in the stridor of their offensiveness. I know that the effect of Chaucer's grossest recitals varies with the tastes of individual listeners; certainly this repulsiveness appeals to Old and New World tastes diversely. Only in the last half century have Chaucerian students had access to unexpurgated editions in Middle English. I recall my repeated frustration when a student: we read editions of the original works that resorted to textual gaps or suspension points when the action waxed hot. I still find the euphemisms of standard translators really more tasteless than Chaucer's honest, if homely, idiom.

Yet, qualified scholars can produce satisfying editions of Chaucer for children! I refer to *The Story of the Canterbury Tales,* by F.J. Harvey Darton and others, of 1914; and to *A Taste of Chaucer*, by Anne Malcolmson, of 1964. Such condensation, or deletion of crucial stuff, may be rational practice; I tend to believe that it is. After all, editors must omit a good deal to produce for children acceptable Shakespeare classics or high-minded Bible stories. But at some stage a youth must reach man's estate. It is then that he may consult, if he likes, unexpurgated modern editions of both Shakespeare and the Holy Bible. But even today no adult, whether young or old, can reach unbowlderized Chaucer except in the East Midland dialect. It comes to this: today's reader must become a specialist in order to grasp Chaucer's exact meaning! To savor his choicest diction, however, pays rich guerdon for even the hardiest effort.

Himself keenly aware of the degree of his realism, Chaucer in several places enunciated applicable critical principles. In *The Canterbury Tales* he laid out a justification of his artistic ends and a defense of the rawness of his portraitures. More than once the artist Chaucer spoke of endeavoring to match the language to the action, by this means describing in ugly words a foul act. To some large extent, he succeeded. Two or three apologetic digressions in *The Canterbury Tales* precede the full apologia at the end, the famous *Chaucer's Retraction*. The author claims in it that all he composed was "writen for oure doctrine" and that he revokes (takes back) all he had told that "sownen into synne" (1082–85). For myself, I look upon the *Retraction* as a semi-serious literary convention. Chaucer's disavowal is at one with the excuses in *El Libro de Buen Amor* of the slightly earlier apologist, Juan Ruiz, Archpriest of Hita.[9]

What Chaucer tried to do in actual practice was to equate deed with diction, speech with speaker. The rustics in the Miller's and the Reeve's tales speak an idiom redolent of the soil. They are plainspoken people. The bourgeois Merchant and Wife of Bath employ equally rugged expressions but flavoring less of the country. The patricians display a recognizably loftier speech in *The Knight's Tale* and in *Troilus and Criseyde*. The plots here involve as much eroticism as ever, but a heavy euphuistic overlay now screens the obscenity. Such an overlay allows for rich puns and double entendres, which Chaucer introduced more often than traditionally supposed.

Shakespeare as supreme punster excelled at shadings of word sense. He did so because legal restrictions on theatrical dialogue forced him to shroud his obscenities in euphuisms. His play, *Much Ado about Nothing*, peaks in an eponymous double entendre, "Notes, notes, forsooth, and nothing" (II, iii, 59). These words may indicate that the title could also be pronounced *Much Ado about Noting,*[10] which phrasing better fits his plot. Londoners regularly pronounce "nothing" something like "nutting," an apt phoneme yet more typical of the dramatist. Puns of this order abound in Shakespeare; the indecorous instances can be consulted in Eric Partridge's *Shakespeare's Bawdy* (New York, 1955). To a lesser degree, Chaucer likewise employed, not abject coarseness, but shades of sense—as already noted with "queynte" in *The Knight's Tale*, with "deth" in *Troilus and Criseyde*, and with *"bele chose"* in Alice's *Prologue*. To begin to understand Chaucer fully, one must perceive that he abandoned himself entirely to smut in his fabliaux alone; there he had to reproduce the broad tone of this genre to please contemporary tastes. His facility with fabliaux was the shallowest aspect of his genius. To read him more widely is to find a stylist of many voices.

One voice he had for the Court. He long lived at the Lancastrian Palace, the Savoy, on the generosity of John of Gaunt. Chaucer briefly lived in Aldgate, possibly through the patronage of Alice Perrers, domineering mistress of aged Edward III.[11] The Lancastrian author served his sovereign and Parliament wherever he was required; in England, in France, in Spain. He had a second voice for personal friends like Bukton and Vache, to both of whom he addressed verses. He had yet another voice for lesser notables, like Mayor Walworth of London, who owned many a Southwark brothel, standing near the inn where Chaucer waited, ready to go on the pilgrimage ("In Southwerk at the Tabard as I lay" [GenP 20]). Finally, he had a fourth voice for the poor and the simple, for the "povre Persoun of a Toun" (GenP 478) and his lowly brother, the Plowman, "A trewe swynkere and a good was he" (531).

It is this humble voice which unexpectedly calls to us when we as youths first read Chaucer the forbidden. Once heard, this voice as we grow older reverberates even louder in our ears and lingers on with us. Chaucer is no pornographer. He not once endeavors to excite us sexually or incline us towards vice; he often enough turns us from obscenity by ridiculing it. We do not want to emulate the Merchant's actions with his young wife; his lust for her nakedness appalls us, considering his age. We do not aspire to outdo the Wife of Bath in her conquests; her promiscuity sounds almost repulsive; and we pity her inability to understand that she turns serial marriages, legal though they be, into sin. *The Pardoner's Tale* is a corker, but that intolerable business tacked on at the end about the man soiling his breeches just about gags me; the Summoner's portioning the flatus into twelve does gag me. This discreditable sort of filth, Chaucer at his worst, figures small in the total. Far more often, Chaucer's indecency communicates something a good deal more lasting than momentary sexual arousal and stimulation.

One could even say that Chaucer was a moralist; in fact, some critics insist on it.[12] Admittedly, he was religious enough, but I regard him as the best example among English authors of liberal-mindedness. I cannot imagine a reader who studies Chaucer sympathetically not feeling very much the same way.

At the outset I described Chaucer as multivoiced. Such a personality garners from life those experiences requisite for the verbal production of a variety of plots, characters and styles: all those ingredients indispensable to the maker of literary art. A realist must have recourse on occasion to frankness, to ribaldry, and to bawdiness. The license must extend to obscene puns and to rowdy double entendres. Everyone accepts this as a legitimate exercise in the case of Shakespeare; most readers do not concede as much to Chaucer. The time has come when enlightened criticism must place Chaucer alongside his Elizabethan successor as a fellow genius in artistic realism, the greater for having blazed the trail. Majority reaction to Shakespeare's aloofness seems to derive from the distance that Shakespeare keeps between his reader and himself. The acute separation of voice and ear prevents emotional involvement of the hearer with Shakespeare's bawdry. Chaucer, conversely, registers so immediately as a warm and human storyteller that he draws his reader to the acme of involvement. The reader experiences shock and at times revulsion at earthy words, risqué sallies, and indecent acts in Chaucer's telling. Shakespeare's parallel usages, in his dramas, separated from us by height of physical plane and loftiness of epic subject, never catch us up as closely.

An intimate identification of the reader with Chaucer highlights the medieval Londoner as the realist par excellence. To him, verism becomes a ruling principle that encompasses minor elements like obscenity and bawdry. They are simply subservient particulars. In the whole body of Chaucer's art, realism as a universal surmounts everything.

NOTES

[1] For editorial aid, I need to name Miss Corrine Peschka and Mr. Richard Escontriás, whose services were made available to me through the University fund, Organized Research. This topic was suggested to me by my friend, Dr. Harold F. Harding, H. Y. Benedict Professor of Speech. All quotations are from F. N. Robinson (ed.), *The Works of Geoffrey Chaucer* (Second Edition, Boston, 1957). The notion that Chaucer had more than one voice or three specific levels of meaning lies at the heart of two new schools of Chaucerian criticism; see, respectively, Arthur W. Hoffman, "Chaucer's Prologue to Pilgrimage: The Two Voices," *ELH*, XXI (1954), 1-16; A. Leigh De Neef, "Robertson and the Critics," *ChauR* II (1968), 205-34. I prefer to regard broad-minded Chaucer as an author who played on words in much the same fashion as Shakespeare, not as a slave to a formula à la Edmund Spenser or, say, Marie de France. Aimie Brière succinctly expressed a commendable observation when she stated that in Chaucer "toute pruderie est absente" ("Le théâtre à Londres," *Revue des Deux Mondes,* Nou. sér. (1968), p. 166).

[2] On the motif of women's preference for inferior men, see *Hamlet's Wounded Name* (El Paso, Texas, 1964), pp. 33-44. In a later paper, I plan to deal further with the Manciple's handling of the inferior lover.

[3] "Chaucer's Bilingual Idiom," *SFQ,*XXXII (1968), 1-6.

[4] W. F. Bolton, "The Topic of the *Knight's Tale,*" *ChauR,* I (1967), 224.

[5] "Chaucer's Bawdy Tongue," *SFQ,* XXX (1966), 214-22; I have now written a new but as yet unpublished paper on "Criseyde's Playful Uncle."

[6] Eric Partridge, *Shakespeare's Bawdy* (New York, 1955), p. 101.

[7] G. DeWitt Sanders, J. H. Nelson, M. L. Rosenthal (eds.), *Chief Modern Poets of England and America* (New York, 1962),I,211.

[8] Peter Heidtmann, "Sex and Salvation in *Troilus and Criseyde,*" *ChauR,* II (1968), 250.

[9] George Ticknor found Chaucer like the Archpriest of Hita in several particulars, including a "mixture of devotion and licentious immorality" (*History of Spanish Literature* (London, 1863), I, 77). Sometimes the Archpriest seems disturbed by the bawdiness of his own plots (*ibid.,* I, 72n.7).

[10] Thomas Marc Parrott (ed.), *Shakespeare* (Revised Edition, New York, 1953), p. 493. In his comment, Parrott also cited line 57: "There's not a note of mine that's worth the noting."

[11] "Chaucer and Dame Alice Perrers," *Sp,* XXI (1946), 222-28. My latest researches tend to connect Perrers with Chaucer again in her role as the probable stepmother of Cecily Chaumpaigne. Alice Perrers is also my candidate for the historical prototype of the Wife of Bath.

[12] D. W. Robertson, Jr., *A Preface to Chaucer* (Princeton, 1962); Bernard F. Huppé and D. W. Robertson, Jr., *Fruyt and Chaf: Studies in Chaucer's Allegories* (Princeton, 1963); and Bernard F. Huppé, *A Reading of the Canterbury Tales* (New York, 1964).

Reprinted from *Arlington Quart.,* II (1969), 121-138.

24

Reviews

On Rereading Chaucer. By H. R. Patch. Cambridge, Massachusetts: Harvard University Press; London: Humphrey Milford. 1939. Pp. xiv+269.

On first reading Chaucer even a casual reader must be immediately impressed by the author's sterling qualities of good spirit and health, and that this first impression is correct Professor Patch amply testifies in his new book. In more than one passage of brilliant critical insight he advances far towards proving that among the poets Geoffrey Chaucer is the supreme humourist of our English tongue. From this study of the comic spirit one receives a deeper understanding and wider appreciation of the individual genius which produced the *Canterbury Tales.* For if there is in the depiction of the Canterbury pilgrims a subtlety which is French and also occasionally a German grotesquery, it is Chaucer's individual genius which has fused these elements into an art at once international and universal in its appeal.

The element of humour is a thread of gold in both the greater and the lesser works. It dazzles when the oft-married Wife of Bath is unable to fathom why the Samaritan woman's fifth man was not her fifth husband as well, and it gleams not wanly amid the barren spaces of the *House of Fame* in the discourse of the talkative eagle. There is even humour in *Troilus and Cressida,* especially where Troilus, peering down from heavenly heights, laughs at his earlier follies; for here it is the spirit of humour, of seeing things more in correct proportion, which serves to cancel the pain of what otherwise would be an unbearably cynical conclusion. This sense of proportion was undeniably strong in Chaucer: he could write almost romantically about chivalry in the *Knight's Tale,* although as one of the Canterbury narrators he preferred to tell himself the ludicrous story of Sir Thopas. Moreover, and this should encourage the rereading of Chaucer, Professor Patch observes that there is almost a humour of sources, that the poet often took passages from serious works to gain a comic effect, that sometimes he apparently means the joke for himself alone. Certainly no demoniac urge or divine frenzy seems to have impelled Chaucer; instead he appears to have experienced a sense of joy, of fun in writing.

As explained in the "Preface," three of the ten essays in *On Rereading Chaucer(i.e.* Chaps. IV, VII, VIII) have appeared hitherto in American periodicals. Although the discussion for the most part centres on the theme of humour, Professor Patch has not focused the volume on one lone thesis. There are accordingly not a few other topics which deserve every reader's attention.

A second theme argued in *On Rereading Chaucer* is that behind all Chaucer's works there may be found a moral conviction or moral aim. This argument is not unsupported by evidence and comes as a welcome antidote to the popular conception of the poet as a mere entertainer. In the satiric tales there can hardly be questions as to the moral purpose. Moreover, in the chapter entitled "Chaucer and the Common People", Professor Patch appears fundamentally sound in holding that Chaucer saw something not wholly "Merry" in England, that he was kindly disposed in his view of the lower classes, and that he was keenly aware of existing injustices when asking the King in *Lak of Stedfastnesse* to cherish his folk and hate extortion.

Although, as Professor Patch states, Chaucer would have drunk his drink with any one of them, which Canterbury pilgrim would he have sought for intimacy? In seeking to discover moral purpose in Chaucer's nature, Professor Patch suggests the Clerk as most likely: both were fond of study; both might be touched by a pathetic tale. Again, the poet was fond of youth. But was Chaucer, like the Clerk, serious, philosophical, moral? What of that other young gentleman, the Squire? One cannot forget that Chaucer himself has sometimes been considered the Squire's prototype: both were fond of writing poetry, and both were not ascetics but young men very much in touch with the times.

In fact, as for evidence that Chaucer was in any respect a moralist, it might rather appear that he disapproved this type of personality in labelling Gower and Strode, respectively, as moral and philosophical. However this may be, Professor Patch further contends that Chaucer's "poems of Courtly Love were meant to celebrate devotion, not of the secret lover for his *amie,* but, within the bonds of matrimony, of perfectly domestic attachments." This is a very pretty picture, but such poems of faithless love as the *Complaint of Mars,* the *Complaint of Venus,* and *Anelida and Arcite* do not at all fit the frame. For another thing, although Chaucer was doubtless no libertine, it is equally unlikely that "in his private life he was after all pretty much the hermit." It is one thing to hold that Chaucer was a reformer, social and political no less than moral; but it is quite another to hold that he was a moralist.

In the chapter on "The Court of Love" Professor Patch, after treating Gaunt's family and the *Book of the Duchess,* declares that he also could "work out a very neat interpretation of the *House of Fame* and the *Parliament of Fowls* with reference to the family." There is little if any evidence for this declaration. In view of poems referring to such diverse personages as Graunson, Bukton, and even Queen Ann, it accordingly may be seriously questioned whether or not any appreciable number of Chaucer's poems may be linked even tentatively with the interests of one family group. However, since Professor Patch seems deeply impressed with the Lancastrian influence, it appears a striking oversight that he nowhere so much as mentions Shirley's contemporary or almost contemporary testimony that the *Complaint of Mars* was written "at the commandement of the renommed and excellent prynce my lord the duc John of Lancastre."

In general, Professor Patch's remarks are most to the point where he discusses philosophy, as in the *Troilus,* or satire, as in *Sir Thopas,* or humour, as in the *Wife of Bath's Tale.* The commentary in *On Rereading Chaucer* is largely impressionistic, but is impressionism of a high order: pleasing in good taste, sparkling in wit. Whatever may be the sources of Chaucer's moral view of the world, Professor Patch has established that his humour is modern, for although Chaucer is deeply critical, it is a criticism which wounds little and heals much. One of the great masterpieces of all time, the *Canterbury Tales* when read and reread is ever that tonic rare which exhilarates even while it chastens.

Reprinted from *RES,* XVI (1940), 198-201.

> Chaucer's "Troilus". A Study in Courtly Love. By Thomas A.
> Kirby. University, Louisiana: Louisiana State University Press.
> 1940. Pp. xiv+337.

In a volume of over three hundred pages Thomas A. Kirby offers the fullest exposition yet attempted for the thesis that *Troilus and Criseyde* is "the finest courtly love poem ever written" (p. 284). This obviously ambitious and yet praiseworthy study is divided into three loosely arranged sections. Part One (90 pp.) discusses Ovid, the Troubadours, Chrétien de Troyes, Andreas Capellanus, Italy and *Il dolce stil nuovo* as founders of that mediaeval system known as courtly love. Part Two (30 pp.) treats this erotic system in Boccaccio's *Il Filostrato.* And Part Three (166 pp.) elaborates on courtly love in relation to Pandarus, Criseyde, Diomede, and

Troilus.[1] Citing in the Preface (p. vii) the poet's "And if that I at loves reverence, Have anything in eched for the beste" (III, 1,405-6), Professor Kirby argues, then, that at all stages Chaucer was aware of the courtly love tradition represented in these earlier writers as well as in Boccaccio, and that accordingly the *Troilus* is synonymous with all that is evoked by *l'amour courtois.*

As for the origins of courtly love, especially Chaucer's conception of it, this new study affords much suggestive material, but appears somewhat to neglect several sources which are fairly contemporaneous with, and therefore more likely to have effect upon, the composing of *Troilus.* I refer to the *Roman de la Rose,* which is mentioned, but too hurriedly handled, and more specifically to such uncited materials as *La Cour Amoureuse,* connected with Charles VI of France, and the *Puys* established in Paris and other cities, where love subjects were discussed. Perhaps Chaucer was likewise influenced by the legend of Pygmalion, whom he certainly mentions. Further reference doubtless should have been made to those old courtly figures of Lancelot and Gawain, to whom Chaucer also alludes. Similarly, in tracing the origin of the confidant or confidante as a figure in the courtly love setting, something more might have been said about the Oriental background of this type of pander. Furthermore, Eastern analogues of the *Squire's Tale* make it clear that Canace's mistress was nothing less than a confidante.

Howsoever great or small was Chaucer's knowledge of panders-- whether this derived from literature or, as a matter of speculation, from actually observing the conduct of illicit love affairs between such notables as Gaunt and Katherine Swynford, or Edward III and Alice Perrers--the important point is that pandering is at least not fully appropriate to an ideal situation of courtly love. Professor Kirby, however, proceeds farther than any other investigator towards establishing this figure as a legitimate member in a circle of clandestine lovers. But even in doing this, it is not undismaying to have Professor Kittredge in one instance mistaken in his view of Pandarus (p. 117), and in another instance to quote with approval a passage containing these same words by this Professor (p. 181).[2]

Such tiptoeing through the complexities of evidence as this last extends to Professor Kirby's interpretation of Criseyde,[3] if it does not indeed almost everywhere encroach upon his characterizations of the chief figures in this tale of mediaeval love. This procedure might be interpreted as proper scholarly caution if it did not permeate even the numerous virtual paraphrases of the Chaucerian text. To put it frankly, the reader may feel, not unjustifiably, that the interpretative discussion is not only unduly extended, but also all too often not so much impartial as downright flavourless. A clear stand should be taken in the argument. It is true that the contemporary scholar, bound to respect older opinion wherever possible, may well find it a problem to view Criseyde's infidelity from a standpoint either fresh or unbiased. Yet we who live in this present generation should find it not difficult to estimate her upon an almost naturalistic basis.

Is Criseyde's infidelity so incomprehensible, after all? Those were times when besieged Troy might any day be sacked. She was daughter to Calchas, first traitor and master leaver of them all; she was a lonely woman, widowed, and yet more lonely since, mayhap, childless; she was lacking somewhat in "corage" and waxed ill at letters; there is the matter of that Horaste reported by Pandarus; although fresh from an *amour* with Troilus, she told Diomede she had not known love since her husband's decease; and it is a pity, but it is true, that she appears an opportunist, successful and capable. But was she not of human flesh in feeling not unyielding when a nobleman sought her, especially when he clothed his desire by the fugitive agency of an uncle whose opinion she would be obliged to note with respect? If frailty's name is woman, it is circumstance as much as character which attaches the name to Criseyde!

Professor Kirby makes more important contributions in delineating Troilus and Diomede. Throughout Troilus seems an early Romeo, naïve, sentimental, uninitiated; yet it appears equally clear that the poet was not satirizing Troilus, that he did not favour Criseyde, that indeed Chaucer was creating a romance for nothing at all if not for the ultimate glorification of the holiness of true love. In this new study it is also importantly established that for forceful contrast Geoffrey Chaucer consciously depicted Diomede as a mundane foil to the ethereal Troilus.

Thus, although there is nothing essentially new in linking *Troilus and Criseyde* with the great romances of the world's literature and all that this implies with respect to the erotic theme, Professor Kirby's task of interpreting Chaucer as a great exponent of courtly love could not have been accompanied with so much success without a deep knowledge of poetic conventions in tongues and times now old--without a mature judgment of psychological behaviour in characters complex, diverse--yes, without a wisdom which patiently explores even galling detail to bring to light those little tributary gleams which lead from the outer corona to the very heart of truth itself.

Reprinted from *RES,* XVI (1940), 463-465.

The Canterbury Tales of Geoffrey Chaucer: A New Modern English Prose Translation, Together with the Original Middle English Text of the General Prologue and the Nun's Priest's Tale. By R.M. Lumiansky. With a Preface by Mark Van Doren, and Illustrations by H. Lawrence Hoffman. New York: Simon and Schuster, 1948. Pp. xxix + 345.

The recent appearance, in Professor R. M. Lumiansky's idiomatic translation, of early England's greatest poet, Geoffrey Chaucer, should inspire a large part of the literate American public to read, perhaps for the first time, the undeniably engrossing stories which compose the richest of all medieval collections--the imperishable *Canterbury Tales*. This new work is furbished to capture readers. It has a short preface by the well-known critic Mark Van Doren, and a display of startling colored drawings by the modernistic illustrator H. Lawrence Hoffman. Eulogies of Chaucer from fifteen authors lead the novice to Lumiansky's excellent introductory observations. A thoughtful appendix contains, for the curious, the "General Prologue" and "Nun's Priest's Tale" in Chaucer's Middle English.

Young teachers may believe that colleges are fit places to use profitably this most modern version, although only yesterday high school students, with occasional inaccuracy, quoted the poet's own tongue. Though admittedly a traditionalist, I can recall in twenty years of teaching most success when Chaucer was read in the original. If a translation in present-day English is demanded, Lumiansky's work may be recommended as reasonably clear and accurate: "Wel nyne and twenty in a compaignye" becomes (fittingly) "a group of twenty-nine people"; "A Kynght ther was, and that a worthy man/That fro the tyme that he first bigan/To riden out, he loved chivalrie" becomes (less satisfactorily in its changed tense) "There was among us a brave knight who had loved chivalry...from the time of his horseback rides"; and "A Monk ther was, a fair for the maistrie," becomes (misleading, I think) "There was a Monk, an outstanding one." Lumiansky throughout affords an *impression* of the original, not its meaning to the letter. Though the spirit of Chaucer's personality is lost, Lumiansky's readable book demonstrates that *The Canterbury Tales* is eminently worthy of perusal for its plot, action, and characterizations. Chaucer's prominence as a spinner of first-rate yarns is thus brought home anew. For this reason, I believe that Lumiansky has accomplished something worthwhile. The reader who wishes to turn to corking good stories in a language readily understandable will find Lumiansky's book the best on the market.

The revised *Modern Reader's Chaucer* (1936), a noteworthy labor by the late Professor Tatlock and the poet Percy MacKaye, fully translates Chaucer's complete poetical works, whereas Lumiansky treats only *The Canterbury Tales* and these incompletely. The Melibeus and the recitals of the Monk, the Parson, and the Prioress are the four summarized. The first three he discounts as "moralizing"; the last, "for another reason." Censorship of the Prioress is surprising. For six centuries readers hitherto have not been alarmed by Chaucer's strictures on the fanaticism of the Jews who murdered the little choirboy. Yet Lumiansky now would introduce a *cause célèbre,* declaring that "For most of us, 'The Prioress' Tale' is ruined by the similarity between this sort of story and some of the anti-Semitic propaganda which was current in Nazi Germany, and which is still in operation, not only in numerous foreign countries but also here at home."

Is this not an inadvertence to link Chaucer with Nazi Germany? The average American "here at home" is reasonably broadminded, so why deny him the full text? Nothing can alter today the intention of the Prioress' criticism; but the whole truth includes the fact that Chaucer reported what history taught him, namely that these particular Jews murdered Hugh of Lincoln, a lad of twelve, in the year 1255. It is elementary; but let us, like the Dark Ages, be sufficiently liberal to examine *The Canterbury Tales* as it was written, with smut about the Miller, disapproval of the cruelty of Griselda's Italian husband, as well as pity for the little choirboy. The people in Chaucer's timeless world, as large as life itself, are not a race-- English, Italian, or Jewish--but the human race of a magnificent comedy.

Reprinted from *MLQ,* XI (1950), 246-247.

Medieval Skepticism and Chaucer. By Mary Edith Thomas.
New York: William-Frederick Press, 1950. Pp. 184.

The title *Medieval Skepticism and Chaucer* is arresting inasmuch as it suggests, affirmatively, the rather startling idea thet Chaucer may have been a skeptic. But, after perusing the book, a reader is likely to conclude what he and everybody has long believed; namely, that Chaucer was not a skeptic but a tolerant moral thinker and just about the most humane poet in the English tongue. Frankly, the title is a misnomer, the term *medieval* being too comprehensive for the thirteenth and fourteenth centuries, the period treated by Dr. Mary Edith Thomas. Perhaps a better name would be *The Literature of Skepticism in the Later Middle Ages,* a title more descriptive of the contents. The initial inaccuracy is unfortunate since it alerts the reader for others.

In regard to skepticism, Dr. Thomas speaks often of the later medieval disbelief in immortality. She garners quotations from many sources to display that infidelity was widespread; but she omits Corliss Lamont's *The Illusion of Immortality* (1st ed., 1935; 2nd ed., 1950). Had she consulted it, she doubtless would have qualified her assertion that in Chaucer's time and its foreground "skepticism became an element in the climate of medieval thought" (p.132). The questions were there from the ancient world. Moreover, the age of Chaucer was not marked by such great religious doubts as to justify her claim that "it was in the later Middle Ages that these problems came to be discussed among laymen as well as clergy, among the folk as well as scholars" (p. 132). The scholars and clergy were pretty nearly uniform in their orthodoxy, for belief was their doctrine, and their bread and meat. Nor were the laymen and folk infidels. The commoner was not docile, as proved by the Peasants' Rebellion; but he did not revolt similarly from the "collar" of Holy Church. The Age of the Reformation came long after Chaucer.

What of the statement of the hero in *Aucassin et Nicolette* that "into Hell would I go . . . [since] there go the beautiful courtly ladies"? Dr. Thomas believes that "in the thirteenth century it must have startled many listeners." On the other hand, in speaking of his destination in either Heaven or Hell, Aucassin clearly subscribed to a belief in immortality. Would Hell suggest to an English ear a horrendous fate? Many a knight in the Hundred Years War would have preferred the domain of the goddess Hel, reserved for women, to Valhalla, the home of slain heroes. Aucassin was gay but hardly an infidel.

Dr. Thomas is right about Chaucer: "Indeed there is reason to believe that Chaucer was in the main a good Catholic" (p. 95). The trouble is that she is inconsistent: "Chaucer gives expression in various passages to uncertainties and doubts which if they had been carried to the extreme of denial would place him among the infidels" (p. 5). The main references are to the *Legend* and to the *Knight's Tale,* where "the ideas are largely borrowed from Boethius" (p. 6)-- in other words, they are not Chaucer's own. Moreover, in his sketches of the churchmen she wrongly classes him as "anticlerical" (p. 5), because, for one thing, Chaucer in his reference to the Monk declared: "I seyde his opinion was good" (183). Of Chaucer's "smut," to which the Church might object even today, nothing is reported; instead, Dr. Thomas follows her mentor, R.S. Loomis, in viewing the poet as a lukewarm believer, a Laodicean. There was, however, nothing lukewarm about Chaucer's splendid humanity, and he inspiringly remains as a preeminently liberal mind.

Reprinted from *MLQ*, XV (1954), 74-75.

Chaucer Life-Records. Edited by Martin M. Crow and Clair C. Olson. Austin: University of Texas Press, 1966. Pp.xxxvi+629.

The long-awaited *Life-Records*, edited by Martin M. Crow and Clair C. Olson, now issued abroad by the Oxford University Press and domestically by the University of Texas Press, ranks as a landmark in bioliterary research. *Chaucer Life-Records*, equal in merit to *Sources and Analogues* (1941) and the eight-volume *The Text of the Canterbury Tales* (1940), exhibits scholarship as it soundly comes of age in the American Southwest. No other English poet, not even Milton or Shakespeare, can be studied today in so varied biographical detail as Chaucer. *Chaucer Life-Records* is at once a useful reference for all libraries serving theme-writers and also the indispensable companion for graduate students of English.

Materials in the volume represent the searchings of both British and American scholars and the time required spans several lifetimes of assiduous and passionate devotion to research. *Chaucer Life-Records* incorporates the total findings of a succession of savants: the pioneer collecting of R.E.G. and E.F. Kirk; the later discoveries of Miss Lillian Redstone; the yet later fruits of the intense and well-organized "Chicago gang" directed by Manly and Rickert; and finally the recent industrious activities of, first, Crow, and then Crow and Olson. Martin M. Crow alone devoted fourteen years to the final completion and eventual publication of the volume. The result is as definitive a biographical source book on a medieval writer as we are ever likely to see. A deliberate, exhaustive "ransacking" of every European depository of documents might or might not yield a few fresh items, data to match with the "new" information included on Chaucer's Spanish mission through Navarre in 1366. But since the harvest from the all-important British archives has been scrupulously reaped, Crow and Olson have produced a work which must be appraised as authoritative.

Perhaps the most significant contribution of *Chaucer Life-Records* is that at last the basic materials are assembled for the writing of a full and classic biography of the poet. To date, there has been no truly standard biography of Chaucer to compare with the serviceable ones on, say again, Milton and Shakespeare. Crow and Olson's compendium will now enable investigators to follow the record of Chaucer from its beginnings past its end into the careers of his children, notably his distinguished son Thomas. Even so, the challenge of writing a definitive life of the poet may require a like span of years and the similarly combined efforts of still another elite team like Manly and Rickert, or Crow and Olson. This is because the documents in *Chaucer Life-Records* are rich with suggestions about Chaucer's activities and teeming with names of intriguing friends and impressive associates. These fields offer more hope for meaningful finds than a continued search for further relevant data on the name of Chaucer himself or that of his wife. But the appetite of scholars is insatiable: Crow and Olson present 150 items unknown to Kirk; yet after this unexpected feast, the editor A.C. Baugh (*Chaucer's Major Poetry* [New York, 1963], p. xiii) still hungers, expectantly, for a fuller account of the poet's wife Philippa, whom I first identified as Philippa Pan' (*MLN,* LXIV [1949], 342–43).

The general plan of *Chaucer Life-Records* rewards the reader's time and pains, but it is a compact volume weighted with countless details and specialized information. At that, *Chaucer Life-Records* improves tremendously on Kirk's bare gatherum, which was almost impenetrable until indexed by E.P. Kuhl (*MP,* x [1912-13], 527 ff.). *Chaucer Life-Records* has a number of aids, such as footnotes, tables, and an index. The whole amounts to a limpid interpretative commentary divided into chapters which detail how the documents have been evaluated and understood by Chaucerian scholars over the centuries. The commentary affords excitement for both apprentice and veteran students as they delve into a breathtakingly enormous Chaucerian bibliography. A commendable feature of Crow and Olson's staggering achievement in utilizing over 7,000 note cards is their fairness, humility, and honesty in referring to other investigators. For example, F.N. Robinson's edition (*The Works of Geoffrey Chaucer* [Boston, 1957], p.xxvii) asseverated without mention of source that Chaucer may have had Alice Perrers, Edward III's mistress, as patroness; *Chaucer Life-Records* (p. 5, n. 3) properly refers to *SP,* xxi (1946), 222-28. A praiseworthy conservatism characterizes their sane judgments in the thirty-one chapters that set forth the vivid records of Chaucer's active life in categorical sequence.

It is the responsibility of a scholar, not to create and not to destroy, but to perpetuate his ideas. Manly and Rickert did so with Crow and Olson. May these be able to do the same with their students in the task of compiling and publishing the life-records on Chaucer's ancestors, which are now in Crow's custody. The finest scholorship transcends one man, often one generation, as did *Chaucer Life-Records.*

The sole major omission in the footnotes that appears crucial to the chronology occurs on page 51, note 1. The entry there being discussed is from the *Chroniques* of Jean Froissart, which Manly (who echoed Nicolas sans credit) read as Froissart's mistaken "blending" of data from documents of 1377 and 1378. Yet it is clear enough to me that at least Crow's first French quotation (p. 50) refers to 1377, particularly since this date is corroborated by other contemporary historical proofs (*RES,* xi[1935], 204-209; xiv [1938], 63-67). It may be worthwhile to note that Eustache Deschamps' *Ballade (MLN,* LII[1937], 33-34) is not excerpted in *Chaucer Life-Records* (but see pp. xiii and 27n.). He and Froissart are, so far as I know, the only two major contemporary French poets to cite Chaucer by name. Nobody has ever questioned the veracity of Deschamps, and since Froissart sojourned at various times in England, his testimony cannot be impugned on the basis of present evidence. All men are fallible, therefore perhaps Manly slipped; indeed this appears more likely than that Chaucer's friend Froissart did.

The last remark may well smack of old hat, but the new discovery in *Chaucer Life-Records* of Chaucer's mission in 1366 through Navarre, a separate Spanish kingdom after 1328, contains prime meaning. The date was 22 February 1366, a terminal point of Chaucer's so-called "lost years," the period of 1360-66. Scholars have generally placed the poet in Ireland during these years, in the company of his patron, Prince Lionel, or his friend, Sir Richard Stury. Could Chaucer have been making, instead, various European jaunts on the Continent and past the Pyrenees? Relative to this, Crow and Olson show unexpected restraint in opining nothing. These two dedicated scholars have restricted themselves to the presentation of mainly evidential materials in their first-rate source book. If anything be amiss, it is that the authors hardly appreciate their own strength. They say, for example, that the 150 additions to the collection of hitherto published life-records do not materially change our understanding of Chaucer. I believe they do. The document from Navarre (p. 65) certainly does. Moreover, the sheer total of 493 entries in *Chaucer Life-Records* that depicts his full official responsibilities could be construed as explaining why Chaucer lacked the necessary tranquility to recollect memories or generate original themes. This fact bears on why he had to resort to transcribing the manuscripts of others, with the result that he early became known on the Continent, in Deschamps' phrase, as a *"grand translateur"*. All in all, Crow and Olson can be credited with a significant scholarly contribution to Chauceriana.

NOTES

[1] The volume is further and somewhat fully equipped with concluding sections of Abbreviations, Notes, Select Bibliography, Index, and an Appendix of Translations. Of unquestionable service to both beginners and advanced students, these translations of antique dialects (Provençal, Lombard, *et al.*) afford a feature which should be more often employed in books of scholarly character.

[2] The statement about Pandarus and Villon on p. 175 is misleading, otiose.

[3] The date of publication of Professor Kirby's book (1940) apparently precluded the possibility of a reference to Arthur Mizener, "Character and Action in the Case of Criseyde," *P.M.L.A.* (March, 1939), LIV, 65 ff.

Reprinted from *JEGP,* LXVI (1967), 441-443.